EXPLORING VILLAGES

TO MY HUSBAND

EXPLORING
VILLAGES

by

JOSCELYNE FINBERG

ALAN SUTTON
1987

ALAN SUTTON PUBLISHING
BRUNSWICK ROAD · GLOUCESTER

Copyright © Joscelyne Finberg 1958

First published 1958
by Routledge & Kegan Paul Ltd

This edition published 1987

ISBN 0 86299 346 6

*Cover photograph: Little Gransden and
Great Gransden, Cambs. Aerofilms Ltd.*

Printed in Great Britain
by The Guernsey Press Company Limited,
Guernsey, Channel Islands.

Contents

Illustrations

FIGURES

Plates

Author's Note

I have spent many happy hours carrying out the kind of investigation I have endeavoured to describe in these pages, but in writing of so many different aspects of village life I have naturally been indebted to the work of many scholars, especially those whose books are included in the select reading lists at the end of each chapter. The documents I have used in the text are mainly quoted from these sources. I wish also to thank Dr. E. A. L. Moir for permission to quote from her unpublished work on local government in Gloucestershire.

I

In Praise of Curiosity

CHARMING as many, if not all English villages are, they seldom quite live up to the photographer's account of them. When he trains his camera on a group of cottages with low eaves and massive chimneys and a row of chestnuts in full glory, with a road between, whose only occupant is a sturdy labourer driving a dung cart, he manages to avoid the telephone kiosk at the corner, and the iron bedstead stopping a gap in the hedge; and when he takes a picture for St George's Day showing the church tower and the village roofs embowered in fruit blossom, the council houses and the garage never come within his line of vision. The customers prefer it that way; the villagers themselves rather like to see the old place thus romanticized, and town-dwellers regard villages as places to look at, not to live in.

They come and they look, but how much do they see, even the walkers with time to spare? The theme seems too familiar to arouse any real curiosity. They take a few snapshots and then they go away. If, instead, they could have put on a pair of spectacles which would have added an historical dimension to their vision, how much more rewarding their looking would have been! Even the ugly bits would then have had a place and a meaning, and a landscape which contained an electric pylon as well as a derelict windmill would be richer than one which lacked either of these features. If these visitors only knew (and the villagers themselves are hardly more aware of the fact) they have before them a document on which is written the life story of a community.

How to read that story is the subject of this book; and because

I

this way of looking at the dear, familiar countryside will be for many an expedition into little-known territory I have called it *Exploring a Village*.

The first and most essential piece of equipment for this voyage of discovery is an unlimited curiosity; nothing must be taken for granted. We must begin by asking why there is a village on this spot at all. And to answer this question it will be necessary to look beyond the cluster of buildings. The village only exists as the capital or heart of its little territory, the parish, on which its life depends, and as we continue our investigations we shall become increasingly aware of this fact. The size and shape of village and parish, with the nature of the soil, and the position of roads, rivers, and hills are therefore first scrutinized for evidence about the founding of the village; next fields and hedges, barns, yards and workshops are searched to find out how the people got their daily bread; then, their houses, how they built them, and where they got their materials (where are the forests in which the timber was cut, or the quarries from which the stone was hewn?). The church is made to yield a rich harvest of information on many aspects of village life; how a small community raised the money for an expensive building and why; how they used it, and where the people went to pray who could not see eye to eye with the parson on religious matters. Why churches received such drastic treatment from Victorian restorers, and why the Sunday school, which nowadays occupies the church on Sunday afternoons, often had a separate building in 1830. The village school also comes in for its share of attention. The parish chest is opened and the operations of that mysterious body, the Vestry, are considered. This leads naturally to the parson and the squire, once the rulers of the parish; the village is searched for traces of their doings, and their houses are studied, less as examples of domestic building, than as evidence about the lives of the men who lived in them. Finally the cottages of the poor are examined. They are often among the newest buildings in the village; why is this, and how did the large families we are accustomed to believe were common a century ago manage to live in them? Who built the railway and what difference did it make to the people of the parish? Where did the villagers grind their corn; why is the inn so large? These and many other similar questions can often be answered by close observation. Shops, factories, garages, and allotments are fitted into the picture, for our record is to be a documentary film rather than an album of picturesque snapshots.

In the course of the following chapters I shall endeavour to show what questions need to be asked, the kind of evidence which may be expected, and the inferences which may be drawn from it. There is a sense in which we can only find what we are looking for, and I have therefore used appropriate questions as section headings in the longer chapters. As often as space permitted I have cited villages known to me as examples. But I am not offering rules which can be universally applied; no two villages are exactly alike, and many problems can never be solved. The suggestions here made are intended to form a kind of framework against which the reader can check his own observations, and to stimulate and direct his curiosity.

In order to supply this background of fact it will be necessary to touch the fringes of many more subjects than can be dealt with fully within the covers of a single book, and what I have to say of them will accordingly be brief. No one can hope to know much of an English village without some study of the geography of the parish, yet it would be impossible to explain here the full significance of every feature. There may sometimes be reasons for thinking that a particular site has been occupied since prehistoric times, and I shall therefore try to show where traces of prehistoric men are likely to be found, and describe some of them; I have made no attempt however to sketch in all that archaeologists have to tell us of Stone, Bronze, or Iron Ages. I could not provide a dictionary of architecture to accompany what I have to say on the parish church, nor a history of agriculture in my observations on the parish fields. 'History is about chaps', and architecture, archaeology, and the rest are used here only for what they can tell us about one particular group of men. It is no part of my purpose to tell my reader how to distinguish between twelfth- and four-teenth-century work in parish churches; there are numerous books already in existence devoted to this subject, and probably a detailed guide lying about in the nave. I want him to ask himself 'Why then and not before'? or 'Why so little'? and suggest a possible answer.

The catastrophes and triumphs of national history are seen

through the diminishing glass of everyday life in remote places, but none the less become more real if we can discover, let us say, exactly how the people of Stow on the Wold or Margaret Roding coped with the religious upheaval of the sixteenth century, and the civil disputes of the seventeenth.

Although we are mainly concerned with things which can be seen and touched, it would be absurd to rule out of consideration what can be learnt from the map. Accordingly we shall pay full attention to the names of places and things, and such other information as maps provide.

A large-scale map of the whole parish is, indeed, indispensable for this type of investigation. It should be of the scale of six inches to the mile, though the two-and-a-half inch scale map is more convenient if any long-distance walking has to be done. The popular one-inch map is almost useless for our purpose; it is too small, and omits much necessary detail. Anyone who is fortunate enough to get a sight of an old map of his parish, an estate map or a tithe map, or even the first edition of the Ordnance Survey Map, will find it useful and fascinating. For many counties also large-scale maps were published during the last century; there is a series by Greenwood which is well worth looking at.

These last, and a number of standard books, such as the *Victoria County Histories*, and the *Oxford Dictionary of English Place Names*, to which reference will be inevitable, can be found in the reference section of any county library.

I believe that anyone who conducts an investigation of his village on the lines suggested in the following chapters will find that there are many modest historic monuments which survive without help from public agitations or public money, and that if only we understand how to look at it, the whole present still mirrors the past, even though the remotest objects have become a good deal obscured and blemished with age. He will be able to read from the landscape the life story of the place, and in doing so, will have achieved more than a collection of small facts, or a chronicle of unimportant events. He will have increased beyond measure his pleasure and interest in the scenes he will have come to understand so well; and if he puts his findings on record he will have contributed one small piece of true gold to the mosaic picture of the nation's history.

4

II

All Shapes and Sizes

THE site of every one of our villages must once have been a subject of anxious thought to somebody. The face of the landscape has changed so much that it is difficult to imagine it as the first settlers saw it, and the fortunes of some of our villages have fluctuated so much that it is hard to picture them as they were only two hundred years ago. But much more may still be learnt from their lay-out and general appearance than the casual and incurious passer-by would think possible.

The purpose of this chapter is to consider the site and the ground-plan of the village, and to see what these may be able to tell us about its past. We shall ask first:

Why is the village in this precise spot?

The nature of the soil is all-important to men who must live on what they grow, and though prehistoric man had to settle on land which he could clear with primitive tools, our Anglo-Saxon forefathers could go where they liked and knew how to choose good land. But where in the chosen territory was the settlement to be? Water was perhaps the first consideration. In England there is not usually much difficulty about this, but the presence of a good spring may often be the determining factor in the choice of a site. A line of villages along the side of a river valley is a common feature of the landscape, and there are many obvious reasons for preferring the valley to the hilltops, but the position of the villages will be related to the level of springs which give an adequate supply of water all the year round. The founders did their job well enough as a rule, but the demands of our enormous population, among other causes, have so lowered the water level that many wells and streams once full of water are now shrunk, or dry, and country places suffer from a drought unknown in prehistoric times.

Shelter from the wind is not hard to come by in heavily wooded country. Most of England was heavily wooded before man got to work on it, and continued to be so throughout the period of settlement. The names of vanished forests frequently appear on the map on land almost totally cleared, and the names of smaller tracts of woodland often only survive attached to farm or lane.

Security from hostile visitors might be more difficult to achieve. For many centuries the inhabitants of these islands preferred to settle out of sight of the sea for fear of pirates, and in troubled times they avoided the main roads.

These considerations may not have affected the lay-out of the site, for by no means all of our villages give the impression of having been built in accordance with any preconceived plan. Some grew up haphazard, others have grown so much in course of time that the original shape has been obliterated. If we are to become intimately acquainted with the past of our village and find out what happened to it, we must ask:

What was the original ground-plan?

Roughly speaking, there are four types of village. First, there are the villages grouped about a central open space, a green or a square. Secondly, there are villages grouped round a central feature usually the church; these are sometimes called 'round' villages. The 'street' villages, where the houses are all strung out along the roadway, form the third group, and the fourth is made up of those which seem to be entirely shapeless, their first settlement and later growth equally a matter of chance. Each of these typical forms can tell us a little about the foundation of the village.

Not many village greens are found in the higher and wilder parts of England, but they are fairly common elsewhere. In the lowlands of the north, especially in Co. Durham, there are a large number, which conform to a particularly well-defined and regular

6

pattern. The green is a large rectangular grassy space, either nearly square, or very long with a road running down the centre. No buildings are allowed upon it, except occasionally the church, the school, or the smithy, but the village pump is usually there, often enclosed in a little conduit- or well-house (Fig. 1). The principal farms of the parish, which alone enjoy the ancient common rights, stand side by side, interspersed with cottages round the perimeter, and behind these again runs a ring road, usually called Back Lane, from which the various roads, and tracks, branch off

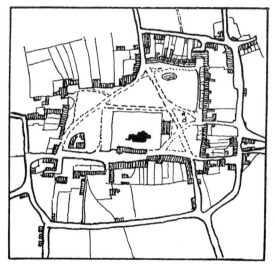

Fig. 1. A village green in Co. Durham. Heighington.

into the fields of the parish. Examples of this plan may be seen at Heighington in Co. Durham and Milburn in Cumberland. Finchingfield and Writtle in Essex are villages with greens of the less formal and symmetrical type more common in the south of England.

Most of the Durham examples are large villages with a long history. In the twelfth century their inhabitants were grass farmers, pastoral husbandmen depending for their livelihood on sheep, cattle, and dairy products. Most of the villages stood upon land which in a primitive state would not require a great deal of clear-

7

ance; the constant grazing of large flocks and herds would be adequate to keep trees and scrub under control. These facts taken together suggest that they are very ancient pastoral settlements and that the greens were originally designed as pounds into which the villagers could drive their beasts for safety, or at any rate greater protection, from wild beasts and cattle thieves. It can not be assumed, however, that every village with a green belonged originally to a pastoral people. The plan is a good one for an agricultural community too, and in fact it is more common in the parts of England which always grew good corn than in those where dairy-farming and stock-raising were the rule.

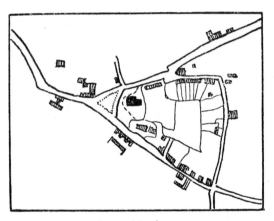

FIG. 2. Northaw.

The villages with 'squares' are very similar in plan to 'green' villages. The central open space is by no means always a rectangle. In Hertfordshire a triangular shape is more common, and the villages which have that plan, e.g. Northaw and Aldbury, are in country where dense forest had to be cleared before any settlement could be made. Here again we seem to see traces of an enclosure to protect cattle from wild beasts, but where land was so precious, the enclosure was small. This plan is also found in the once forested districts of Middlesex, Surrey, and Sussex (Fig. 2).

That the greens were, and continued to be, meeting places where all the public business of the community was transacted, hardly needs to be said. Preaching crosses were sometimes set up

8

on them where mass was said, and the priest taught, and baptized, before churches began to be built, and the greens were splendid places for markets, fairs, races, sports, and dancing. So convenient a plan was not likely to be given up where there was room for it. The open space is still jealously preserved in many of these villages today, and the villagers take toll of fair vans making use of them.

Where the growing village has had nowhere else to expand the green has sometimes been sacrificed, so that a central block of

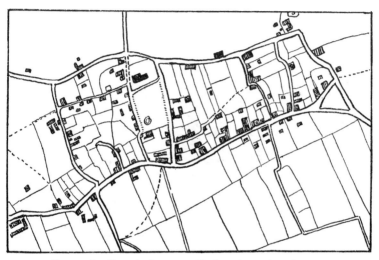

FIG. 3. A village built over a 'furlong': Marham-le-Fen.

houses stands with a lane running between them and the older homesteads on the perimeter. Where the village streets form a rectangle, a green may be concealed under the houses in the centre, but there is another possible explanation. The village may have started as a small settlement with one street, with its ploughlands lying beside it, but as numbers increased and the inhabitants enlarged their fields, they may have used a part of the field nearest to the village for new homesteads. Since the furlongs, as the field divisions were called, were usually rectangular in shape and divided into narrow strips, the streets and lanes reflect this pattern. Such a plan may be seen at Marham-le-Fen in Lincolnshire (Fig. 3).

9

In those parts of England where village greens are most uncommon, on the Welsh border, and in the western counties generally, the second of our village types, the 'round' village, makes its appearance. Often crowning a hilltop, the homesteads are grouped on a ring road round some central feature, the church, or an ancient earthwork, occasionally even a pond. This type of village is not unknown in eastern England; there is one at Bringhurst in Leicestershire (Fig. 4), for instance, but it is so much

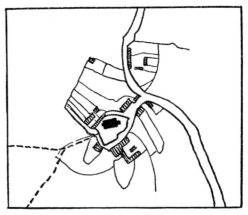

FIG. 4. A 'round' village: Bringhurst.

more often found in the west, and especially in Wales, that it is considered to be of Celtic origin, and where a village has this ground-plan, there is that much reason for thinking that it may have existed in Roman, or even prehistoric times. The church is the most common central feature; where it stands in a circular church-yard, it may well be on the site of a far more ancient holy place, as it obviously is when it stands on, or close to, a barrow or pre-historic grave or ringwork.

A vast stone, or menhir, standing or lying among the graves, or incorporated in the churchyard walls, sometimes provides the proof. At Rudston in Yorkshire, for example, there is an enormous stone 23½ feet high, standing next the church, and another of triangular shape in the circular churchyard wall. The larger stone has a rough cross carved upon it, probably engraved there in the Dark Ages when it was the practice of Celtic missionaries to sanctify pagan shrines by marking the stones with a cross. We can be fairly sure, therefore, that Rudston is even older than this; the name of the village means rood-stone.

At Ashmore in Dorset the central feature is an embanked pond just like those which are sometimes found in the abandoned prehistoric villages of the chalk downs. Ashmore means the pond by the ash, so evidently the pond, which is man-made, gave the village its English name.

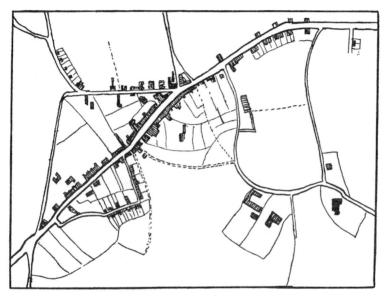

FIG. 5. A 'street' village: Codicote. Notice on the right, the church, manor house and farm on the site of the original settlement.

From the centre of some of these round villages, the roads, lanes, and tracks which connect the village with its fields and with the outside world, radiate like the spokes of a wheel in a manner which suggests that their position is not accidental. There are traces in early Welsh laws of tribal regulations which might well produce an arrangement like this if they had any effect on the physical plan of settlements.

We now come to the most common of our village types, the 'street' village (Fig. 5). The houses are strung out along the road;

cottage doors open straight on to the highway, or on to a narrow verge of grass or rough ground; farmhouses are usually at right-angles, presenting their gable ends to the street, with their yards and barns beside them. These villages are of all ages and are found all over the country. In many cases the lie of the land has dictated the plan—in a narrow valley, or on a steep hillside, a long, straggling settlement might be the only convenient arrangement. More often, however, we can say that the road was there first, though it might have been no more than the sort of track the nomadic early settlers first trod out.

Many of the roadside settlements of Roman Britain, especially those on the great main roads, were abandoned in the troubled time of the Saxon Conquest, but whenever a government was strong enough to remove the terror of hostile armies from the English roads, villages sprang up again at cross-roads, at river crossings, wherever somebody thought he had something to gain from passing traffic. From the Norman Conquest onwards, and sometimes even before, villagers whose forefathers had made their settlements in the woods, hidden from the dangerous highway, found it worth while to transplant themselves into new homes by the roadside, leaving the old site to become derelict. Trade was undoubtedly the motive of these migrations, and sometimes the new village blossomed later into a market town; nearly always it had some benefit from better communications with the outside world. Street villages are often well-built, comfortable-looking places, even though today, they may concern themselves little, if at all, with passing traffic. It would not be difficult to find examples in most counties of each of the three types of street village; those where the lie of the land has dictated the plan, those which have sprung up by the roadside, and those which have come into being as the result of a migration from an older site. I will mention a few in different parts of the country. Bourton-on-the-Hill in Gloucestershire is a beautiful village lying along the main road from Oxford to Worcester. It was already in existence in the eighth century. Moreton-in-Marsh, a few miles away, is about as old. It lies at the junction of the Oxford–Worcester road with the Roman Fosse way. The lord of the manor obtained the grant of a market for it in Henry III's reign, and though it never grew up into a town, it became the centre of a district. The inhabitants live by trade, there is a handsome market hall, and all express trains on the London–Worcester line stop at the station.

These two places grew up from the beginning by the roadside, but in the eastern counties, nearer to the coast on which enemies so often landed, there was far more reason for avoiding the main roads in the centuries which saw the founding of most of our villages, and so roadside villages sometimes have a parent settlement near by. (A good example is Whitwell in Hertfordshire, an offshoot from St Paul's Walden.) More often, the parent settlement dwindled away until only the church and perhaps the manor house are left.

To illustrate this from the numerous examples which could be given, we will take the case of Codicote, also in Hertfordshire (Fig. 5). To the enquiring mind, the street of this village immediately suggests a question. There are hardly any farm buildings and no church; only a few tiny shops, and one good inn, yet the cottages are numerous. How did the inhabitants live for whom they were built? This was originally a tiny settlement, probably a forest clearing. The villagers moved on to the main road and set up a weekly market and an annual fair in the time of Henry III, but these never flourished enough for the village to develop into a town, and by the end of the eighteenth century they were extinct. The village had then developed a new source of livelihood and was holding a weekly market for straw platt to supply the hat-making industry. This manufacture, for which Luton is especially famous, was carried on in villages all over the surrounding country, and evidently Codicote was a local centre. Very little straw is plaited in England now, and unless the road enables the inhabitants who work elsewhere to reach their destination more easily it no longer contributes anything to the life of the village. The parish church is on the site of the original settlement, half a mile away. Redbourn in the same county has a rather similar story. The church is in a tiny hamlet called Church End, about a mile west of the little town or large village on Watling Street. Great and Little Harrowden in Northamptonshire probably have the same sort of relation to each other. The name, derived from the Saxon word for a heathen shrine, makes it certain that one of the two villages dates from pagan times, and we can guess that Little Harrowden, the roadside settlement with the smaller church is the younger of the two. Newton Poppleford in Devon is a fine street village in the parish of Aylesbeare, of which it is probably the new-*tun*. If so, it is a bigger place than its parent. At Bow in North Devon the fourteenth-century parish church was built midway between the new village and the old settlement at Nymet Tracey, which is two and a half miles away.

Our last type of village is that with no observable plan at all. The houses are scattered over the site in groups, intersected with lanes and pathways, perhaps in odd terraces on hillsides, or dotted about beside a stream.

One may guess that many of these villages are younger than those with a coherent plan, and that the people who made them were not quite so closely bound together by necessity or kinship as the earlier colonizers must often have been. Sometimes, indeed, we know that this was so. Middle Barton, for instance, in Oxfordshire, came into being in the fourteenth century, long after the neighbouring village of Steeple Barton, which contains the parish church. The remains of the older village, the street, the mill, and the foundations of the manor house can be seen in the fields near the church.

Mining and industrial villages are usually shapeless. The need to cram a large number of houses into a small space, often in hilly, broken country, usually makes any of the types of plan we have been considering unsuitable for a new settlement, and obliterates the shape of an old one. Avening in Gloucestershire is an example of this. An ancient place, it probably once lay neatly along the road, but cloth mills and their workers' cottages now sprinkle the hillside in haphazard fashion. The mining villages of Devon and Cornwall usually present a similar, though less comely, picture.

All these types of villages, except the mining villages, and sometimes the round villages, are the centres of their parishes and to them the term 'nucleated' has been given, a term which is perhaps confusing today. It is not a metaphor taken from atomic physics, but has the same sense as the name nucleus, given to a small colony of bees. Originally nearly all the inhabitants of the parish lived in the village itself, had their farm buildings and cattle there, and from there, as from a hive, went out to work in the village fields. All this has been changed in the last two hundred years, but in the midlands, in parish after parish you will find outside the village, not a single farm, hardly a cottage, built before the last quarter of the eighteenth century, unless it is a lodge or a toll-house.

Outside the midlands, the classic open field country, things are not so clear-cut. In the fens, for instance, village clusters are smaller and there are many isolated ancient farmsteads. There men went from the parent village to carve out a new life for themselves and settled on the land they won from the waste. In Gloucestershire there are large clustered villages, with splendid farm buildings in the village street, but often there are hamlets in the parish as well, with as long a history, each of which originally had its own field system. In Devonshire too there are some clustered villages in a countryside full of small hamlets, and farmsteads which stand alone, where once there was a little community of three or four peasant holdings.

Another question, then, presents itself:

Is this a nucleated village or is it merely the most important settlement in the parish?

In Cornwall, and west Devon, in Herefordshire, and indeed all over the West Country, the village as the lifeblood and centre of a territory of several thousand acres, disappears.

Wherever the taming of the wilderness was especially difficult, whether because the country was mountainous, or densely-wooded, people settled in small groups rather than in large clusters. Probably in such country only enough land could be cleared to support a few people through the winter; often the land was too poor to attract anyone who commanded large resources and had a numerous following. Sometimes perhaps the settlers embarked on the work of clearance as a sort of speculation to see if the soil was worth cultivating. That this last occasionally happened is suggested by a passage in the Laws of Ine (688–94) King of Wessex, which lays down that if a man wishes to leave his land he must show half of it settled, and he may take with him only his children's nurse and his smith. This regulation seems to be designed to control the activities of colonists, and it is fair to suppose that it would not have been made if there had not been some nomadic and wasteful use of land.

Where the country proved to be poor and unprofitable, unless, at a later date, mineral deposits were found, no access of prosperity or increase of population has come to overlay the poor and arduous beginnings. In such districts the modern map shows the pattern of the original settlement and we can almost surprise the founding fathers at their work. A hamlet, dignified by the presence of a church, gives its name to the parish. The church seems sometimes to have been built at a convenient meeting-place for the inhabitants of the lonely hamlets and isolated farmsteads of which the parish is made up, but more often, perhaps, it was built by the local landowner near his own home, and the 'church-town', as it is sometimes called in Devonshire, remains small and unimportant. Where the situation is convenient and the region not too poor, it may have grown into a small village since the building of the church made it the parish centre.

The scattered type of parish is not confined to the highlands of the west; it is found, for instance, in Hertfordshire where the forest was so dense that it could only be cleared piecemeal, and much of it remained untouched until the tenth century. Then the Abbot of St Albans made a drive to get more of his territory under cultivation, and a number of new villages came into being in the neighbourhood of Sandridge, Cashio, and Bushey. The land round Barnet and Hatfield was cleared still later and covered with tiny settlements.

The term hamlet, which is used here to denote a very small settlement—perhaps six dwellings, more or less, grouped together, it sometimes also used of any rural settlement, however large, if is has not a church, and is not the centre of a civil parish. Either use is really an anachronism when one is dealing with the beginning of our villages, for then the population was so small and so thinly spread that only a few royal manors, or centres of large estates, were anything like a moderate sized village of today, and the rest, whether or not they contained the habitation of the local thegn, or a church, were all of them about equally small and insignificant.

So far we have considered the basic shape of the village mainly as evidence for the founding of the village. The next question we must consider is:

BLANCHLAND, NORTHUMBERLAND. The village grew up at the gates of an Augustinian abbey founded in 1165, of which the gatehouse is visible in the middle of the village street (centre). Part of the abbey church (right centre) is in use as a parish church, and the guest house is an inn. The quadrangle in the foreground, said to be on the site of the cloister, consists of cottages put up for lead miners in the eighteenth century.

SEVENTEENTH-CENTURY FARM BUILDINGS at Taynton House, Glos. They were built between 1695 and 1700 by a thriving yeoman. The group includes barn, oxhouse, and "mill house" which housed his cider presses and probably a horsetrack. The buildings are all of rose-red brick, roofed with Cotswold slate.

What can the ground-plan tell us about its later history?

The pattern of streets and lanes is sometimes the only visible record of a departed glory. Few places could have less appearance of life and importance today than the village of Lydford in Devonshire. The church and the Norman castle mound with the ruined shell of the keep are all that seem to remain of what was once the centre of West Devon, a strong point in the defence of the peninsula against the Viking invasions, an important market, one of the earliest towns, the 'capital' of Dartmoor (nearly the whole of which lies in Lydford parish), where the tin miners kept their prison, 'one of the most annoious, contagious, and detestable places wythin this realm', as one prisoner described it. But if we explore the site more carefully, we can find in the small lanes running at right angles to the road, leading nowhere, and having no practical use today, the line of vanished streets; and, running across the neck of land on which the village stands, there is an earthen rampart, in its great days doubtless crowned with a wooden palisade, which provided the only artificial defence-work needed to secure this very strong natural site. Military considerations determined the position of Saxon boroughs like Lydford. Naturally they tended also to become trading centres, as Lydford did, but they were often badly situated from the commercial point of view. Towns thrive at cross-roads and river crossings and on main thoroughfares; forts in those days were placed on promontories with only one line of approach. Lydford, until the bridging of the famous gorge, was a completely dead end; so, when its military importance disappeared after the Norman Conquest, the town was unable to compete with better placed rivals; and it dwindled in the course of ages into a tiny village.

The rapid growth in the number and wealth of towns in the twelfth and thirteenth centuries induced many landowners to embark on the gamble of town creation, not by laying out new sites, but by establishing markets and persuading traders to settle in existing villages. Geographers know the conditions on which the success and prosperity of towns depend, but many medieval landlords had no idea that the game had any rules at all, and in some of our villages traces remain of unsuccessful speculations, particularly in those cases where a town did come into being and flourish for a time. There are over fifty of these abortive towns in Devon, where landowners seem to have been remarkably optimistic.

Buntingford in Hertfordshire was a successful result of the third attempt to found a town in the neighbourhood, first at Chipping, a hamlet three miles to the north on Ermine Street, then in the village of Buckland two miles further on. Both these efforts failed, and a hundred years later, in 1360, Buntingford itself was established. Placed at a cross-roads, and planned so that both north-south and east-west traffic would pass along the main street, it succeeded where the attempt to transform the ancient village had failed.

The case of Dymock in Gloucestershire is an interesting one. This tiny village in the centre of the daffodil country, a quiet group of houses set among orchards, has a church fit in size and dignity for a small town. Here, too, the lines of ancient streets can be detected in little lanes leading off the high road, and having no meaning today. As long ago as the thirteenth century, when the fine church was still newly built, Dymock was eclipsed by Newent, four miles away. The Welsh drovers bringing their cattle to Gloucester used to spend the night at Newent, and a flourishing market grew up there, to which the other little town could offer no counter-attraction.

The superior attractions of a rival and the unsuitability of the site; to these may be added as causes of decline the attentions of the enemy and the caprices of the sea. The small village of Newtown in the Isle of Wight was once a little port depending mainly on fishing and salt-making for its livelihood. It had four broad streets in the Middle Ages, but already in 1598 the town was very much decayed and had 'no good houses standing'. The author of this report gave an economic reason for this collapse, but tradition held that it was the result of French raiding. The place continued to have some importance, however, as a parliamentary borough, returning two members, and no doubt it was for electioneering purposes that the little town hall was built in the eighteenth century, in the middle of one of those fine, broad streets. Eventually the borough was disfranchised and even the church fell down. Today the town hall stands on the wide grass verge which occupies two-thirds of Broad Street, half High Street remains, containing about six cottages and the little chapel which has replaced the church, and the other half of High Street, Gold Street, and Town Gate Lane are grassy, tree-lined tracks, flanked by derelict cottage gardens.

FIG. 6. The Town Hall, Newtown: Isle of Wight.

Winchelsea, founded as a fortress and harbour by Edward I, is no more than a large village today. It was laid out on a strictly rectangular pattern and furnished with handsome gateways. The church was planned on a most ambitious scale, and a town Winchelsea was for several centuries, though such military importance as it ever had vanished, and the silting of the river made the port unusable. As a smuggling centre it enjoyed an Indian summer, and every old house and cottage is provided with ample cellars. Certainly it is not the plan alone which provides the evidence of past greatness here, but it remains an interesting feature of the place.

When towns decay, tradesmen move away, the town hall (if there is one) gets boarded up, and the people turn back to the land for their bread; but if a village does not thrive the result may be still more drastic. At Hardwick, in Northamptonshire, there are only seven houses beside the church, and the place has lost all semblance of community life. In any of the Midland counties, where large clustered villages are the rule, one would expect to find signs that a village of this sort was once a more considerable place, and such signs are not lacking at Hardwick.

Signs of men's handiwork similar to those which may be seen at Hardwick occur in many deserted village sites all over England, where grassy mounds beside a mysterious gully are all that remains of a once busy street. These mounds, if you dig into them, are heaps of stone and rubble with occasional fragments of medieval pottery; they are ruined cottages; one may even be the church, though this is often a visible ruin. The village street may still be a cart track, but even that has frequently vanished, and where the houses were not built of stone, but of some less durable material, the site may have been levelled out so much that even an air photograph does not reveal it. The name, however, quite often survives, sometimes in a corrupted form, attached to a field or plantation, or, more often, to a farm. At Stutchbury, again in Northamptonshire, for instance, there is a large farm on an open place where lanes converge; perhaps it was once the village green, although there are no signs of old buildings. Yet this was a village in the time of Domesday Book, and the next parish is still called Helmdon with Stutchbury. At Astwell, close by, a castellated manor house, the manorial fishponds, and a mill, remain of what was once a separate parish. At Charwellton, in the same county, the church survives, as well as a farm and a mill, beside the field where traces of ancient habitations heave up the grass in odd shapes, and the old approach road emerges from a cornfield. This is because the villagers seem to have migrated to another settlement on the main road two miles away, and they still use the church.

Such remains as are visible at Church Charwellton are a fairly common feature of the original settlements of the roadside villages which have been described earlier in this chapter. Helmdon, already mentioned, may be taken as a typical example. It is recorded in Domesday Book, but it is probably much older, since the original site lies just below a very ancient thoroughfare, now called the Welsh Drove. Here, on the side of a valley, stands the church with a modern rectory, and in a field close by are to be seen

the mounds and ridges which are probably the remains of the
original village, for the people of Helmdon now live a quarter of
a mile away. On the other side of the valley a village of comfortable stone-built cottages and handsome farms grew up beside a
newer road, in the seventeenth and eighteenth centuries, and the
coming of the railway at the end of the nineteenth century caused
another group of houses to spring up in the valley-bottom. This
village may be said to have had, at different times, three different
centres.

Most of the deserted and shrunken villages were abandoned
for economic reasons. When there was a shortage of labour after
the Black Death had decimated the population, the villagers may
in a few cases have left because they were able to get a better living
elsewhere; but more often they were evicted by landlords anxious
to turn poor arable land to greater profit by sheep-farming. During
the fifteenth and sixteenth centuries much land was enclosed for
pasture, and many villages disappeared.

In the eighteenth century a landowner who found the hovels
of his tenants too near for comfort, and pulled them all down,
usually made some provision for them outside his grand new
park, where they would not spoil the view from the terrace. So it
happens that traces of an old village are sometimes visible within
the grounds of the squire's house. At Birdsall in East Riding, for
example, the ruins of the church abut on the terrace, and the lines
of the village streets show faintly in the grass. We only know
through the existence of an old map that another Yorkshire
village, Hinderskelfe, lies buried in the gardens of Castle Howard.
Some rich and enlightened landlords made beautiful villages, of
which Milton Abbas in Dorset is a well-known example; others
planned them in accordance with some private fad, as did a banker
named Harford at Blaise Hamlet near Bristol where the houses
there are so arranged that none can overlook his neighbour, in
order to make gossip impossible. For some of these new villages
a new church was provided, but usually the old one continued to
serve the parish although isolated in the park.

It was not in order to beautify, but to enrich his property, that
the local squire, George Cary, founded the famous Clovelly. He
describes what he did in his will, dated August 9th 1601. 'I have
of late erected a pier and quay in the sea and river of Severne upon

the sea shore near low water of the said seas . . . and also divers houses, cellars, warehouses, and other edifices, as well under the cliff and on the salt shores of Clovelly aforesaid, and also near above the cliff there, which standeth and hath cost me about £2000 and which place was of none or very small benefit before my said exertions and buildings.' The small harbour which he made, the only safe anchorage on a long stretch of dangerous coast, flourished, and a village grew up in the gully of the diverted watercourse which gave access to the shore.

Most of our coastal fishing villages are young compared with the inland settlements; many came into existence about the same time as Clovelly or a little earlier. Fishermen before that had landing places and fishing rights on the shores, but they lived inland, hidden from the sea. This is well illustrated in a document dated 1309 describing the customs of Stokenham in Devonshire. Stokenham lies about two miles inland of Start Point. The fishermen of the village had then three landing places or fishing stations on the long stretch of open shore between Start Point and Slapton. Today there are three hamlets of fishermen on this same stretch, Hallsands, Beesands, and Torcross, and the latter, which by 1850 had grown into a tiny resort with bathing facilities, is certainly on the site of one of those earlier landing places. Staithes in Yorkshire first appears as a village in 1415, but the name means landing-place, so it is probable that the men of the nearby villages, Seaton and Hindewell, had been using it long before. Mevagissey in Cornwall seems to have come into being about the same time. Probably, in every case, the lord of the manor made a quay or breakwater as a speculation, and the village grew up round it.

When the fishing villages round our coasts had come into being the tally of England's villages was nearly complete. Some settlements were built to accommodate miners, and industrial development changed the shape and plan of many others; but now the roll is made up. A few villages have been created within the past twenty years in Northumberland, where the Forestry Commission is transforming the moorland wastes, and small settlements are being built for their workers because there are often no existing villages near enough at hand. But these are exceptional circumstances; among all the current plans for social improvement and new housing, the founding of new villages, self-sufficient little communities of a thousand souls, more or less, forms, and can form, no part.

BOOKS TO READ

The Making of the English Landscape. W. G. Hoskins. Hodder and Stoughton, 1955.
The Lost Villages of England. M. Beresford. Lutterworth Press, 1954.
'The Origins and Forms of Hertfordshire towns'. W. Page. *Archaeologia*, Vol. 69.

III

Taking Possession

H ow did it all start? In the last chapter we saw villages planned
to provide security for the village herds, villages springing
up to take advantage of road traffic, difficult country settled
almost yard by yard, easy country peopled with large close-
clustered villages, and so on. We may have learnt why the
founders came there, something of how their sons and grandsons
prospered to the thirtieth generation and more, but we have yet
to discover, if we can, who these founders were. The questions we
are going to ask are: Who first settled here? Why did they come?

We must now go outside the village and take a look at the
parish, and indeed the whole region in which it lies. The answers
to our questions will depend primarily on the geography of our
neighbourhood. If we are on heavy clay, for instance, which in
prehistoric times was waterlogged and densely wooded, we can feel
fairly sure that there was no settlement there before the coming
of the Saxons. On the other hand, if the soil is light and easily
cultivated, we may look for traces of early man. The significance
of prehistoric earthworks and standing stones in the village has
already been touched on in the last chapter, and we must find
out what the archaeologists have to say about the whole region.
Then we must study the roads of the district: how ancient are
they? And the rivers, are they navigable? Place names are also
of importance. They may be said to be our oldest documentary
evidence, and when their testimony can be understood, it is incon-
trovertible. The names of villages, farms, hills, rivers, woods and

field all have something to tell about their past. Finally there is
the evidence of recorded history.

The purpose of this and the following chapters is to provide a
general background against which the search for the origin of a
particular place can be made. I shall describe very briefly how the
land began to be peopled, and what evidence exists to enable us
to identify the earliest settlements, that is those made before about
A.D. 600. It will be necessary in this section to devote some space
to the Saxon Conquest because this, while it obliterated much
that we long to know, also provides a datable point in the story
of our villages as the coming of the Romans does for some of our
towns. We can say 'This place has a Saxon name which it cannot
have acquired before about A.D. 450'; although the coming of the
Saxons may not be the beginning of the story.

Everybody has a mental picture of the map of England, and a
rough idea of its physical features. In the west and north the land
is high and wild with deep valleys and rapid rivers. In many places
the volcanic rocks have burst through the smooth surface of the
hills, and in others the cliffs of long-vanished seas are still scoured
by wind and rain. On the hills the soil is poor and thin; the valleys
are narrow, their sides heavily wooded. Everywhere the Atlantic
weather beats in. This is sometimes called the highland zone, and
roughly speaking it lies west and north of a line drawn from the
Humber to the Dorset coast (Fig. 7). To the east and south are
the lowlands, where the country wears a gentler aspect. The prevailing wind breaks its force and sheds much of its moisture in
the first impact with the hills to the west, so the climate is milder.
The chalk hills spread their ribs over the south, encircling London,
and reaching northwards into East Anglia; and, less spectacular,
but not least important, the oolitic limestone belt lies across the
breast of the land like a garter ribbon, from the shoulder about
the Humber, to the tip a few miles from Portland Bill. Between
all these ranges of hills lie broad fertile valleys, and the rivers
which drain them are smooth waterways, navigable to small craft
far inland. And up these rivers came the founders of our villages.

The first settlers had come long before, arriving from the south-
west. They did not linger on the low ground, in the dense water-
logged forest which spread all over the clay of the valley bottoms,
but made their way wherever terraces of gravel and silt afforded a

25

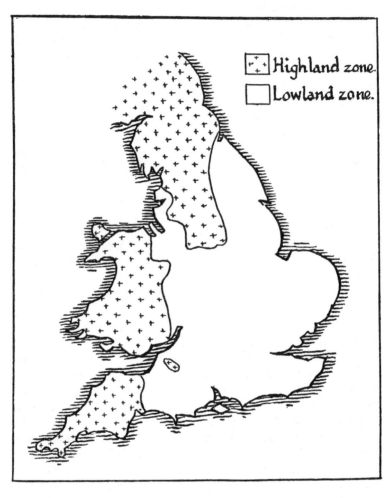

Fig. 7. The highland and lowland zones of England and Wales.

clearer path to the uplands. They were herdsmen, not cultivators. Their pigs and cattle could feed on the hills where forest gave way to scrub, and could be reduced by their stone axes, and still more by the constant grazing of their beasts. After a time they were followed by the first tillers of the soil who spread east and north over the high ground. The impressive graves which they made for their chieftains, the long barrows, the great stone circles and stone avenues that they set up, and their hilltop earthworks, show that these were well organized and powerful people.

We know little about their settlements, but it was these Stone Age men who first began to tread out those ancient routes, which we call the prehistoric trackways, as they moved about looking for fresh pasture for their herds. Always keeping to the high ground, above the line of springs which occurs at roughly the same level on each hillside, they avoided the morasses and the dense jungle below, and if they had to cross a stream, chose the narrowest part of the valley.

These Stone Age men have left traces of their presence all over the uplands, and some places where they flourished particularly, notably on the Cotswolds, are far away from the sources of the flint they needed for their tools and weapons. Flints brought from Cumberland were used for weapons in this region, and some of the giant pillars at Stonehenge came from Pembrokeshire, so we know that they traded with men living many miles away and were able to move about freely on their hilltop tracks. These were not roads in any modern sense. They were not confined between hedges, nor surfaced in any way, but they were through ways, so much trampled by men, and still more by cattle, over an area sometimes as much as a quarter of a mile wide, that they could easily be followed. In some places where a track rounds the spur of a hill the whole slope may appear on the skyline indented like the teeth of a saw, presumably because the level they moved at varied according to the wet or dry season. Where the ground was soft, and the track led downhill, the soil would gradually be carried away, and a hollow way worn out between ever-higher banks until the underlying rock was reached, and the path would resemble a steep country lane of today. Stretches of many of these trackways lie under our modern roads, and it is a fascinating game to pick them out on the map.

One of the best known is the Berkshire ridgeway which, beginning near Avebury, runs along the edge of the downs, passing by the Uffington White Horse and the remains of a long barrow known as Wayland's Smithy. Eventually it links with another track coming up from Salisbury Plain to cross the Thames at Streatley. Beyond this it climbs the Chilterns, and follows the line of the Chiltern scarp, past Ivinghoe Beacon to Dunstable. There it has less of the character of a true ridgeway, in that it follows a course along the middle of the hillsides. The track crosses the Hiz at Ickleford, a mile and a half north of Hitchin, passes north of Baldock, through Royston, Ickleton, and Newmarket; crosses the Lark at Larkford, and fades out in the neighbourhood of Thetford. Some of it lies under modern motor roads, some under green lanes, some across open downs. Only for short stretches is its course at all doubtful.

This is the famous Icknield Way, so-called at least since the Middle Ages; but its existence as a thoroughfare for many centuries before that is attested by much archaeological evidence. The prehistoric sites it connects, the ancient earthworks built across it, its use from ancient times as a boundary, all tell the same story: it is about three thousand years old. This was the highway used by the flint miners of Norfolk to trade their products with the people of Salisbury Plain; the long barrow men moved eastwards along it. Here came the itinerant bronze founders of a later period; and it was certainly a thoroughfare in Roman times. The Anglo-Saxon invaders filtered into the Thames Valley along it, and in A.D. 871 the great army of the Vikings rode this way from East Anglia to Reading; it is possible that William the Conqueror on his first march northwards after the battle of Hastings may have moved along a part of it.

The Icknield Way was only one among many trackways trodden out by the earliest settlers, some of them covering long distances, others purely local, cattle tracks or paths leading down to the springs from the high ground on which they made their homes. Very slowly the country was being opened up.

About 2000 B.C. the Bronze Age farmers began to arrive, bringing their improved implements and settled habits of life with them. We do not know if they came looking for land or for tin, but they found both. It was these bronze-using people who began to exploit the mineral wealth of the country. Bronze is an alloy of tin and copper, and though the rich veins of copper ore in the Cornish and Devonian hills lay too deep to be reached by prehistoric man, the tin was readily accessible in the stream-beds. They developed a flourishing industry in the south-western peninsula.

They planted their villages high on the bleak wastes of Dartmoor and Cornwall and some of them remain to this day. Only an archaeologist can distinguish between hut and stone shed; the low massive walls of each little building, made of stones, large or small, gathered from the moor around, are almost intact though overgrown with whortleberry and heather; the doorposts still stand, and only the roof of furze thatch, supported on poles, has disappeared.

The Bronze Age peoples seem to have been 'little men', farmers, miners, and traders; they settled wherever the soil was light and clear enough of heavy timber for them to cultivate it with their primitive tools, their bronze axes, their wooden ploughshares. On the whole they preferred the gravelly terraces which break through the stiff clay of the river valleys in places, but their villages were numerous on the very light sandy uplands of East Anglia and Lincolnshire, and wherever they found the minerals they knew how to use. In the lowlands of England, hardly any traces of their settlements remain above ground, because they lived on lands which have mostly been under the plough for centuries, but a village of the Early Bronze Age has been unearthed in the Orkneys. At Skara Brae there were about six stone-built rectangular houses, with some built-in stone furniture, and a communal workshop, huddled together against the weather. The alley running between them was roofed, and there was even quite an efficient system of drainage.

The new settlers seem to have mingled peacefully with the stone-users already inhabiting the country, and they were not entirely submerged when, later, the men of Iron arrived. The Iron Age people who began to move into the south-west about 300–400 B.C. were a vigorous and warlike people akin to the Brigantes who took possession of Northumbria about this time. They built and inhabited the great hill-forts which are especially conspicuous crowning the heights of East Devon and Dorset, and they extended many dating from the Stone Age, notably Maiden Castle in Dorset. They occupied Devon and Cornwall, without stamping out the native population.

Fortunately one of their villages has survived and can be visited. This is Chysauster in Cornwall. It has been very fully excavated, and eight houses can be seen grouped in pairs along the cobbled street. The houses are rectangular in plan, stonebuilt round an unroofed courtyard. There were garden plots behind the houses, and small arable fields. The people were smelters of tin, as well as farmers. Close by is the Iron Age fort called Castle an Dinas, overshadowing the village much as a Norman castle mound sometimes does. Perhaps this was the habitation of the conquerors; the tin industry which continued to flourish after their coming, in Cornwall at least, may have remained in the hands of the indigenous population.

This village is the showpiece among the numerous Iron Age remains in Cornwall, but not far off, at Castallack in the parish of Paul, traces are to be found of a settlement of different type: a circular enclosure with the remains of buildings outside. These circular enclosures, locally called Rounds, are thought to have been the meeting-places, moots, and possibly temples, of Celtic villages. It is probable that the ruins adjoining this one are of the same date. These have traces of gardens and small fields adjoining, but the Round seems to be the focus of a more extensive enclosure, an immense continuous granite-built bank which encloses an area of about sixty acres, now broken up into fifteen small fields. This is almost certainly an ancient cattlefield belonging to the settlement.

The Iron Age men were Celts and with their coming our story really begins. A few of their settlements, certainly, and probably more than can ever be discovered, have been continuously occupied since they made them in pre-Roman times. Caesar tells us that in that part of Britain of which he knew anything, which was also the richest, the inhabitants lived in scattered farmsteads and very small clusters. Where the population was so small how could individual settlements be very big? We have seen that at Chysauster only eight houses, and at Skara Brae only six, have come to light. But it is difficult to imagine that the whole population of these settlements were so well housed. These may well represent the dwellings of the most important villagers. There were certainly some larger settlements. The lake villages of Glastonbury and Meare contained many more inhabitants.

The Celts were energetic and successful farmers. Many square miles of their field banks show up on the chalk downs of the south. They even terraced the steep slopes in many places. These terraces are called lynchets, and many of them will be found marked on the Ordnance Survey Maps. Where they occur in Cornwall, at Chysauster, for instance, the terrace wall is often a field bank faced with granite, made before the field above was levelled by constant ploughing. Perhaps the best examples, however, are to be found on the chalk downs, where they appear very frequently. There are splendid examples at Fore Down near Eastbourne, and at Cessbury, Woolbury, and Lilbury in Sussex, which are undoubtedly pre-Roman. Here the banks are usually faced with flints picked up off the fields; they may be anything up to about thirteen feet high, and seem to have been begun, at any rate, unintentionally, by leaving an unploughed turf balk as a field boundary, against which the downward drift of the loosened soil gradually piled up, and levelled out.

The Celts extended the area of settlement in the river valleys too, mingling more or less peacefully with the previous inhabitants, although inter-tribal warfare must have been a constant menace to well-ordered agricultural life. It was presumably for defensive purposes that the dwellers in the lake villages at Glastonbury and Meare in Somerset chose their remarkable sites. These were boggy islands in the marshes, ground so insecure that a foundation of logs, brushwood, rubble, peat, and clay, had to be laid over the whole area, which was enclosed by a palisade bound together with wattle. The Glastonbury village contained about ninety huts, not all of them dwellings, and some of them in the course of time had as many as nine floors laid one on top of the other, on account of subsidence. The villagers were prosperous, however, and as well provided with comforts as any of their descendants were to be for a thousand years.

In their search for ore the iron workers penetrated the densest forests. They began to work it in the Weald of Kent, in the iron-stone belt of Leicestershire and Northamptonshire, and in the Forest of Dean, and as they hacked down the trees to feed their forges the farmer was ready to raise crops on the land they cleared.

Under Roman rule this process of colonization was, of course, accelerated. The military roads cut through the virgin forests, so that regions hitherto separated by a wall of jungle found themselves in easy communication with each other, and the stimulus of civilized organization quickened the aboriginal tempo of British life. Roads were not the only engineering works undertaken by the Imperial Government. Embankments were made to improve Romney Marsh and dykes were cut in the East Anglian Fens.

In prehistoric times the Fens were not the swampy wilderness they later became. It is thought that towards the end of the Roman period the land level of the whole country sank; and the climate also had changed in the hundred years before Christ, to become the damp and dreary one we know today. So the great rivers which meander across the flat country to drain into the Wash—the Ouse, the Nene, and the Welland, with their tributaries, and the Witham further north—must already have been sources of trouble, as well as convenient highways. Probably the Car Dyke, the most considerable Roman engineering work in the Fens, was made to serve both as canal and drain.

There are plenty of traces of Romano-British fields and drove roads round the Fenland and especially near the Car-, and other very ancient dykes, but very few habitation sites have been found. The most probable explanation of this is that they lie under existing villages. Fowlmere in Cambridgeshire, for instance, is a 'round' village of the Celtic type described in the last chapter and is not likely to have acquired so foreign a character at any time since the Saxon conquest.

On the estates of the villas, which, after roads, are perhaps the best-known manifestations of Roman civilization in this country, the best farming methods of the classical world were introduced. Some of the villas were owned by the state, but more, probably, were in the hands of a prosperous landed gentry. They were all economically self-supporting and grew their own breadcorn, but sheep farming on a commercial scale was carried on where the country was suitable, indeed towards the end of the Roman period some of the villages on the chalk were abandoned, and their fields returned to pasture. This need have been no hardship

LINGNOR, STAFFS. A "green" village. The long narrow fields behind it are probably strips enclosed from former open field (see page 85). The continuous hedge at the bottom of the slope suggests the boundary of a furlong.

DEPARTED GLORY. Hazelbadge Hall, Derbyshire, is now a farmhouse. The fifteenth-century windows and the coat of arms above them reveal its former dignity; extreme left in shadow is a range of farm buildings added to the house.

to the villagers, though it was probably unpopular at the time. The country was still very thinly peopled, and there was plenty of room, and much better farmland, in the valleys than on the downs. It is to this movement that we owe our knowledge of many of the upland settlements. The sheep grazed over them for centuries, without obliterating the dimples in the ground which tell the archaeologist where to look. On ploughland such remains are soon deeply buried, and only chance can bring them to light again. Such a chance occurred at Chew Stoke in Somerset not long ago when a few sites were hurriedly excavated because the valley was about to be flooded to provide a reservoir for Bristol. Besides the foundations of a medieval convent in one field, at a ford over the stream a Romano-British village came to light, and not far off, a farm, which had been first occupied in the Bronze Age, and had blossomed under Roman rule into a small but comfortable country house. This was hastily excavated, the diggers rowing to the site over the rising flood, and only abandoning the work when the water closed over it.

Anyone interested in the history of his neighbourhood should always be on the look-out for opportunities of this sort. When an arterial road is cut, or the municipal authority makes extensive excavations for its own purposes; when the local farmer who occupies an ancient holding, makes a new cowhouse and puts in new drains, some bit of the past may slip out for a moment from under the blanket of the ages only to disappear for good unless there is someone at hand to catch and record it. It was in this unofficial way that the temple of Mithras in London was recently uncovered, but even a single coin or a few broken potsherds can be very revealing. Such finds should be taken to the local museum where they can be dated, and a record of their existence made, even if the finder wishes to keep them.

This excursion into prehistory may seem to be irrelevant to our subject—the visible traces of the past in the villages of today, but it is necessary to show where, if anywhere, the habitations of our so distant forefathers may be found. The kind of country where prehistoric man loved to settle, sometimes called the areas of primary settlement, together with the expansion brought about by Roman civilization, has been described in order to help the reader to overcome the instinctive feeling we have, confronted by something ancient, that it 'just growed', and to stimulate in his mind, when he wanders down the village street, a curiosity about its first beginnings. It didn't just grow, someone chose it. Who was he and why did he come here? It is possible in some cases at least to find a probable answer.

By the time Domesday Book was compiled very nearly all the villages on the map today were in being, and the population is not likely to have been much more than twice as great as it had been in Roman times. It would be natural, therefore, to suppose that at least half those Domesday villages were in existence before the Romans departed, but the immense disolcation of life caused by the Saxon conquest has to be taken into account. Moreover we have seen in the previous chapter how often within the historical period the centre of population of a village may shift.

In considering the beginnings of our village, then, we shall ask first:

Did anyone live here in prehistoric or Roman times?

The first step is to consult the $2\frac{1}{2}$ inch Ordnance Survey Map of the district. This will show the site of any archaeological finds—villas, villages, earthworks, cemeteries, flints, and so on. Then the local museum should be visited—all county towns and many market towns have museums. There, some of these objects will be on view, with details about the finding of them which will be interesting and informative. There may also be new finds not recorded on the current edition of the map. The explorer who is not afraid of a little heavy going can find a good deal more information in the public library. He should go to the Reference section. There he can consult the Victoria County History in which there is usually a descriptive list of sites in the county. Some of these lists were made many years ago and more evidence is always coming to light, so it is worth while to take a look at the contents list of recent volumes of the Transactions of the local Archaeological Society which will probably have something to say about more recent discoveries. The Ordnance Survey Map of Roman Britain published in 1956 will give the general picture. The makers of this map, however, included nothing which could not certainly be dated within the Roman period, and this is a grand defect from our point of view, for it is not doubted that there were many small places, especially in the west and north, where the furniture of Roman civilization—the characteristic pottery, coins, etc.—never penetrated.

Supposing that in these investigations we draw a blank, there remains the possibility that the name of our parish may be of Celtic origin or conceal a Celtic element. These names become more common the further west we go; on the eastern side of the country they are very rare. The answer to the question: *Does the name of this place show any Celtic traces?* must be sought, again, in the library. On no account should the imagination be set to work; the modern form and spelling of place names can be extremely misleading, and any attempt to deduce a meaning from them is bound to be worthless. While a few names do retain their original form, this can never be taken for granted. The very simple-sounding name Churchdown, which belongs to a village over-shadowed by a large round hill on the outskirts of Gloucester, may be taken as an example. It is formed of two elements of which the second, *down* is, in fact, what it seems; it is the Old English *dūn*, meaning 'down' in the sense of hill. But *church* isn't church at all, it is *crūc*, the British word for hill; so the two halves of the name both mean the same thing, and the name as a whole suggests that the *dūn* got tacked on when the British language was dying out and *crūc* was no longer understood as a description of the prominent landmark by the Saxon part of a mixed population. There are a number of similar bilingual names.

This British element *crūc* appears in several place-names with an English translation. There is Croichlow in Lancashire, Crichel in Dorset, and in an Old English charter we have an explanation. A grant is made of land near a hill 'which is called in the British language *Cructan* but by us *Crycbeorh*'. This Somerset village is now called Creech St Michael. Since Somerset was conquered by the Saxons in the seventh century we have written records of several of these name changes. Leigh near Glastonbury was called by the British *Lantokai*, Biddisham near Axbridge was called *Tarnuc*. In Cornwall Kilkhampton had an English suffix tacked on to the Cornish *Kelk*. Another charter calls the Creech St Michael already mentioned *Cyricestun*, so evidently the new names took a little time to settle down, and did not always stick. Bede, who wrote towards the close of the eighth century, often gives the name of a place in the two languages, and sometimes neither can be identified today. In one case, however, we can follow the whole process. He refers to the city called *Legaceaster*, which he says the British called *Caerlegion*. The Romans, who founded it, called it *Deva*, and we call it Chester. In Gloucestershire the Saxons christened the upper reaches of the River Coln Tillath, but it was the Celtic or pre-Celtic name which survived.

Bilingual names strongly suggest that the villages which bear them are of Romano-British origin, if not older, but there is another group of names still more explicit. These are the Waltons. This name has three possible meanings and it is not easy to distinguish which is meant. There is a wall-*tun* on Hadrian's Wall. The name can also mean wold- or wood-*tun* or Welshman's-*tun*, *wealh* being the Saxon name for a Briton. Sometimes the early spelling decides which is meant, sometimes a close study of the terrain is necessary to decide whether either of the other two meanings is more likely to be correct. This same element appears in the Walworths and Walcots, and names of similar kind, and they are found all over the country.

Information about place-names is to be found in the volumes of the *English Place-Name Society*, and every County Reference Library is sure to have its own county volume, if there is one. Where there is none, the *Oxford Dictionary of English Place Names* will provide the answer. The Place-Name Society volumes are fuller, and deal not only with the village itself, but with most of the other names in the parish. The society also publishes two introductory volumes which discuss more fully the common elements of names, such as *tun*, *well*, and *ham*, and this makes fascinating reading. It will be found that natural features have Celtic names more often than villages. Rivers, especially, even on the eastern side of the country, very often have Celtic names. The place-name evidence for the survival of Romano-British settlements is certainly meagre. Over by far the greater part of England the names of villages are of Saxon origin and refer either to natural features, or to a Saxon personal name, or to both, and one might think that the names the Anglo-Saxons gave to their villages would have been the same if they had been moving into an empty land, an uncultivated desert.

It has been argued that this or something like it was just what they did; that continuous raiding by ferocious pirates on the coasts, and later on by marauding warbands of Saxons and Picts inland, had killed or driven off most of the population, and much of the land had returned to waste by the time the Saxons came to settle down on it. Some villages on the downs apparently survived independently for some time, co-existing with a Saxon settlement in the valley, but signs of continuous occupation are rare indeed. If this were a true picture, it would be unnecessary when trying to find out the age of the village to consider anything except the geographical evidence which indicates what land was most suitable for settlement, and most accessible from the sea. But even then we should have to consider the network of roads which covered the country when the Saxons arrived.

This network was formed of two distinct elements. There were the main trunk roads built by the Roman engineers and designed primarily to provide for the rapid movement of troops and government officials from the channel ports to all parts of the country, and to a lesser extent, from one region to another. But these rationalized lines of communication overlay a far older system. The ridgeways, the ancient trackways already mentioned, as well as a complex of short local tracks, accommodation lanes, drift ways, drove roads and the like, evolved through thousands of years by men going about their daily affairs, covered the country, and it was about them that the habitations of the people were mainly clustered. They served the villas as well as the villages. In effect they were the 'B' roads of Roman Britain and were sometimes surfaced accordingly.

Is the village served by one of these roads?

The villages which lie on either side of an ancient track or Roman road are likely to be earlier settlements than those which lie directly on its path, for the roadside settlements were unsafe places to live in during the Dark Ages, and they were nearly all abandoned. When times improved the inhabitants of villages hidden down side lanes sometimes moved on to the road in the interests of trade and often fresh settlements sprang up (Fig. 5). Villages which are apparently unconnected with any ancient line of communication, road or river, often represent later conquests from forest or heath.

A Roman road will nearly always be so described on the map; straight stretches of road not so marked are probably the work of eighteenth-century planners. The principal features of a prehistoric ridgeway have already been briefly described. The existence of such a track may be surmised when a road is seen to keep to the high ground above the spring line for several miles. It is a through road, and often a lonely one because the places it was meant to connect have vanished, and throughout its course it will very frequently constitute the parish boundary of numerous villages lying below it, each with its own lane leading down from the ancient highway. The road was there first and formed a natural and easily recognizable frontier when the territory of the village was marked out. Of the numerous examples that could be quoted I will mention only one. The parish of Bygrave in Hertfordshire is bounded on the north by the Icknield Way, on the east by a green lane, possibly a boundary ditch, and on the south-east by a stream. At the eastern end the boundary comes to a point on another stream. A Roman road crosses the parish at this corner, and since it would form as natural a frontier on this side as the Icknield Way does on the north it is conceivable that the territory of the village was already defined before the Roman road was built.

Having considered the possibility of a Roman-British or prehistoric origin for some of our villages, it is necessary to say that the continued existence of these native communities, even in complete subjection to the Anglo-Saxon conquerors, has been much disputed. In the past it has been generally held that in the Midlands and the south-eastern areas of England very few of the Celtic people remained, and those uprooted and dispossessed, 'displaced persons' to use a familiar phrase; and that over most of the country the Saxon triumph was so complete, the flood of immigrants so overwhelming, that the land may be said to have been resettled, and the pattern of Roman Britain wiped out. Where evidence of some survival of Celtic life has come to light, historians have been most hesitant to take it at its face value, and have sought alternative explanations.

No one, however, can pretend to know exactly what happened in so dark and undocumented a period, and now these views are being challenged. In spite of the great lack of archaeological and philological evidence for Celtic survival, the improbability of the extinction of Romano-British settlements is very considerable, when the conditions of the conquest are considered. If the Saxons replaced and expanded a settlement which had taken two thousand years to make, if they built up a civilization from scratch, so that within three hundred years it was strong enough and wealthy enough to withstand the continuous Viking assaults which were as fierce as, and far better organized than, their own had been, it was a formidable achievement indeed. Did the Saxon warrior, in the intervals of campaigning, or when he got stiff in the joints, apoplectic with heavy drinking, or crippled with wounds, beat his sword into a ploughshare, and apply himself to the heaviest work that a man can do? On the face of it, it is more likely that when he had defeated a local British magnate in battle, or caught him unprepared, he would parcel out the enemy's lands and people among his followers, and take over a going concern; sometimes a village in full working order, sometimes one which had been burnt and from which the inhabitants had fled, leaving the corn standing. Others again may have been deserted for several years and their fields almost obliterated by thistles and brambles. Where the villagers remained behind, would their condition be so very different from what it had been before? True, they had now an alien lord, but the fact that he was on the winning side may have made it easier to get on with the business of extracting a living from the soil.

Once the possibility of continuity is admitted a most interesting field of investigation opens up, to which the amateur determined to find out just what happened in his own village can make a real contribution.

Many of my readers will have visited the Roman Villa at Chedworth in the Cotswolds. Here there is no sign that the Saxons took over. The modern village is a mile and a half away in another valley. The villa was abandoned, and in the course of time the ruins of the house were completely buried under several feet of woodland soil. They were discovered by a shooting-party whose terrier, digging for a ferret, scratched up some fragments of a tessellated pavement. We can guess where the fields were, because all round behind the house rise steep hills and in front lies the narrow valley of the Coln, with land suitable for tillage; and we can guess that the house was approached by a road leading down from the ancient track which runs along the ridge above. It is a typical example of what used to be regarded as the almost universal fate of Roman settlements. But if on leaving Chedworth we take the valley road leading north we soon come to Withington, and here a very different picture presents itself. There was a villa here too. It was served by a road leading from the same ancient track which continued in use into historic times, and can easily be followed on the ridge above the village; and again it is possible to make a safe guess about the fields of the villa. To the north of the site the Coln valley broadens a little, and here, on level ground, lay the largest of the medieval fields of the village, called Northfield; here, too, says the modern farmer, lies the best land in the parish, the only land that really invites tillage. The presence of the villa at the southern end of the area, and of Bronze Age and early Saxon remains in a hamlet at the northern end makes it relatively certain that here too lay the Roman fields. But between the Northfield (divided since 1819 into the usual modern chequerboard), and the villa site, not a quarter of a mile from the latter, lies the village; a village already large enough only about a hundred years after the Saxon conquest to support a small monastic community. Was this a new Saxon settlement on derelict land, or did they take over the village with its British peasants, who until the conquest had cultivated the land for the Romano-British owner? The case of Withington has been studied in detail, and with the aid of documentary evidence a very strong case for continuity has been established. Here we are only concerned with the fieldwork, with the kind of evidence the land itself may supply if asked the right questions; questions which must be asked if the true origins of our villages are to be uncovered.

Sometimes the point of departure will be a place-name. All over Devon there are places, usually farms or small hamlets, with names like Yelland, or Yoldeland. What do they mean? Here, as in Somerset, we have written records to help us. An ancient document refers to a certain estate as 'Hyple's Old Land', and this can be identified with a farm now called Treable. This is a purely Celtic name compounded of *trev*, a homestead, and *Ebell*, a personal name. Old land here, and probably, therefore, in other places, meant land which had formerly belonged to a Briton. A study of this particular estate and its boundaries shows that the owner was left in undisturbed possession long after the Saxons had conquered Devonshire. Either he, or another of his race and name, may have given his name to Ipplepen in the same county. Here the fieldwork consisted of tramping the boundaries described in a charter of 976, and comparing them with those of an earlier one dated 789. Let me quote some of the boundary marks in the two charters which it is possible to identify on the ground today. 'From the Greenway to the Wolf pit,' 'from the landslip to Greendown,' 'from Green Down on the highway to Putta's post,' 'the head of Hurra's comb,' 'south to the old ditch and along the ditch to Ecca's stump.' Place-names, the lie of the land, and coincidence with a modern boundary make identification possible. The Greenway is a road now called Crediton Lane, the Wolf pit and the landslip are recognizable, Putta is commemorated at Puddicombe, Hurra at Hollycombe, called Horracombe in early maps, Ecca at Eggbear. The old ditch is still there for anyone who likes rough walking to see; the highway is the modern A.30. The boundary points are differently described in the two charters but on the ground they are found to coincide, apart from minor variations, with each other and with the parish boundary. The greater part of the parish of Cheriton Bishop represents the estate of Hyple the Briton, on whose land a coin of Hadrian's reign has been found. The village and church are not on the site of Hyple's home farm, but then there is no real village, only small scattered groups of houses, and so it may well have been in Hyple's day.

The impact of the coming of the Saxons was differently felt in north and south, east and west, but over much of Britain a considerable part of the native population may well have survived in the native villages.

The Saxons first came here as raiders. As far back as the third century the Romans had been forced to constitute a military command to deal with them, and to set up a system of fortifications from the Humber to Southampton. Later they had to devise another system of combined operations to protect the western seaboard from the Irish; and Hadrian's wall more or less successfully contained the Picts. But the enemy was always at the gates and whenever the defence was weak he broke in in search of plunder. To pirates Britain was an attractive proposition. They could land anywhere, and move quickly about on the well-kept roads before beating a quick retreat. So long as the army was there to frighten them off, they were a nuisance rather than a serious menace, but with the weakening of the garrisons, and the final removal of the Roman army, they grew bolder and ranged at will over the country. No wonder that the luxurious but undefended country houses, the villas, easily accessible from the main roads, became unsafe to live in, and their civilized but unwarlike owners removed themselves to the towns.

With the tillers of the soil it was different. The absentee owner would still expect the revenue of his estates. The villager had no other resources, and if one year the crops were burnt and some of the animals driven off, he had no choice but to hope that next season he would be luckier. He and his like would develop, too, a technique for dealing with the emergency. In the fifth century the woods were never far off, and man and beast could take refuge in them. To the natives even the most unreclaimed forest must have been familiar ground, visited for hunting, for fuel, and for its harvest of wild honey, but in the Saxons the forest inspired a superstitious awe, and was, moreover, unlikely to yield much spoil; there was also the danger of an ambush. In short the raiders would keep mostly to the roads, or at least to the open country, although they often slipped into the country up the rivers, and it was by the rivers that they finally chose to settle. No doubt they often killed and burned, but when they had passed, the survivors could creep out of the woods and pick up the threads of normal life again. Gutted huts could easily be re-thatched, and if only a smaller area of the fields could now be cultivated there were also fewer mouths to feed. When anyone came to collect rent or taxes, the recent calamity would be a very good reason why little should be forthcoming. Under such conditions the man who grows the food is in a strong position. We know that the villas were abandoned; we do not know, and it does not seem very likely, that the same fate overtook the Romano-British villages.

Life became poor and precarious, all the materials of civilization gradually fell away, the comfort and the ornament, but institutions cannot be carried off, only undermined, and that is a slow process. The Britons long retained the consciousness that they were Roman citizens, and while the older generation of the governing classes died out, migrated westwards, or even left the country in search of the old stable and prosperous conditions, their sons and grandsons, who had never known the comfort and security of effective Roman rule, set themselves to defend their proud heritage of Christianity and civilization. It was probably this, almost as much as local patriotism, which inspired them at first. For about a hundred years the issue hung in the balance.

Their forefathers had been efficient warriors, and during the Roman period the country had produced more than its share of military leaders with enough force of character to get themselves elected as usurping emperors, but since the army had gone each tribal capital was left to rely on the local militia, and though there must have been many men with military experience in the country, these would be mostly retired army officers and soldiers, used to the routine of well-organized army life, and not necessarily suited, even if they were not too old, to be leaders in the kind of guerilla warfare which had now to be undertaken. It must have been a heartbreaking business, endeavouring to control marauding barbarians, who were not interested in pitched battles, who would dissolve when one came up with them, only to reappear a little later, cohesive and ferocious as ever, further up the road. Even a well-armed and stout-hearted local force would find it impossible to come to grips with them. What was wanted was a mobile field army able to seek out and strike quickly, to pursue and mop up the enemy as they scattered. There may have been such a force operating from Richborough early in the fifth century, but if so it was soon withdrawn, and in 446 the Britons made their last vain appeal for help to Rome. This request has been regarded as a sign of weakness and lack of ability and initiative in their own defence, but it was an obvious and practical step. They were a Roman province, they had paid their taxes, and were entitled to the protection of the Imperial army.

The political outlook was certainly black, but organized life could still be carried on. When St Germanus visited Britain in 429 at the request of the British church, he seems to have moved about among people living normal lives in town and country. He preaches and baptizes, and stays with the local magistrate at Verulam. In one district there are raiders about. St Germanus had begun life as a soldier, and he assisted the Britons not only with his prayers, but by organizing and leading an ambush which surprised and routed the enemy. He came again ten years later, and on that occasion his visit was entirely untroubled by the barbarians.

But if the magistrates still presided in the tribal capitals and the harvests were still gathered in the fields, the character of life was rapidly changing. Most of the inhabited regions of the country were still divided from each other by natural barriers of mountain and forest. These had been cut through by the Roman military roads, but even in the age of peace and prosperity, a road book now called the *Antonine Itinerary* had recommended more devious routes avoiding some of the most inhospitable tracts of country pierced by a direct road. By now the countryside must have been infested with bandits of every sort and travelling dangerous. Communications between the regions was becoming difficult and intermittent. In the isolated self-governing units the successful leader of a local force would soon become the most important person in the district, in short, a dictator. A man of high character, sprung of a thoroughly Romanized stock, might scruple to call himself king, but in the west and north the local rulers had no such inhibitions. The petty ruler of a Welsh tribe would see in the collapsing state of Britain the opportunity to extend and increase his power, and the obstacles in his path would be his neighbours as much as the common enemy.

Such a one was Vortigern. We know little enough about him, but we know this. He was a Welsh prince who had obtained some sort of precarious authority over a part of southern England, and it was to protect himself against the hostility of a rival as well as from the intrusions of the Picts, that he invited a band of Saxons, led, according to tradition, by Hengist and Horsa, to settle in Thanet as his mercenaries. His fellow countryman, Gildas the monk, writing of these events a hundred years later, describes this as an act of horrible treachery, but whether Vortigern was showing the imprudence and treachery so common and fatal in Celtic princes, or whether he was following the Roman custom of settling barbarians in frontier districts with the obligation of defending them—we cannot now tell.

44

The date of this event is still disputed by the experts, but tradition describes it as 'the coming of the Saxons'. Three boats, capable of carrying about forty or fifty warriors each, were enough to bring in this historic army, and this was the normal size for a band of this sort, but reinforcements followed. The way now lay open, and summer by summer the settlers came in whose coming is recorded, not in ancient documents, but on the face of the landscape.

At first, however, Vortigern's policy was a success. For a few years the Saxons did all that was required of them, and something like peace and prosperity began to return. The raids of the Picts, to whom Christianity was now bringing news of an immortal destiny, and a more civilized way of life, were in any case becoming less frequent and far-reaching. Then Hengist and his men fell out with their employers and savagely revenged themselves. After defeating the Britons in several battles and driving their army out of Kent, they ranged over the country ravaging and burning wherever they went. The army had fled towards London, but the way along the North Downs was open, for the ancient Harrow way led straight into Salisbury Plain, whence roads and trackways branched in every direction. This central core of southern England became the battleground where Briton and Saxon strove for mastery and this region probably suffered the worst devastation. Local rulers lucky enough to be out of the main stream fortified themselves against both the contending parties. There are quite a large number of dykes and fortifications remaining from this period, in the Pennines, for instance, and there are earthworks apparently barring the passage of the Icknield Way in East Anglia. Many of the Saxons who were moving into the Thames Valley used this highway, and the people who lived in the deep forest fastnesses of the Chilterns threw up ramparts along its course to defend themselves, and seem to have remained unconquered long after the surrounding country had acknowledged Saxon lordship.

It is easy to understand why no trace should remain above ground of many of the settlements which are known to have existed along the main roads in Roman times. Who would want to live on a road down which might come Aelle, with his three sons and their followers; the people who crowned their conquest of Sussex by storming the fortress of Anderida and killing every man, woman and child in it? The Saxon settlers called the Roman roads 'army paths' and they and the British villagers were equally careful to live as much out of sight of them as possible. To the tillers of the soil, Saxon immigrant or native British, it must have mattered little whether the passing army was led by Hengist or Vortigern or even Arthur; all spelt ruin to him. At best his stores would be ransacked, his beasts driven off. Similarly on the coast, men turned their backs on the sea, and built their villages up inland valleys hidden from the eye of cruising pirates.

It is not easy to draw the picture of a movement which has left no written record at all. The evidence we have is so scanty and difficult to interpret that the experts refuse to commit themselves to more than a few, a very few, tentative conclusions. It is rather like one of those children's puzzles which consist of numbered dots on a sheet of paper. You follow the numbers round with a pencil, and an elephant, or a fish, or a funny man emerges. The experts have put in the dots, and numbered a good many of them, but they warn you that if you attempt to draw the picture, the result is sure to be wrong. And yet it is a fascinating theme and fundamental to our story.

In this chapter we are exploring the parish, the territory of the village, in order to find a clue to its origins. We are asking Why and When and Who? Out of the villages which may be presumed to have acquired their modern names within a hundred years or so of the Saxon Conquest it will very seldom be possible to say in a given case 'here the Saxons massacred the inhabitants and took over their fields and herds', or 'here they simply made the natives their slaves', or 'here they destroyed everything and moved on', and 'this and this remain to prove it', but about their doings after their arrival it is possible to be a little more definite. Archaeologists can tell us something, place-names perhaps rather more. We know for example that the suffix *inga* was added to the name of the founder of a family or tribe to denote its members— for example the Kentish royal house was called the *Oiscingas* from Oisc, son of Hengist, the founder of the line. These tribal and family names were often applied to the district they controlled in Germany, whence the Saxons ultimately came. That it was so in England is proved by numerous names of this type, such as

46

Hastings, Lancing, Patching in Sussex, Sonning in Berkshire, Epping and Roding in Essex, Spalding, Billing, Peatling in the Midlands. The suffix was sometimes also attached to the name of some natural feature to denote the people living about it. This type of name however would not serve as each group established more settlements, so it is safe to infer that they represent the earliest Saxon villages.

Places which are called after some heathen god or temple are at least certain to have been in existence before the inhabitants became Christian and may therefore be mentioned as possible indications of very early settlement. Such are Wednesbury, Wednesfield, after *Woden*, Thundersfield, Thundersley, after *Thunor*, Tuesley and Tysoe after *Tig*, Harrow from *hearg*, the Saxon word for a heathen temple. But names of this sort do not necessarily show that the villages so-called were new Saxon creations, and not places taken over from the native inhabitants. On the contrary, the districts where they are most numerous are generally those which we know to have been thickly inhabited in the previous centuries. Names of this type are mainly confined, as might be expected, to the lowland zone of Britain, and are thickest round the south-eastern shores and up the slow rivers which penetrate the heart of midland England.

The settlement of Kent, Sussex, Surrey, and Hampshire was the direct result of Vortigern's policy. The people who pushed up the rivers from the Wash into East Anglia and the south midlands, or outwards from the Humber basin into the midlands and the north, were of a different race, and came uninvited, profiting by the undefended coastline, and apparently also by the indifference of the local population where Vortigern and his like were not in control. On the east coast a steady trickle of immigrants began to flow in, perhaps as soon as the Roman garrisons had left.

The Conquest of Britain was a long and piecemeal business, however, very different from the well-planned and overwhelming military operation which brought the Romans here. It was not to be complete for another two hundred years, even in England. After their first successes the Saxon advance was halted. This must have occurred about A.D. 500, and for the next fifty years they had to content themselves with the territory already acquired. They were forced to begin a far harder and longer cam-

47

paign than any they ever fought against the Britons: the conquest of Nature.

Their earliest homes had been easily won. They had settled on land by nature easy to cultivate, and already tamed by man. Now their vigorously expanding population needed more and more land for the plough. Some of the more restless spirits among them went oversea and founded new settlements on easier terms in the Rhineland. The majority that remained entered upon an inheritance of dense forest and waterlogged heath, and for centuries the labour continued with axe and spade, felling, trenching, burning, the threat of starvation never far removed, till they had changed the wilderness into rich and fruitful fields.

Thus it was that by 577, when the men of Wessex made a decisive enlargement of their territory in the west, the process of taking over and assimilating the native settlements was over and the pioneer work already begun.

BOOKS TO READ

The Personality of Britain. C. Fox, 1943.

Roman Britain and the English Settlements. Collingwood and Myres, Oxford. 1937.

History of the Anglo-Saxons. R. H. Hodgkin, 1945.

The Beginnings of English Society. D. Whitelock. Penguin Books Ltd., 1952.

Roman and Saxon Withington. H. P. R. Finberg. Occasional Paper No. 8. Leicester University Press, 1955.

IV

A Goodly Heritage

GEOGRAPHERS tell us that before men came here nearly the whole country was covered with forest; that for early man it was hardly a question of seeking open country on which to settle but of choosing a part of the forest where the trees and undergrowth were less dense or gave way to scrub and could more easily be cleared. For many centuries the population was so small that there was enough of this type of land for everybody, and though the search for minerals might provide an incentive for exploring and settling more inhospitable country, and the change of climate which occurred round about the beginning of our era might make the exposed uplands less attractive, even in the most favoured regions there remained unreclaimed waste round every settlement into which the population could expand. For a long time after the Saxon Conquest there remained great tracts of country, the plains of Lancashire and Cheshire, and North Warwickshire, the Trent basin, the weald of Kent and Sussex, besides the high moorlands, where man had hardly set foot and certainly never lingered. The appearance of the countryside today is no sure guide to its original condition. Some counties, such as Kent and Essex which once had great forests, are still rich in timber, whereas in the midland shires woods and trees are scarce. The Ordnance Survey map is much more helpful, and provides two kinds of evidence: the size and shape of the parish often tells us something about the nature of the country, and the local names frequently tell us this and much more besides. The parish boundaries themselves have a meaning too, which can only be fully appreciated by someone who has fully explored them and knows the kind of country they run through.

In this chapter, then, we shall deal with the questions:

What do the village names tell us of the country?
What do they tell us of the people?
What is the shape and size of the parish, and the position of the village in it?

What do the village names tell us of the country?

There is a whole class of descriptive names which can make the primitive landscape of forest, heath, and fen grow again in our imagination, and another complementary group which shows man at work upon it. Such names as Acton (the place by the oaks), Oakenshaw, Elmstead, Elmham, Aldershot, Mapledurham, Willey and Willoughby recall the forest of oak, elm, and alder, maple, and willow on the low ground; Ashton, Berkhamstead, Birkenshaw, Birkin, Buckholt, Buckhurst, Bockhampton, the woods of ash and birch and beech which grew on the hills where the underlying rock was capped with clay; eagle and raven hover above, (Yarcombe, Cranage, Creacombe, Crasters), deer, fox, and badger roam the undergrowth (Hindlip, Rogate, Foxcote, Fewston, Brockholds) and in the deepest thickets lurk the bear, the boar, and the wolf (Borley, Boarham, Ulpha, Woolpit, Woolley); besides all those which mention trees or forest beasts, are the names containing elements which mean a wood or woodland clearing. These are *ley, leigh, holt, shaw, hanger, thwaite, green,* and *hay.* There is plenty of evidence too for marsh and heath. *Fen, ful- Venn moor more* all mean water-logged ground, and the bird-names such as Cranleigh, Crakemarsh, Heronswood, Bitterne, and Gosford recall the natural population of these wastes. Perhaps most common of all are the *-ey* names such as Witney, Athelney, Sibsey, Eyton Osey, Sandy, Iford, Eyam, Mersea; many of which we should never suppose to have been islands, surrounded by bog if not by water, if the name did not tell us so. Heathfield, Chatfield, Bromfield, Bremilham, Branshot, tell of land cleared of broom, furze, and bramble.

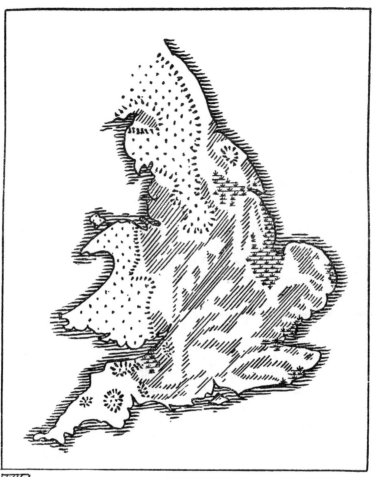

▨ Areas naturally densely forested.

▦ Fen and marsh.

▧ Mountainous wastes.

FIG. 8. What the settlers had to contend with: the principal areas of forest, marsh and moorland.

From the hilltops the landscape of England remained for centuries an ocean of green forest with islands of cultivation in it (Fig. 8). Into these islands the settlers crowded, as can be seen from the small size of parishes generally in the favoured regions. For example in the river valleys with their gravelly floors, and the thin, sandy uplands of East Anglia, areas which were equally popular in the Bronze Age and with the earliest Anglian settlers, the parishes are very small and some of them were once even smaller. Only when the easy land was fully occupied did men push out into more difficult country. Between the closely-settled river valleys of Essex are the large parishes (Finchingfield is one of them) which, with their numerous scattered hamlets, are characteristic of land reclaimed from forest everywhere.

The progress of this colonization was slow and intermittent. It continued until the Black Death in 1349 put an end to the need for constant expansion. It is often reflected in groups or pairs of villages with the same name. Pairs of villages are too common to require illustration, but take a look at the shape of some of their parishes. The villages are often close together right on one side of each parish, clear evidence, if any beyond their names were needed, that they were two branches from one stock. The original territory has been divided to support the second community which sprang from the first. Groups of villages usually follow a river valley from which they take their common name, e.g. Margaret Roding, Abbas Roding, Leadon Roding, White Roding, High Roding, Beauchamp Roding, Bespers Roding in Essex; Tarrant Crawford, Tarrant Gunville, Tarrant Hinton, Tarrant Keynston, Tarrant Monkton, Tarrant Rawston, Tarrant Rushton, Tarrant Neville in Dorset. Most of the distinguishing names were evidently given after the Norman Conquest; indeed, of the Rodings, only two are mentioned in Domesday Book so that the set may be said to show clearly how gradual was the colonization of the whole valley.

The forests were slowly reduced. In the eighth century, when the King of Mercia built his great frontier, still known today as Offa's Dyke, stretching from the Dee to the Severn estuary, there were districts where no demarcation line was needed because the forest was so dense that not even marauding Welshmen might be expected to penetrate it. A century later the great tract of wood-

land which occupied the weald of Kent was still 120 miles long
and 30 miles broad; its colonization is recorded in such names as
Seven*oaks*, Mid*hurst*, Cran*leigh*, Uck*field*, and Craw*ley*. In the Midlands *Oak*ham, Ruge*ly*, *Ash*by-de-la-Zouche, Fothering*hay*, tell
of the reduction of the great forests which clothed the midland
clays. Even in 1066 much still remained to be done. The Chiltern
forests were only just beginning to be cleared. The villagers of
Flamstead and Aldenham held their land not for a rent but by the
service of protecting travellers on Watling Street through the
dense woods in the neighbourhood. Abbot Leofsin, one of the
last English abbots of St. Albans, cleared much woodland, and
the villages of Abbots Langley, Cashio, Bushey, and Rickmans-
worth were founded about his time. Barnet and Sarrat came into
being after the Conquest. The clearance at Barnet was probably
effected by wholesale burning; there are other names, Brent and
Brentwood in Middlesex, Swithland (a name of Scandinavian
origin: a grove cleared by burning) in Leicestershire, which carry
the same suggestion. The work in Hertfordshire was still not
complete. As late as the thirteenth century the abbots of West-
minster divided their vast manors of Wheathamstead and Hatfield
into holdings of 120 acres, of which settlement traces can be seen
in the numerous small hamlets and the large parishes in the neighbourhood of these two places. Clearance was still going on in
the midland forests. Woodhouse Eaves in Leicestershire began
about this time, and indeed the thirteenth century saw the creation
of many small new settlements on the edge of wood and waste,
some of which were destined for a brief existence, while others
still flourish today.

The work of reclaiming fen and marshland could not be effected,
as was the clearance of the forest, by the individual exertions of
single families or very small groups of people. The making of
embankments to keep out the tides or river flood-waters could
only be undertaken if a fairly large body of men were available for
the work. The fens therefore present a picture, first of co-operative
enterprise of which the great churches of the region are the most
obvious record, and then of the beneficent exploits of dawning
capitalism which produced the landscape we see there today.

From the earliest times islands of higher ground rising above
the level of the surrounding bog in the great marshlands had

Fig. 9. Village Churches of the Fenland.

attracted settlers, for the soil on this higher ground was fertile, and the summer pastures which the marshes provided were greatly valued. The shape of parishes round the edge of the fens clearly indicates the importance attached to the grazing grounds. Along the slopes of Lincoln Edge, the ridge of oolitic limestone which crosses the north-east of the county, each parish contains its share of fen and downland so that some of them are as much as ten miles long and barely a mile in width. The same feature can be seen on the Essex, Suffolk, and Cambridgeshire borderland, and north of Cambridge there is a place where several parishes meet to share a small patch of fenland.

At first only such parts of the marsh as were naturally dry enough were used, but after a time an effort would be made to enlarge the grazing grounds by making a dyke to keep out the high tides. Then, as silt washed up by the sea made new pastures beyond the dyke, the herdsmen and dairymaids would camp out during the summer months in huts and cabins put up on the dry ground of the dyke itself. In time these temporary abodes became permanent settlements and they, in their turn, built new dykes and drains further out in the marsh, but such names as North Cotes, Summercotes, and Marsh Chapel show that they began in this way; as the names Catfoss, Fangfoss, and Wilberfoss in the Humber basin show that, though the villages which bear them are older than Domesday Book, the drain on which they stand, and to which '*foss*' refers, is older still.

The men of the Holland villages were combining together to make dykes and drains for the purpose of creating new pastures as far back as the twelfth century and probably earlier. The splendid churches which stand up so nobly amid the flat black fields of the fenland were built out of the wealth these marshes provided, the pastures and to a less extent the fisheries, long before the seventeenth-century engineers began the work of draining them on scientific lines which endowed the people of the fens with an even better heritage—the richest arable land in England. Even in this artificial landscape, where everything except the sky is the work of man, some traces of the aboriginal countryside may be found. Bicker, the *village by the shore*, now far inland, marks the head of a creek which was once wide enough to constitute a kind of frontier; places lying south of it have mainly Danish names, while those on the north seem to have remained in English hands; the Isle of Ely, the Isle of Axholme, and the Isle of Thorney were all in truth islands once.

On the Somersetshire levels the original character of the countryside has been less completely altered than in East Anglia. Much of the land is still given up to rough pasture and osier beds. We seem hardly to need such names as Sedgemoor, Athelney, Muchelney, and Meare to tell us what it was once like. The drains in this neighbourhood are called rhines, and as some of them are named after St. Dunstan they have probably been in existence since the tenth century. The monks of Glastonbury had already begun work on the marshes before this and they became experts in land drainage.

The foregoing pages show, I hope, how often a village name will reveal what the founders had to contend with, so that name and situation combined will give us a fairly clear indication of the period and conditions in which it began. Quite as often, however, the name has nothing to say about the physical aspect of the place, but tells us who the early inhabitants were, and this too will sometimes enable us to place it chronologically.

What, then, have the place names to tell us of the people?

We have seen how such a village name as Churchdown may call up a picture of bilingual England, a country where two peoples are settling down uneasily together, one race having gained the political mastery without as yet obliterating the language and culture of the conquered; how the name Rudstone, given by a Saxon-speaking people, reflects the coming of Celtic Christianity in the fifth century to a Yorkshire village built on the site of a still more ancient shrine; while another group of names provides some of the best evidence we have for Saxon infiltration.

Unfortunately village names are not all equally informative. There is a very large body of names (everyone will be able to call numerous examples to mind) ending in *ton* or *ham*, names such as Gillingham or Walsingham, Withington, Kensington, and Trumpington, which tell us only that at an early period in their history they were known as the homestead or village of such a one, and we do not know whether this individual was the founder or even if he was resident. Alwington in North Devon, for instance, was the *tun* of Aelfwynn, wife of a tenth-century nobleman, and she certainly did not live in the village, she gave it away. It is very seldom possible, as it is in this case, to identify the eponymous personage, but we might perhaps infer from names of this type that the villages were not inhabited by communities of free peasants, as has sometimes been declared, but by tenants or followers more or less closely bound to their landlord. *Ham* names are thought to be generally older than those with the *ton* element because examples are known of *ton* names given as late as the eleventh century. In by far the majority of cases the personal element in a village name will be a Saxon one, but where this is not so it is all the more interesting. Normanton, for instance, indicates a settlement of Northmen (from Norway) in the east midlands right outside the area where they mostly settled. The disposition of Scandinavian names gives us far more evidence about the Viking settlements than we could get from the written records of the period, which have much to say of Danish depredations and exactions, but very little of their settlements. The Anglo-Saxon Chronicle records briefly that in 876 Healfdene shared out Northumbria among his followers 'and they began to plough it', and later entries mention the parcelling out of Mercia and East Anglia. It is by studying the names of villages that we can fill out the picture. Scandinavian *by* and *thorpe*, *thwaite* and *booth* correspond to English *ton* and *cot* and *leigh*. Scandinavian personal names are numerous; Grimsby, Thuresby, Algarkirk, and there are names which contain elements from both English and Scandinavian, and English names whose pronunciation and spelling have been modified by Norse or Danish influence—*bridge* or *ridge* become *brigg* and *rigg*, *church* becomes *Kirk*, e.g. Kirkstead, and so on. It is mainly by the study of place-names that historians have learnt that while the Danes sailed across the North Sea and settled thickly on the eastern seaboard, the Norsemen went round the North Cape and descended upon the west coast of Scotland and upon Cumberland and Westmorland, Lancashire, and Cheshire.

Another group of names tells us of the occupations of the early inhabitants. The settlers at Herdwick, Butterwick, and Chiswick were dairy farmers, the *stocks* and the *stokes* began as dairy farms in the summer pasture of their parent settlements, e.g. Chard and Chardstock, Basing and Basingstoke. Shapwick and Shipton are names found in parts of the country where sheep rearing was once the most profitable, or the only possible, form of husbandry. Barton and Berewick, Rayhall and Wheatley originally meant corn farms. (The names Barton and Berewick, however, had a complicated history and came to mean sometimes an outlying portion of an estate, and in Devon, the home farm of the manor.) Many of the *wich* names, Nantwich, Droitwich, and Sandwich, are associated with the production of salt. The name Newton is self-explanatory, but others seem specially designed to confuse. Newport and Littleport in Cambridgeshire, Lamport in Somerset, are not near any navigable water. In fact *port* is the Saxon word for a town and was often given to roadside markets; what we call a port was a *wic*, e.g. Norwich, Ipswich, or a *hythe*, e.g. Greenhythe, Rotherhythe, Hythe (on Southampton Water).

A third group of names enshrines the patron saint, e.g. Martins-thorpe in Rutland. The element *stow* and in the west *lan* often indicates a name of this type, e.g. Felixstowe, Bridstow, Edwinstow, Stow on the Wold (formerly Edwardstow). *Stow* names are common in the south-west, frequently associated with the name of a Celtic saint, who is usually supposed to have founded the church there. Occasionally there is some foundation for this belief, but in general it would be as reasonable to suppose that St. Bernadette of Lourdes had visited all the churches dedicated to her; in the distant past, as now, people cherished special devotions to particular saints, and monastic houses spread the cult of their patrons by founding churches in their honour.

The social status of the inhabitants is indicated in such names as Didcot, Charlton, Knighton, Bowrish, and Galmton, where cottars, ceorls, cnihts, geburs, and tenants paying a rent called *gafol* are commemorated.

The significance and interest of place-names can hardly be exaggerated. Although the *Oxford Dictionary of English Place Names* provides a valuable key to the subject, the work, compiled by a foreign scholar necessarily without local knowledge in most cases, is not always accurate. The volumes of the Place-Name Society with their longer lists carry the subject a good deal further, but there is still room for the man on the spot to explore and record. Field names, too, though often without interest, sometimes record vanished features which once had importance in the life of the village: Forges field, for instance, where the gallows (*furcas*) stood. The name may recall a vanished farm, sometimes the home of a family of more than local interest. There is a field in North Devon called Galsworthy, which is all that remains of the place where the author's family first flourished. Readers of the Forsyte Saga will remember the use Galsworthy makes of this in one of the closing scenes of *Swan Song*. The name may record the site of a lost village, or make possible the definition of a boundary. There was a point in the Anglo-Saxon boundary of a North Devon village which could not be identified until the oldest inhabitant remembered that a certain field had once borne the name Trendley, recognizably the 'Trendlebury' of the ancient document.

The mention of a boundary brings us naturally to our third group of questions.

What is the size and shape of the parish, what is the position of the village, and how does the boundary run?

We may begin by drawing together the facts which have already emerged about the size and shape of parishes.

The regions most favoured by the early Anglo-Saxon settlers and their predecessors are still marked out by the dense clusters of small parishes in them. These coincide with light, easily worked soils.

The large parish is characteristic of difficult country—heavily wooded, marshy, or mountainous—brought into cultivation relatively late in our history. Moorland parishes remain very large to this day unless the discovery of mineral wealth—coal, iron, tin, or china clay—has brought an increase of prosperity and population, and caused them to be divided. In the lowlands, where dense woodland was the obstacle to settlement, the value of the underlying soil was more variable, and consequently the density of the parishes varies too, and the contrast between the largest and the smallest is much less extreme.

The position of the village is important. If it is in the middle of the parish the parish is likely to be older than others, perhaps grouped round about, where the village is near one boundary or even in a corner. These are probably younger settlements colonized from the centre, their territories carved out of the fringes of the original estate with additions from the waste beyond.

It must be explained that the parishes, now civil units, but originally purely ecclesiastical, are of much more recent origin than most of the villages. Their boundaries, however, normally coincided with those of existing estates. (The case of Cheriton Bishop in Devon which has virtually the same boundaries as a Romano-British estate has already been mentioned.) The pattern first laid down has of course been modified, mainly by subdivision, but a great deal of it survives, and over the greater part of rural England the parish boundaries of today are things of immemorial antiquity. As such they deserve to be studied in detail; how they run, what landmarks they make use of; what considerations influenced the people who drew them.

These lines which seem at first to cover the map with a meaningless network prove on closer inspection to be full of significance. Perhaps the boundary follows a river, and we find that it runs not up the middle of the stream but up one bank. This probably means that the people on the other bank were there first and established control over the fishing. Further up it may leave the river to strike across country, not by some broad and well-marked valley, but up a much less easily identified one near by. That clearly defined valley probably already had, or was capable of having, good pasture in it, which it would have been unpractical to split in half. In another place, running across a common it goes out of its way a little to give the parish cattle access to a waterhole or stream. If it follows a road we can be sure that that road is an ancient one; if it follows a lane, that may be an old road, or, if it is only a short stretch with little apparent purpose, it may even be a boundary ditch. The great earthworks, such as Offa's Dyke, that kings made to define their frontiers, are easily recognizable when we come to them, but the more modest structure that a small community might undertake to mark out its frontiers in a place where no natural features would serve, a trench perhaps six or eight feet wide with the soil thrown up on one or both sides, is not so easy to distinguish from a lane, and indeed is often used as such. I have seen one of these boundary marks in North Devon which consisted of a trench eight feet deep with a bank on one side, running between two fields; it was still, after nine hundred years, an impressive landmark; there was a rivulet running down it which kept it scoured. In most places such ditches are not so easy to see.

However good a map reader one may be, it is impossible to understand the behaviour of a boundary, or even to recognize one of these ditches, from a study of the map. It is absolutely necessary to go and see what it looks like on the ground.

Boundaries of the type we have been describing were almost certainly drawn across the waste land, which lay around the fields of the early settlements. Where the cultivations of two villages were expanded till they absorbed the waste and touched each other, the boundary between them will reflect the shape of the original fields. These were divided into roughly rectangular pieces called furlongs, and the boundary zigzags back and forth as it passes between the interlocking furlongs of the two communities.

In this way it may be said to reflect the farming practice of the people, as it does also on a favoured hillside, where a number of communities have settled, each grazing their cattle and sheep during the summer in the valley and on the hills in winter, and growing their corn round the village on the lower slopes. Here boundaries run up and down the hillside, enclosing an area many miles long and sometimes less than a mile wide. The parishes of this type on Lincoln Edge have already been mentioned, and a similar lay-out may be seen on the northern slopes of the Berkshire Downs, in the Vale of Pickering, and in many other places where like conditions prevail.

The boundaries of these parishes, and of most others in closely-settled regions, must have been made by agreement between the proprietors of various territories, recognizing the claims of each village community to its share of pasture and woodland. We know of juries and public officials meeting on the spot to draw the line across a piece of disputed ground centuries after it first began to be used by the people round about. The boundaries of a large moorland parish, however, containing a number of tiny isolated communities, may well have been created by the king to form a suitable estate for a nobleman or monastic community, with the sole consideration of providing the recipient with territory adequate for his support. A perfect example of this type of parish is Tavistock in Devonshire, whose boundaries are those of the estate originally granted for the foundation of a Benedictine monastery. A large area was allocated for the support of the community, lying principally between the Tamar and the Tavy; but the whole peninsula between the two rivers was not granted to the monks, for the southern end of it contained silver mines. The boundary was drawn across a narrow neck of land just north of the silver workings so that they should remain in the king's hands.

The explorer who has followed us thus far will now be in a position to begin the making of a parish map on which to record his discoveries. The outline can be traced from the six-inch Ordnance Survey map, and will at first consist only of the principal natural features, rivers and streams, significant hills, and the parish boundary. Roman roads and ancient trackways, if there are any, the site of the village, and the ancient farms and hamlets may be added. By the use of symbols, coloured inks, etc. it will be possible gradually to make a map which will record the fortunes of the village with its territory over the centuries.

In the next chapter, which will mainly be concerned with the villagers' daily bread, we shall try to fill in some of the blank spaces on the map.

BOOKS TO READ

The Domesday Geography of Midland England. H. C. Darby.

The Domesday Geography of Eastern England. H. C. Darby.

English Place Name Elements. A. H. Smith. Cambridge, 1956.

The New Lands of Ello. H. E. Hallam. Leicester University Press. Occasional Paper No. 6.

Devonshire Studies (especially *The Making of the Agrarian Landscape*). Hoskins and Finberg. Cape 1952.

V

Daily Bread

ROUND the village green, or along the street, or scattered about the site, stand the homesteads of what was once a compact, self-sufficing community. Today many of the cottagers may go miles away to work, and some of the houses are occupied by professional people, business men, or even American servicemen, but in past times almost every inhabitant of the village would have got his bread by supplying the needs of his immediate neighbours. The farmers and their labourers are still there; but formerly there was also a body of craftsmen which has now almost disappeared.

In addition to the five farmers, six husbandmen, nineteen day labourers, and one shepherd who lived in the large Dorset village of Puddletown in 1724, there were three blacksmiths, a wheelwright, a miller, a carpenter, a cooper (barrel maker), two thatchers, a glazier and plumber, a bricklayer, a plasterer and tiler, a weaver, a wool stapler, a worsted comber, a tailor, a clocksmith and gunsmith, a shoemaker, a barber, a chandler (general merchant), a shopkeeper, a butcher, a baker, and an innkeeper. This may be compared with an incomplete list for the village of Bealby in Lincolnshire, which had, about the same time, a blacksmith, a miller, a carpenter, a dish turner, a weaver, a fuller, a tailor. The inhabitants of Rillington, a village in the Vale of Pickering, numbering about 683 in 1823, included fourteen farmers, two blacksmiths, two wheelwrights, a ploughmaker, a brickmaker, a bricklayer, two tailors, five cobblers, five grocers, a butcher, a flour dealer, a brewer, a shopkeeper, a watchmaker, two victuallers. In 1840, when the Rillington list was almost unchanged, the neighbouring village of Scampton had six farmers, two gardeners (nurserymen), a miller, a millwright and joiner, two wheelwrights, a butcher, and two cobblers.

These are typical English villages. In stone country there would be stone masons and quarrymen instead of brickmakers and layers, elsewhere thatchers instead of tilers. A few of the craftsmen had a larger market for their goods than their own village, but farming was the principal industry, and all the trade carried on in such villages was subordinate to agriculture. They were in no sense rival industries such as once flourished in many places, and sometimes flourish still, for example the furniture making in the Chilterns, the basket making of Furness, and the Severn fisheries where the fishermen still use coracles no different in construction from those of their Bronze Age ancestors, and wicker traps which may be as ancient, and which have certainly gone by the same name, 'putchers,' for a thousand years.

The six husbandmen of Puddletown were smallholders, small peasant farmers who formed a class of society intermediate between the yeoman farmers and the day labourers which has now disappeared. Their farmsteads were mere cottages with perhaps a small barn and few sheds attached, most of which are gone; but the farmsteads and fields of the yeomen provide the most eloquent record we have of the working lives of generations of ordinary people.

Measured by historical standards, farm houses and buildings are seldom very old; there are many Victorian farmhouses, and a fair number date from the seventeenth or eighteenth centuries; few have a longer history than that. Most of the farm buildings will probably have been built in the last hundred and fifty years, though the continuity of local building traditions often makes it difficult for any but the most expert eye to place them in point of time.

The oldest thing about the farm, as of the village itself, is often its name. This may recall some medieval or Tudor occupier whose buildings have long ago become part of the earth itself below the foundations of his successor's house. The site of the farmstead, if it is within the village, is not likely to have shifted. Not so the farmer's fields; size, shape, and use will have been changed and changed again, for although the produce of his industry satisfies man's most elementary needs, which are not subject to changes of fashion, nor left behind by the march of progress, the farmer's methods, and even his raw material, beasts and plants, are by no means immutable; they have a long history of change and development which has left a visible record in farmstead and field.

From the ages of settlement down to the great ploughing up of the land in the 'forties of the present century the story of agriculture, and to some extent of the villagers dependent on farming for their daily bread, is epitomized in the rolling and unrolling, and rolling back again, of a green carpet. The process of colonization described in the last chapter rolled aside the carpet of forest green and khaki heath which had covered the land before man's coming, and put in its place the brown and gold of tilled fields and ripened corn. Until the early fourteenth century the area of arable was always expanding, villages overflowing into new settlements, and the plough being gradually driven further up the hillsides—further than it ever was to be again. In those days men farmed mainly for subsistence, that is, to produce everything they needed to support life, and only a few necessities such as salt and iron came to them from without. The only produce they had that was readily marketable on any scale was wool, and the clip of many small flocks and some big ones added up to such a total that England became the largest wool producer in Europe. By the thirteenth century 'wool to England' was the French equivalent of 'coals to Newcastle'. The fifteenth and sixteenth centuries saw the apotheosis of the sheep, when villages were wiped out and cornfields obliterated to provide raw material for the golden fleece; in the seventeenth century many men, in the midland counties especially, turned their attention to cattle raising; the green carpet was back, with a vengeance! Except in the neighbourhood of expanding cities like London, the return of the plough was slow, but as the population increased during the eighteenth century, so did the acres of arable. Corn became once more a valuable and protected commodity, until towards the close of the century the demand of the new industrial towns for bread, and the pressure of foreign war, combined with the evolution of new farming methods to burst asunder the old framework of rural life.

The green carpet rolled back once again, and everywhere it was corn, corn, corn, and beef and mutton to supply the bread and meat and beer on which the industrial army marched. This is called the age of high farming; it occupied the greater part of the nineteenth century. Then cheap corn and meat from the new world stole the market from the English grower and back came the grass again. Our own century has seen violent fluctuations in this as in other matters. In two world wars every available acre was ploughed up to feed a population largely deprived by the enemy of its usual sources of supply, and land which had been under grass ever since the Black Death was made to yield corn crops again; while between the wars unused and decaying pasture, raddled with bracken, thistles, ragwort, and hawthorn seedlings, covered many fertile acres. Much of this story, too, can be found written on the face of the parish landscape.

On the farm buildings themselves hardly more than two centuries have left their mark.

Why is it that the old order has left so little record in the farmstead?

Two buildings alone remain from the more distant past, one still in use, the other obsolete: the barn and the pigeon-cote.

The *barns* are often the oldest buildings on the farm. Some of them, on manor farms, date from as far back as the fourteenth or fifteenth centuries, and are of immense size, magnificently constructed of stone and timber. Large and prosperous indeed must have been the farming interests which required such buildings. A medieval manor farm might have three or four barns, ox stall, sheep shed, and piggeries; but the peasant farmer probably required little else in the way of farm buildings besides a barn since he usually kept his beasts under the same roof, and if we may believe contemporary writers, sometimes even in the same apartment as himself.

> 'At his bed's feete feeden his stalled teame,
> His swine beneath, his pullen o'er the beame.'

The oldest farmhouses in Devonshire have the living-room and stable on either side of a passage running through the middle of the house, a common entrance having once served both beasts and men. Figure 10 shows a typical midland plan. The barn served as granary, storehouse, and workshop; here corn was stored and threshed, and the equally precious hay kept safe from wind and weather. Animals could be penned there if necessary, the sheep sheared and the wool stored. No farm could do without a barn, however flimsy its construction might be. Under the early Stuarts even the smaller farmers enjoyed great prosperity. They built

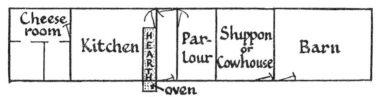

FIG. 10. An old Leicestershire farmhouse (now destroyed).

themselves new and better houses, fine barns, and separate accommodation for their beasts. Many of these old stables and ox-stalls remain, but they do not house much stock, for in corn-growing districts little provision is made for dairy and store cattle (that is, animals fattening for the market).

And here we come to the principal difference between farming under the old order and under the new. The turning point, sometimes called the Agrarian Revolution, came between 1750 and 1810, and the most important changes were the introduction of crops, notably turnips, and the improvements in grass farming, which made it possible to bring a herd of cattle through the winter on arable farms. The development of scientific stock breeding, the greatly increased yield from the ploughed field, the break-up and cultivation of the ancient waste land, would hardly have been possible without this.

What we have referred to as the old order, the routine of farming in closely-settled corn-growing districts, which this great revolution swept away, had gone on virtually unchanged for centuries. The tenth-century farmer, returning to his fields in 1700, would have found their lay-out almost unchanged (unless his was one of the parishes which had become a sheep ranch), and most of the principles of husbandry by which he had ruled his life reigning still; the difficulties which had beset him still troubled his descendants. The chief of these, how to maintain the fertility of his fields, and how to feed his livestock in winter, had, if anything, become more acute. The increased population put more pressure on land which centuries of undernourishment had rendered less fertile. The farmers' search for suitable dressings for their fields has left its trace on the landscape: marlpits 40 feet deep, which were dug to extract the loamy substance that was supposed to benefit the land, are common in Sussex, Surrey, Essex, and Suffolk. From Devonshire came the practice (called

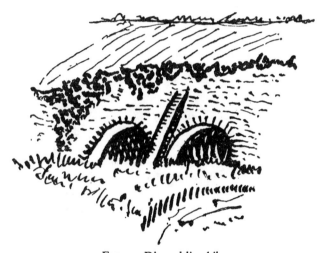

FIG. 11. Disused limekiln.

Denshiring) of paring off and burning the surface of the fields to provide a dressing of ashes. The feeding of livestock was the core of the problem.

As there was never enough hay available, and what fodder there was had to be kept mainly for the plough oxen, few cattle besides these were kept. There would be enough cows to provide replacements for the plough teams, and some young beasts not yet old enough for work. As winter approached old, maimed, and unprofitable animals were killed and salted down: this was generally done at Martinmas (November 11th). Pigs lived mainly in the woods. In spring and summer they flourished on bracken and fern roots and the like; the autumn harvest of beech mast and acorns kept them going at least until Christmas. The sheep which provided milk, butter, cheese, and clothing was never sacrificed. Pasture from which cattle can get no food can still be grazed by the close-nibbling sheep, and for the rest they were folded on the fallows where their droppings were valuable, and fed on pea and bean haulm, oat straw, and a little hay. On big commercial sheep farms they were housed in winter and handsomely fed.

Fig. 12. Two Herefordshire dovecotes.

Until the eighteenth century the roast beef of Old England was a luxury dish for a festival; everyday fare would be more likely to consist of worn-out ox, heavily salted, or ancient ewe. Foreigners admired the English method of making these veterans fit for the table. The animals were bled, fattened, and bled again. No wonder that bullock's blood was a favourite stain, polish, and wood preserver in Tudor England. This is the story behind the pigeon cote. Our forefathers, even the rich men who could eke out domestic supplies by hunting, shooting, and fishing, were always short of fresh meat, and to remedy this vast numbers of pigeons were kept. Their depredations in the cornfields were tolerated for the relief they brought to the winter diet. The lord of the manor was usually the only one to own a *dovecote* (Fig. 12), but there was nothing to prevent smaller men from having birds roosting in their barns. This is the meaning of the rows of small holes in the gables of some old barns, and of the queer little buildings, round or square, with large openings in the roof, which sometimes remain in the grounds, or farmyards, of manor houses. It is the explanation also of such field names as Culver Close, or Culver Park, which indicate that a dovecote (*columbarium*) once stood there. Some of the dovecotes are medieval and few were built after the seventeenth century, for as soon as there was enough butcher's meat available the pigeon became the farmer's enemy, and too mean a dish for a rich man's table.

Some dairy farming there was in spite of the shortage of cattle, but in many parts of the country most of the milk came from the sheep.

The *foldyard*, a square enclosure sometimes surrounded by buildings, but often with only a wall on one or two sides, is a feature of most farmsteads (Fig. 13. 1). The barn may form one side of the square, a milking parlour or cowhouse another, and one side will consist of shelters and pens. These enclosures, and their appropriate buildings, were all created after the coming of the turnip and the grass ley. Some of the early *cowhouses* are abominable buildings because there was a theory then current that cows throve better in a damp, dark fug, but they began to be, as they are today, nearly the most important building on the farm. Since milk is too perishable to be marketed on a large scale without very rapid means of transport, cheese and butter were still the main dairy produce, and most farms had a series of rooms included in, or adjoining, the house, *vessel shed, scullery, press-* and *drying-rooms,* for their manufacture. The waste from the dairy went to the pigs with the kitchen swill, so the *piggeries* are usually close to the house where the women could easily look after them.

The foldyards were used for wintering cattle, fattening bullocks, and rearing calves. The animals lived on hay, turnips, and other roots, and trod the vast quantities of straw with which the ground was spread into manure. The farmer was now able to give his fields the nourishment they needed; the age-long problem of providing sufficient manure was virtually solved. This was so important a consideration that farmers often built foldyards away on the hills so that the muck might be carried down to the fields instead of up; hence the pens with their range of shelters and perhaps a small barn, sometimes still in use but more often derelict, which you will find on many uplands.

FIG. 13. 1. Barn, foldyard, and cattle pens.
2. The threshing floor.

Yields of grain were enormously increased by these innovations, and as more land was brought into cultivation the farmer was often obliged to build a new granary. This sometimes formed the upper storey of the *cart-shed*, and even if it was a separate building, it was always raised from the ground, either on pillars, or in the case of light timber structures, on staddle stones, to protect the grain from rats (Fig. 14). Near the granary was the rick-yard, a clear open space where the hay and corn were stacked, again on staddle stones or on a foundation of brushwood. In the old days most of the straw had been left in the fields to provide autumn grazing for livestock.

FIG. 14. Granary and cartshed.   Granary in timber country.

Another change, far less important, but not less worthy of notice, was completed at the same time. The hard-living ox, patient, strong, and undemanding when alive, and good to eat when his day was done, which had drawn the plough ever since the day when using an animal for the purpose was first thought of, gave way to the horse. In some districts, notably in eastern England, this had happened long before. The horse is not so even-tempered, nor so healthy; he requires four shoes instead of only two, and better feeding and housing than his predecessor: he is not an economical animal to keep, nor easy to breed, but as his pace is a little faster, and he feeds much more quickly, he can get through more work in a day, and for some kinds of work is more suitable. The lady whom Defoe saw in Sussex drawn to church by a team of oxen was evidently an eccentric, but it was a commonplace many years later for the carriage horses of modest gentlemen to do farmwork in their spare time. I quote from *Pride and Prejudice*. 'But my dear (says Mrs. Bennett) your father cannot spare the

horses, I am sure. They are wanted in the farm, Mr. Bennett, are
not they?'

'They are wanted in the farm much oftener than I can get them.'
So Jane was obliged to ride to Netherfield and her sister to walk.

Mr. Bennett's coach was a heavy vehicle, and his horses were
strong, serviceable animals, not like the elegant high-bred Victorian carriage horse, not like Black Beauty, nor yet so heavy as
the Shire horses, Suffolk Punches, and the like which soon came
to the farms. Larger and better stables were built to accommodate
the splendid beasts which thereafter provided the draught power
on the farm, and a *cart-shed* (Fig. 14) to house the great wagons
they drew home at harvest time. It housed the farmer's gig as
well. While these great changes had been coming over the farm,
the roads had been improved, so that a light vehicle, drawn by
one animal, could go on them, and the gig became a convenient
alternative to the riding horse. The farmer's wife, we may be sure,
thought it a great improvement on market days to sit up com-
posedly beside her husband instead of joggling along behind him
in the saddle.

The roads had long been overdue for attention. Bad they no
doubt were in the Middle Ages, but the kings' progresses and
those of nobles and their retainers about the country suggest that
they may have been in better condition then than in the seventeenth century. Care of the roads was a feudal obligation, and
when feudal society broke up, it was one of the first to go. The
roads were neglected and even used as quarries. Wagons and
carts had been used in Devonshire in the Middle Ages, but by
the eighteenth century there was hardly a wheel in the county;
goods of every sort were carried on pack horses, even manure to
the fields and hay to the barn. The turnpike trusts, private associa-
tions of landowners formed for the purpose, changed all that in
Devon and everywhere else, in the later half of the century, re-
pairing old roads and providing new. Many of the roads ascend-
ing steep hills in a series of wide loops were made at this time.
Sometimes you can see the old road, a mere bridle track now,
cutting straight up the face of the hill with a merciless gradient
of 1 in 3 or 4, and a surface with giant ruts, loose stones, and expanses of bare rock, much as it was left when the new road was
made (Fig. 57).

The cart-sheds are full of tractors, floats, and motor-cars today, and the wagon and the gig, if they are still about the farm, will be lying broken and abandoned, together with old tractor parts, old ploughs, and the like, among the nettles in a far corner of the yard.

When the horse became the only, or the chief, draught animal on the farm, the era of mechanized farming had begun. New machines as they came into use frequently brought with them the need for new buildings. The *horse-track* was one of the first. This is usually a four-sided bay, or apse-like projection at the end of one of the ranges, called, in the north, a *gingang* and now generally used as an implement shed (Fig. 15). Originally it housed a wheel turned by an ox, or a horse, walking round and round, and it was used to drive threshing machines, chaff cutters, and cider presses. Such buildings are very common on Devonshire farms where one or two were still in use twenty years ago. The *implement shed*, a long, low, open shelter, was built to house seed drills, cultivators, reapers, and the like. The type of threshing machine still in use in many places brought with it the *Dutch barn*, for the threshing floor of the old barn (Fig. 13.2) was not the place in which to work those cumbrous machines. The Dutch barn is a high corrugated iron structure used for storing hay and straw and often sheltering both the obsolete threshing machine and the combine har-

FIG. 15. Horse-track and fold yard.

vester which has taken its place. It came in at the beginning of the present century, and has not yet become a historical monument; it is the form of shelter still chosen by farmers for their grain silos, grain dryers, and other modern equipment. But the tall silos of wooden slats, put up on a few barns early in this century, and their war-time successors made of concrete or corrugated iron, have already become part of the history of farming. Modern farmers make their silage in concrete-lined pits.

The practice of milking cows in the meadows, immortalized in Thomas Hardy's *Tess of the d'Urbervilles*, came to an end early in this century, and a *milking parlour* was added to the farm buildings. Old cowhouses were sometimes provided with concrete floors, improved stalls, light, ventilation, and running water. Fre-quently, however, new buildings were necessary. Those built before the second German war are mostly of brick, the more recent ones of breezeblocks or precast concrete.

One feature of the farmyard remains to be mentioned. The pond is by no means universal. No Herefordshire farm seems to be without one whether it stands alone or in a village; but in nu-cleated villages one pond might serve several farms. Pond making was a skilled operation, and the stagnant water of the village pond, or the cracked mud basin in a corner of the farmyard, is perhaps as much a record of things past as the ruined dovecote and the empty horse-track.

Enough has now been said to show how the history of farming in the last three hundred years is written large all over the farm buildings, and why it is in the fields that we must look for the earlier part of the story.

Corn is so beautiful to look at, so symbolic of civilization and of life itself, that although townspeople cannot tell the difference between a bad crop and a good one, or even between the different kinds of grain, yet they instinctively think of farming as arable farming, the cultivation of grain; the historian devotes most of the attention he has to bestow on country matters to the history of corn growing; and even a practical farmer will cherish his corn not only for the capital and labour invested in it but because corn growing is in a sense his vocation. He will even sometimes grow it when he knows the produce will not repay his labour. His attitude to his green fields is much more subject to chance, to

regional differences or economic conditions. Yet men were herdsmen first, and to pasture (of a sort) the land returns when man no
longer tills it. The green carpet covers up the past, and peat em-
balms it, but the operation of the plough tends to destroy it, so we
shall find it more rewarding to begin our investigation of the
fields by considering the village pastures.

While the primeval forests remained, with their population of
beasts of prey, all cattle must have spent the night in the stalls of
their owners, and we may imagine them returning in the evening
herded by the village lads, like the buffaloes in Kipling's story
Letting in the Jungle. Later, when that danger was past, the cattle
could lie out in the pastures at night and only the plough beasts
who had no time for grazing had to be fed and stalled at home.

Where were the ancient grazing grounds of the village?

Even in the English lowlands the villages often have a bit of
common somewhere in the parish, usually a piece of land too high,
or too steep, or too poor, to have ever been worth the trouble and
expense of enclosing it (that is, of dividing it with hedges, banks,
or walls, into several fields). Before the commons were enclosed,
all the villagers used to turn out their cattle on them, and when
they came to be divided up everyone who had the right to pasture
there received a piece of land and had the obligation of fencing it
in. As this was an expensive business no one would want to undertake a piece of unprofitable land. The small commons that have
thus survived in many places are all that remain of the extensive
areas of waste which once lay around the village fields nearly
everywhere, and were the permanent pasture of the village flocks
and herds. Nowadays they are usually covered with rough heath,
bracken, bramble, and hawthorn, but in the days when even
cottagers sometimes kept a cow or two and often a few sheep,
geese, and pigs on the commons, and looked to the commons to
supply wood for a hundred purposes, and perhaps peat for firing,
the more useless forms of vegetation must have been kept under
control. The derelict state of most commons is the legacy of the
change-over from a more or less fixed to a convertible husbandry.
In a fixed husbandry certain land is ploughed, some kept as

meadow, mown for hay, and some left as permanent pasture. (Convertible husbandry varies the use to which the land is put: a field may be cropped with grain, then seeded down to grass, grazed for one, two, or more years, or mown for hay, and then ploughed up again. In most districts the modern farmer keeps less and less permanent pasture; his husbandry is fully convertible.) As a rule, if all the land of the parish is fit for cultivation, no commons remain.

Although they afforded much comfort and sustenance to the labouring poor whose sheep and geese provided them with a marketable crop of wool and feathers, as well as milk, butter, cheese, and meat and clothing, the commons seldom provided very satisfactory grazing. In closely settled districts only a limited number of animals might graze in them, but the number permitted was usually too high, and often there was no limit. All kinds of animals grazed together, geese fouled the grass, and pigs rooted it up, sheep, cattle, and horses competed for the struggling herbage (the sheep generally came off best); the young, the weak, and the strong, the healthy and the diseased, all jostled together. Perhaps in the Middle Ages, when the population was small, things were not so bad, but as the number of villagers and their livestock increased through the centuries and the worn grass got no respite the commons slowly deteriorated. Although in the evidence we have for their condition on the eve of their destruction the shrill voice of propaganda and self-interest is apparent, still there can be little doubt that the land was due for a change.

The change came to most places largely as the result of reforms in the second half of the eighteenth century. During this period a long procession of Acts, passed through parliament in response to petitions from the principal landholders in individual parishes, abolished the immemorial rights of all the landholders and ordered the division and distribution of the common lands. These enclosures, as they are called, involved, in very many cases, far more than the carving up of the ancient grazing grounds. We shall speak of them again when we come to deal with the arable fields; but there were common pastures in every parish, and most of them have totally disappeared. Traces however sometimes remain in the names of farms planted in the waste after the Enclosure Commissioners had done their work, such names as

Furzehill, Broompark, Heathfield, and Lew Moor. Occasionally, as we shall see, the size and shape of fields provides a clue.

Important as the common pastures were in the economy of every village, they were never the farmers' only resource. The fallow and the stubble were used for grazing and the number of animals permitted was regulated according to the size of the individual holdings; for example for every 'yardland' (a peasant farm of twenty to thirty acres), three or four oxen and a cow or two with their young, two horses, about one and a quarter sheep per acre with their young, a sow with its young for a short period, and four to ten geese would be allowed. These figures are taken from Leicestershire villages where there was little or no waste. Even in villages where pasture and cornfield alike lay open there were usually a few closes round the farmsteads and by the streams which might be used for pasture. If there is a field near the farm called Oxen Park or Close, this is the pasture reserved for the faithful beasts who pulled the plough. The commons were too far off for them, since their grazing time was limited, and the herbage there too scanty to supply an adequate ration for animals on whose strength so much depended.

Many villages had also a common close, a large field where the number of beasts each commoner might turn out was strictly regulated. This field name often remains. The meadows were most carefully preserved, but after the hay harvest had been carried, the aftermath, that is the fresh grass which grows in late summer in hayfields, provided good grazing. Where the arable land of the village lay in common fields the meadows were usually held in common too, and divided among the landholders when the time came for cutting the hay either by casting lots, in which case a man got a different piece each year, or by doles, in which case he got the same piece. Both lots and doles were unfenced rectangular strips of meadow worked by the holder at the time of the harvest only.

These meadows were usually thrown open for grazing at Lammas Tide (August 1st.). From these practices come the field-names Lammas Meads, and the 'doles' and 'flats'. Here, the number of animals permitted to each farmer was the same as on the fallows.

Among field names the hayfields are generally the *meads* and the *hams.* The hams are found on flat ground by streams, for that is what the Saxon word *ham* means. Here the grass, made lush by the neighbourhood of water and occasional flooding, offered the best promise of a natural hay harvest. As early as the sixteenth century, a system of artificial flooding of riverside meadows was invented. Irrigation channels were cut which not only made it possible to enrich the meadows by flooding them at will, but drained water-logged ground, and made sedge and other unprofitable vegetation give way to grass. This is the true meaning of the term water meadows; they are common in the valleys of the Test, Clun, and Itchin. Some village worthies had grass closes in virtue of their office—Smith's Ham, Barber's Ham, Sexton's Hay are names which may be found among the parish fields.

But however the hayfields might be cherished, in corn country the amount of land on which farmers could hope for a hay crop was usually limited, and indeed, pathetically inadequate for their needs. This was true even in the highland zone where the climate and geological structure on the whole favour a good growth of grass, for there constant rain frequently makes it difficult, even with modern mechanical aids, to save the hay harvest. Nevertheless grass farming in these regions has always predominated, for the farmers usually had access to vast commons, and with their numerous small closes were able to keep grass fit for grazing later in the year than their midland brothers. But how desperate was the crisis which faced the midland farmer in a hard winter is shown by the space devoted in early farming books to such fodder as ivy leaves and tree bark. Heath and furze were encouraged to grow on the commons because they provided a poor but never failing source of food. Even so, six was the average size of a farmer's herd in some parts of Leicestershire in the sixteenth century.

Let us see what difference it made to villages if they lived on the fringes of open moorland, or extensive marsh. Not all such land was common land, even in early times; in the Pennines for instance the moors seem very early to have been divided up into immense estates, and most of Romney Marsh was in private hands. But however it was owned and managed, land which could not be regarded as potential cornland offered opportunities for stock raising, dairy farming, and wool production undreamt of in the closely settled English lowlands, where to get pasture you had to sacrifice corn ground. Our forefathers well understood how to take advantage of these opportunities. Those villagers who lived along the side of Lincoln Edge and made parishes stretching far out into the fen had a great future before them; and so had the settlers on the little islands of high ground in the middle of the waste, the men of such villages as the Tydds, and the Walpoles, in East Anglia.

It has already been explained how the fens and marshes were brought into use as pasture in very early times, each parish having its own, or sharing in, a vast common on which the villagers bred horses, sheep, and cattle and grew rich on their traffic in wool and hides and meat; rich enough to build the great churches of the Fenland which are some of the most glorious in the country.

The Fenman thought that the yield of his marshes could not be improved; he throve on what seemed to others so great a handicap.

'For the first the Fens breed infinite number of serviceable horses, mares, and colts, which till our land, and furnish our neighbours.

'Secondly, we breed and feed great store of young cattle and we keep great dayeries, which afford a great store of butter and cheese to victual the Navy, and a multitude of heyfers, and Scots and Irish cattle have been fatted in the Fens, which affords hides, and tallow.

'Thirdly, we mow off our Fens fodder, which feeds our cowes in winter, which being housed, we gather such quantities of compost and dung that it enriches our pasture and corn ground, whereby we have the richest and certainest corn land in England . . . and can . . . furnish London and the Northern parts in their necessities . . .

'Fourthly, we keep great flocks of sheep upon the Fens.

'Fifthly, our Fens are a great relief not only to our neighbours the uplanders, but to remote countries [he means counties] which otherwise some years thousands of cattle would want food.'

This extract is taken from a pamphlet written about 1640 against the proposals for draining and enclosing the fens to make them suitable for arable farming. It is propaganda on behalf of the commons, but it was not a great exaggeration of the facts. Centuries before, Lincolnshire had supplied hundreds of beasts, sheep, and swine to the royal household and to Parliament.

The pamphleteer finishes up his description with a fine patriotic flourish. 'What is Cole-seed and Rape, they are but Dutch commodities, and but trash and trumpery, and pills land, in respect of the fore-recited commodities, which are the rich ore of the Common-wealth!'

The seventeenth-century drainers did their work; the cornlands were increased and bore fine crops, but the reduced common pasture became overstocked and impoverished; and finally it went the way of all the other commons which had no such record of successful exploitation.

It is evident that Fenland farming in the seventeenth century hardly complied with the general picture of farming conditions before about 1750 which I have been building up in this chapter. The truth is that any general picture which does not show the great variations in farming practice that have always existed between regions, and sometimes even between neighbouring villages, is false. We can point to the cattle ranching of Rossendale in Lancashire, and Blackburnshire in Cheshire, at an early date to the Cotswold wool-country, and to many other sheep-rearing districts to show that specialized farming is no modern invention. Not nearly enough is known about this subject, which offers a great field for intelligent investigation on the spot. There is a connection between this specialization and the principal glories of the English table. Cheshire cheese, the red, the white, and the splendid blue, is said to be the oldest of our noble cheeses. Stilton was invented in Leicestershire, not long after many acres of that county had been laid down to grass for cattle-rearing in the seventeenth century. The marshland farmer, so well provided with every kind of livestock, sold his sheep and cattle, and developed a repertory of pork delicacies, pies, sausages, puddings etc., for his own use for which Lincolnshire, especially, is still famous.

Before we leave the commons we may take a look at one vast area which remains in its primitive state. All the parishes round the fringe of Dartmoor Forest proper, the central portion belonging to the Duchy of Cornwall, include a vast stretch of moorland. There is Petertavy Common, Bridestowe Common, Whitchurch Common, Walkhampton Common, and so on. But the right to pasture on these commons belongs not to these villages alone, but to the whole county of Devon. Some of the farmers in these parishes have in addition the right to pasture in the forest proper, and from time immemorial have used this right as a source of revenue, running strangers' cattle with their own in the forest in return for 'agistment' fees. Graziers doing the same thing on the Lincolnshire commons caused bitter resentment among the smaller commoners, but only the farming aristocracy who occupied what were called the Venville tenements enjoyed the right to pasture on Dartmoor, so there was no conflict of interest among them.

The commons of Devon, and the rights of Venville in the Forest, are still used to some extent today. Ponies and cattle are still rounded up every year and driven into the ancient pounds, Creaber on the north, and Dunnabridge on the south of the moor, for identification, markings, and sale. Creaber pound is a long narrow enclosure on the side of the moor in the parish of Gidleigh, which takes its name from Creaber Farm (a Venville tenement). In Dunnabridge pound the stocks are still there which were used to keep order on what was once a great annual occasion. Formerly every village had its pound into which strays were driven until claimed.

No attempt has ever been made to enclose the commons or the Forest wholesale, but farms or fields bearing the significant name of *Newtake* show where piecemeal efforts have occasionally been made to turn the land to greater profit. Often the wilderness has already reclaimed them, and a few broken banks among the bracken and heather are the record of still more ambitious efforts, made perhaps on the eve of the Black Death or during the Napoleonic wars when corn commanded a good price, and enclosure was the fashion. These Newtakes or Intakes, farms carved out of the fringes of the waste during years of prosperity, and since abandoned, are a feature of the Pennine country too.

In the seventeenth century the first plants of the *brassica* tribe were introduced. Turnips came first, then swedes, then mangolds, and finally kale. Brought in by enterprising men and cultivated with great success by such magnates as Lord Townshend at Raynham and Coke at Holkham in Norfolk, and by gentlemen farmers up and down the country, they were regarded with suspicion by the peasants. At the same time the pioneers were developing a sound system of crop rotation, improving their grassland and their livestock, and doubling and trebling the value of their estates. But their neighbours preferred to go on in the old way. Coke of Holkham reckoned that his ideas travelled no more than a mile a year. For seven years and more, a Yorkshire gentleman farmer tells us, his neighbours watched his success with indifference, but when one of them was at last won over to the new methods, the others quickly followed suit.

To do the farmers justice, the open-field system of farming which was practised over so much of England made experiment and innovation difficult. On the other hand, many parts of the country which were already enclosed did not show much more enterprise: when the new methods finally gained ground, Devon, for instance, lagged behind. However, the desire for improvement conquered at last, the open fields were done away with, the commons enclosed and ploughed up, and the Norfolk four-course rotation became the nineteenth-century farm rule of three.

These changes gave the countryside a new face, especially where the bare prairie-like expanses of the open field gave way to the modern chequerboard of fields and hedges, corn and grass, and the nucleated character of the villages was modified by the departure of some of the inhabitants to new farmsteads and cottages planted on the waste, or even on the old open fields. These farms are very easy to distinguish; the farmhouse and buildings will have been built in the late eighteenth or early nineteenth century, and they often have names recalling current political events, such as Botany Bay, Bunkers Hill, or Trafalgar, to date them more exactly; Northfield Farm will have been built on one of the open fields of the village, and Gorsehill on the waste. Where the enclosure involved most of the land of the parish, cornground as well as pasture, a new lay-out of roads and paths became necessary. Many a stretch of road, straight enough to deceive the unwary into attributing it to the Romans, owes its existence to the eighteenth-century planners.

But this new appearance of the landscape is after all hardly more than a transparent drop scene. If we can light up the stage behind, the concealed set will show through.

What does the network of fields and hedges tell us of the farming history of the village?

The pattern of fields and hedges will be found to vary greatly in different parts of the country. The parishes of the south-western peninsula are made up of tiny fields of all shapes and sizes, varying from one to seven acres, divided by vast banks carrying a small woodland of brushwood, saplings, and even trees on top. In the midlands the fields are generally much larger (ten to fifteen acres is a normal size), more regular in shape, and divided by elaborately-trained hedges of hazel, ash, and thorn. In other districts the field divisions are dry stone walls. The open fields and commons were neatly carved up by the eighteenth-century enclosure commissioners and the individual landholders divided their portions into closes of convenient size and shape for regular cultivation. Large fields are a sign of their handiwork. In the south-west the land had nearly all been enclosed piecemeal long before; much of it had indeed never lain open, and many considerations other than convenience for the plough had governed field shapes: the need for windbreaks in a boisterous climate, perhaps, or the existence of some obstacle, a giant boulder or a tree root, which it was easier to incorporate in the line of the hedge than to remove from the surface of the field. But even in Devon and Cornwall you will find on the high ground groups of large rectangular fields, and that is where the ancient commons were enclosed a hundred and fifty years ago. The local tradition of vast hedgebanks was not abandoned, however, and the new fields have as formidable divisions as the old. It is generally safe to guess that a pleached hedge in the midlands is not more than two hundred years old, but a bank in Devon or Cornwall, or a stone wall in Gloucestershire or the Pennines, may be anything from one to a thousand years old, and some—the Iron Age bank at Castallack mentioned in the second chapter is one—are even older.

In Cornwall, indeed, the field pattern, generally of very small fields of squarish shape, retains the form given it by the ancient Celtic farmers. The Saxons, however, when they won difficult land from the wilderness, usually enclosed it field by small field, so that, as we have already seen, there are numerous parts of the country where they never laid out the great open fields which are regarded as characteristic of their farming. There the field pattern differs little from that of Cornwall. But a close study of field patterns in these regions may lead to interesting discoveries. Round some of the larger villages you may find groups of long narrow fields lying parallel, with a continuous hedge-line along the ends. These are unquestionable indications of open field, enclosed not by eighteenth-century planners, but so long ago that no other record remains of the old method of cultivation.

We can find, then, in the network of fields and hedges about our parish, clear enough indications of the kind of farming that has been practised there in the past. We can often identify the wastes, the meadows, and the cornfields of the old fixed husbandry. Of the cornfields, however, little has yet been said.

The great open arable fields were cultivated in a traditional rotation, and by common consent. However, individual farmers could use their discretion provided their operations did not interfere with their neighbours' rights. They could fence their own land temporarily, and let the grass grow for grazing purposes. (Even before the artificial sowing of grass was understood leys were in use to a limited extent.) But whatever the system, the basic necessities were the same: the fertility of the soil had to be maintained and sufficient pasture had to be kept for domestic animals. Where the land was closely settled these rival necessities were most rigidly adjusted under what is known as the open-field system; where the population was thinly spread and the uncultivated wastes extensive, infield and outfield cultivation gave good results.

It is supposed that both these methods of cultivation came into use in the pioneering days when a small community toiled together to win land from the wilderness, and divided each piece of ground among them as it was won. This seems to be the most rational explanation of the strips and furlongs into which the fields were divided. In open-field villages the cornground was divided into two or three, and sometimes more, fields of over a hundred acres each, and these were divided again by rough turf balks and rides, into furlongs, that is, more or less, rectangular pieces made up of the individual farmer's strips lying intermixed and unfenced. A field might have nine or ten furlongs and each

farmer would have strips in each, presumably because each furlong represents a piece of land reclaimed and divided by joint
effort in the early days of the village history. The shape of the
strips, ideally 220 yards long, is thought to represent the distance
the oxen could comfortably pull without resting; and the width,
the amount of land a team could plough in a day. It was the fencing of these strips by their owners in ones and twos, that produced
the field patterns mentioned earlier in this chapter as evidence of
open-field farming.

Each farmer's land was scattered over the whole parish by this
means, and the system of cropping had to be agreed by all. This
made it almost impossible to introduce new crops, and was the
chief reason why the eighteenth-century reformers were so
anxious to enclose the common fields. The great advantage of the
system was that it enabled a great number of small farmers (the
six husbandmen of Puddletown for instance) to maintain their
independence because a few strips and unrestricted common
rights made a more economic holding than an enclosed farm of
equivalent size.

One of the great fields was rested each year, but otherwise the
same land continuously bore crops of wheat, barley, oats, rye,
beans, and peas, according to local custom and the prevailing
fashion. Occasionally the furlongs had to be laid out in terraces
on the hillsides. Mention has already been made of lynchets in
connection with prehistoric man, but lynchets were also made at
a much later date, and the later ones can be distinguished because
they have the characteristic shape and width of a furlong. There
are fine examples of this at Clothall in Cambridgeshire, and at
Wotton-under-Edge in Gloucestershire (Fig. 16).

There are not many open fields left in England today. The
most characteristic are at Laxton in Northamptonshire, and at
Braunton near Barnstaple. Devonshire is a county where the
characteristic traces of open field are hard to find. At Braunton,
however, while the field has been a little diminished by enclosure,
and many of the farmers have thrown their strips together, its
appearance is little altered, and the furlongs still go by the names
they had in the thirteenth century. There are open fields also at
Westcote in Gloucestershire, in the Isle of Portland, in the Isle
of Axholme, and traces of them in many places. Almost universal

throughout lowland England before the enclosure movement, they have all but disappeared, but they have left a record on the face of the land, and in the names of field and farm: names that contain the elements 'flat', 'furlong', 'shot'; strip fields which indicate very early enclosure; the apparently meaningless right-angle turns and double bends on midland roads, where they pass round the ends of what were once interlocking furlongs; the same feature in parish boundaries; the nucleated village itself,

FIG. 16. Lynchets.

which is the necessary form of settlement for open-field farmers, the road system of the parish as a whole. For indeed it is almost possible with a one-inch map to decide at a glance whether we are looking at open-field country with its characteristic pattern of large villages linked by a few roads, or enclosed country with its intricate network of villages, farms, and hamlets connected by innumerable lanes.

It is in the latter type of country that we are most likely to find traces of that other system of cultivation, the infield and outfield. We cannot carve England up and say that in some sections open-field farming was never practised, or that the infield system is the older method superseded in more advanced regions. Some districts may never have seen either method, in others both existed side by side; nor does the precise method of laying out the corn-ground appear to have depended entirely on the lie of the land.

An outfield, however, was only possible to people who had access to large areas of waste ground, especially well-drained down or moorland, and most of the traces of it which have been discovered are in the Celtic west.

The infield was the arable land near the village or individual farm. It was never so large as even one of the great fields of a two- or three-field village, but similarly divided into strips, the solitary farmer having of course a compact infield of whatever size suited his purpose. This field was continuously cropped, never rested, and on it was expended whatever dung the farm could muster. Since the field was relatively small, and this system is associated mainly with pastoral country, the supply of manure was probably enough to keep the land from being exhausted. The outfield was a portion of the waste temporarily fenced, ploughed up, cropped to the point of exhaustion, and then allowed to return to a state of nature while a new piece was enclosed and cultivated. This intermittent co-operative cultivation of the waste was also practised by communities having compact and individual holdings.

It is not easy to find traces of this system. It was practised all over Devonshire for instance, on wastes which have since been divided up and cultivated in the modern manner, but on the remaining open spaces we may hope to find the marks of ancient cultivation if we know what to look for.

How can we recognize land which has once been under the plough?

It must be said at once that we cannot always do so, for it depends mainly on the manner of ploughing. The custom of laying the land up in high ridges, called ridge and furrow, was still in use in some parts of the country within the memory of people still living, and goes back into the mists of a very distant past. Whenever we find land ridged and furrowed, therefore, we can only be sure that at some time within the last thousand years it has been ploughed. Since ridge and furrow was mainly used for draining it is most prevalent on heavy clays, and there are many parts of the country where there is none to be seen; in others the ridges have been ploughed out in the last twenty years because they are a great inconvenience to tractor drivers and render cross-ploughing

acutely difficult; and, moreover, since the introduction of sub-
terranean field drainage, they have ceased to have any use. Where
they remain, however, they are unmistakable, the surface of the
field is ridged like corrugated strawboard, and the furrows sometimes are so deep that standing in the trough one cannot see over
the next ridge. Ridge and furrow is commonest in the midlands.
It is nowhere to be seen in the Devonshire fields, but there are
some traces on some of the commons, which shows there were
outfields in these places.

In open fields the strips within each furlong all ran the same
way, and so must the ridges. It cannot be assumed that the ridges
we see today fossilize the ancient strips, but where they suddenly
change direction in the middle of a field, or pass under a hedge
or a railway line, it seems probable that they do preserve the lay-
out of the vanished furlongs. There are some splendid examples
of this on the Central Line between Brackley and Rugby, a track
not laid, however, till the second half of the nineteenth century,
and on the Kingham-Cheltenham line in the parish of Maugers-
bury in Gloucestershire.

Where the ridge pattern corresponds to the field shape we may
suppose that the old ridges have been ploughed out and new ones
made after the land was enclosed. Ploughing the ridges out, however, was not an easy matter, and in many parts of Warwickshire
you can see small half-ridges between the great hump-backs,
where farmers began and never completed the task of obliterating
them. William Marshall, who wrote agricultural surveys of a
number of counties at the close of the eighteenth century, tells us
that in his time the farmers of the Severn Vale were endeavouring
to get rid of the deep, sour, bogged furrows by making small
intermediate ridges. They believed, however, in the practice of
ridging—'we must lay her up ridge and furrow or we cannot get
any wheat':—and their ridges can be seen all over the flat fields
of the vale, and even on the Cotswolds, where there can have
been little need of it for drainage. If you examine ridge and furrow
you will find that while many of the ridges are straight, others
of them follow a graceful curve, like an inverted S; even the
hedges of such fields follow the same line. This shape is thought
to be an indication of very old ridges made in the days of the
eight-ox plough. In every field there is a headland—a space at

the furrows' end where the plough can turn. Two horses or a tractor can turn in comparatively little room, but eight or even four oxen needed a very big space in which to manoeuvre. By bringing the team out of the furrows at an angle it was possible to make use of the length of the headland and halve its width. And why an inverted S? Ploughs are made to turn the slice of earth over to the right; a true S could only be produced by a left-handed plough.

Once again it is in the grass fields that all these traces of the ancient plough are best observed. They do not show up well in corn or stubble, though from above, from a railway embankment, for instance, lines of richer green or taller ears among the corn sometimes reveal the ploughed-out furrows. Indeed, a train journey on the Midland line from Stratford to Cheltenham would well illustrate much that has been described so far in this chapter. It is a journey through flat country and on either side of the line stretch ridged and furrowed fields, many of them under grass, broken here and there by orchard and plantation. Every few miles a solid village comes into view, and here and there you can look down into the yards of a post-enclosure farmstead. Where the pattern of ridge and furrow ends, high up on the steep side of the Cotswold scarp, the scrub begins. Turf and bracken, hawthorn and bramble, the natural vegetation of the ancient commons, ramp there as they have done from time immemorial.

We shall look in vain for the story of most of the other village trades. We cannot distil as much history from the carpenter's workshop and the builder's yard as we can from farmstead and field. The record of these craftsmen, indeed, is their work, which belongs for discussion to the next chapter; the workers in perishable materials, the harness-makers, cobblers, coopers, tailors, rope-makers leave fewer visible signs of their activities behind for us, though there may be old tools rusting at the back of workshops and lumber rooms. Collectors do find old wooden ploughs, such as the itinerant plough-maker used to make (in Devonshire he went from farm to farm and could make a plough in a day), latten bells, the arch with five bells attached to the collar of the leading horse in a waggoner's team to warn other travellers of his approach down narrow winding lanes; the clogger's knife, the glazier's 'donkey'. The butcher, the baker, and the chandler are still plying their trades, but their shops seldom supply much material for historical discovery. The rope-maker has given some villages a rope walk, a long alley so-called because there he set up his apparatus and walked up and down twisting his yarn.

In any village a hundred years ago the miller, the smith, and the wheelwright would have been important men. A large village might have two or three smithies, usually very unpretentious little buildings of brick or stone, one storey high, with a little yard in front, where the clients' horses waited their turn to be shod. Even when abandoned, they have a slightly sooty look. The blacksmith of today is more of an agricultural engineer than a smith (except in hunting country), the fire may be out, and the anvil pushed into a corner; but most of the diminished band still ply their trade in the age-old way, with giant bellows and roaring fire. The tools and methods of one branch of the blacksmith's trade, shoeing, have probably changed less than those of any other country craft. The other main branch, the repair of agricultural implements, has developed along with the farm, from the fitting of coulter and share to a wooden plough, or of tines to a wooden harrow, to the maintenance of factory-made machinery, and finally to the repair of tractors. The domestic branch of his trade is not extinct even today. If he has the taste and skill for it, he still supplies the village with wrought-iron gates, hanging signs, fire-irons and so on. In some villages there is a tradition of fine iron work; the churchyard gates, the inn signs, even the door-scrapers, commemorate generations of good blacksmiths.

One wheelwright today can do the work of a whole district, so most of the old wheelwrights' shops have been turned to other uses. Many have been taken over by general builders. A few wheelwrights, however, are still at work. The large shed which forms the shop may contain, besides electrically-driven saws and lathes and a small smithy, the old flywheel formerly used for shaping the naves (as the hubs of wheels are correctly called). The base used for fitting an iron tyre (Fig. 17) to a wheel is probably still in the yard outside, and perhaps the old saw pit, a brick-lined trough, about six feet deep. Two men, one in the pit and one above, performed the laborious work now quickly done by one man with a power-driven saw. The saws for cutting the curved sections of the wheel were specially designed. All the great farm wagons were built in the local shops, and each county had its own type, according to the nature of the country, each design a careful combination of strength and lightness. Even the prettily chamfered edges had a purpose—to reduce weight. The millers' wagons, the carrier's cart, even the bier used for paupers' funerals which is sometimes still standing in a corner of the church, came out of the same shop.

FIG. 17. Millstone, stone cider-press. Iron base used by wheelwrights when fitting an iron tyre to a wheel.

The blacksmith's and the wheelwright's craft can be practised wherever it happens to be convenient; usually, therefore, in the heart of the village. In a county of many hamlets, however, the smith sets up his shop at a cross-roads, a small inn follows to cater for his waiting customers, and another hamlet is born (Fig. 18). The miller, on the other hand, is dependent on natural forces, and must often live and work far from his fellows, on a hilltop or by a stream. His battle with hostile nature is sometimes more dramatic and catastrophic than that of his neighbours. The water mill may be overwhelmed by sudden flood, and the windmill collapse under the force of a gale, or catch fire if the wind gets up unexpectedly and drives the stones too fast. The changeable English climate kept the owner of a windmill forever on the alert, turning his mill into the veering wind, working night and day when it blew hard, regulating the set of his canvas sails. The job of regulating more modern mills, effected by geared shutters, was originally done by hand, so that the sails had to be set low, only just clearing the ground, and it was not unknown for a miller to be brained by his own sails. A fantastic story is told of the mill at Brill in Buckinghamshire. A tinker is supposed to have tethered his donkey to one of the sails and seen it hurled through the air and all his stock in trade scattered abroad.

FIG. 18. The smithy at the cross-roads.

Perhaps it was the fact that he often lived apart, as well as the touch of adventure in his life, that made the miller an almost legendary figure, a likely character for a ballad (the individualist of the Dee and the sinister character in the Berkshire Tragedy were both watermillers), or for a grim joke:

'An honest miller has a patch of hair in his palm.'

Answer: 'Only an honest man can see it.'

He was a key man in the old self-sufficing village community. In feudal times the lord usually compelled his tenants to have their corn ground at his mill, and even occasionally had their hand-querns broken up. The miller paid a rent to the lord and made his profit either by taking a toll of all corn brought to him for grinding or by charging a fee. Whether payment was made in kind or in cash, the bulk of grain is so different from that of flour that his customers never believed he had taken no more than he was entitled to, even after the law obliged him to show a schedule of prices within the mill.

'I know that the miller's pigs are fat, but I don't know where the corn comes from' is another country joke.

The miller was born with the mark of his trade upon him. In defiance of the genetic law concerning acquired characteristics, generations of millers, sons and daughters, boasted of having the miller's thumb, with the spatulated ball which comes from rubbing samples of flour.

Only when corn from the New World began to supplant English grain did the miller's importance decline. The new steam-driven roller mills which came in about 1870 were erected at the ports where the foreign corn was unloaded. In the countryside mill after mill was abandoned, and the empty shells soon fell into ruin. Even the miller's house was often left unoccupied, no doubt on account of its lonely, wet, or windy situation. The few mills that survive, mostly driven by electricity, and occupied in grinding meal for livestock, are those in pleasant situations near to, or in the heart of, a village or town. Others are preserved simply as a record of the past.

Windmills attract far more attention nowadays than watermills, and efforts are made to save hulks which would probably be pulled down and rebuilt if they were still required to work; for the life of a windmill was always relatively short. Most of those still in existence were built within the last hundred and fifty years, usually on the site of a former mill. It was not unknown for a post or smock mill to be transported bodily to a more favourable situation during its working life; hedges would be levelled, ditches filled up, and a team of perhaps thirty-six horses, harnessed six abreast, would drag it to its new position. This would be a historic day in the life of the village, to be remembered by young and old while life lasted. A Suffolk mill from Gedding is known to have stuck in a watersplash while being moved; the mill which formerly stood on the hill at Nettlebed was dragged there from the valley upon two timber carriages, which broke down, fortunately just as they arrived at their destination.

There are three types of windmills, the post mill, the smock mill, and the tower mill (Fig. 19). The post mill, probably the oldest type, is so-called because its main body, a timber structure, revolves on a central post, usually the trunk of an oak. Frequently a circular brick store or cellar, called the round house, is built

94

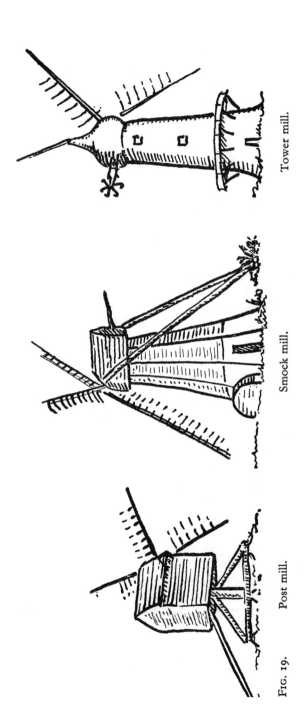

Tower mill.

Smock mill.

Post mill.

Fig. 19.

under the mill itself, which is reached by a long ladder on a wheeled base, passing right over the round house. This ladder frequently carries a fan-tail, whose purpose is to turn the sails into the wind automatically, an operation which the miller had to perform himself before this device was invented.

The smock mill, which takes its name from its supposed resemblance to a countryman's smock, is a many-sided, stationary, wooden tower, with a revolving rectangular wooden cap, carrying the sails at one end, and a small fan-tail at the other. This type may have been introduced by the Dutch engineers who drained the fens.

The third type, the tower mill, is a taller, more solid structure, built of brick or stone with a revolving cap. This is often shaped like a dome in Copenhagen or the Kremlin.

With a few exceptions windmills were used for two purposes only: for grinding corn, and for pumping water. Before the building of oil-powered pumping stations there were over 700 drainage mills in the Lincolnshire and Cambridgeshire fens. An old print shows the North Drain near Deeping lined with smock mills on either side. The Dutch engineers taught the English this use of windmills, but English ingenuity and skill in iron-casting made improvements which in time were adopted all over Europe. The first windmills were undoubtedly corn mills and there is no known reference to them before the middle of the thirteenth century.

The watermill is far older. It was known to the Romans who no doubt brought it to England. Watermills are mentioned in tenth-century Welsh laws, and Domesday Book records the existence of hundreds of them all over England. It is unknown, however, whether the English learnt their use from the Britons or introduced them afresh from the continent. In 1086 watermills were much thicker on the ground in the eastern counties.

There were two types in use from very early times. One was driven by a horizontal wheel with a vertical axle passing through, and turning the upper millstone, without cogs or gears, in a tiny house built over the watercourse. The other type with a horizontal axle is still in use. The first kind, feeble as it was, survived for many centuries in places where there was never much corn to grind, and the ruins of such mills can be seen in Anglesey, the Isle of Man, and Scotland; but in England and Wales no traces of them remain.

The second type, which was much more powerful, had a great future before it. The crude little machines shown in the earliest pictures, some of them looking like Noah's arks on wheels, had in them the germ of England's industrial greatness, for the village grist mill is the parent of a large and powerful family. The Domesday mills were nearly all corn mills, but there was one at least in Somerset which paid its rent in lead, and may therefore have been a stamping mill for crushing ore, such as was common in mining districts two hundred years later. The idea of water power was presently adopted by the fullers. Fulling is part of the cloth manufacturing process, the cleansing and felting of the fabric in water by treading, or—after the invention of the fulling mill at the beginning of the twelfth century—by mechanical beaters. When

Fig. 20. Undershot.   Overshot.

the fullers migrated to the riversides the whole cloth industry followed them, carders, staplers, weavers, and all came out of the towns and settled in the high lonely valleys and wherever else there was power enough to drive the new mills. There they flourished until their product became England's chief source of wealth, a rural industry spread through hundreds of villages in Wiltshire, the Cotswolds, the Pennines, and East Anglia. The machinery of the mills changed little in the course of centuries, but by 1600 men had learnt to improve and control the supply of water by cutting artificial channels and making sluices, and had devised a more powerful wheel. The undershot wheel (Fig. 20) which only developed sufficient power in a very strong current was superseded by the overshot and breast wheels driven by a force of water collected behind the mill-dam and released on to the wheel from above.

The first power looms were driven by water, perhaps from the same watercourse or leat which had driven the fulling mill for centuries; but more often they were placed lower down the valley, where a greater head of water was to be had. Gaunt cloth factories (called mills on account of this origin), with their retinue of workers' cottages, began to go up in river valleys where the trade had long flourished, and in others where the rumble of a mill had never been heard. Cotton mills sprang up by the Lancashire streams, and with their houses and chapel formed new villages and hamlets where not even a farm had existed before. Some of these had a life as brief as their beginning had been

FIG. 21. The weir in the foreground collects a head of water for the mill leat (right). The mill is in the background.

sudden, for the coming of steam drew all or nearly all of this thriving rural industry away into the towns. The factories fell into ruin, but many of the obsolete fulling mills were converted to corn in the great farming boom of the nineteenth century.

Every village had at least one mill, and sometimes more. There were corn-mills everywhere, tan-mills (where mechanical beaters pulped oak bark to extract the tan), edge-tool mills, pin-mills, silk-mills, cloth-mills.

The site of the old mill is very often marked on the Ordnance map, and visiting it you may find anything from a large clump of nettles at the end of a dried-up watercourse to a complete building from which only the machinery has been removed. Sometimes the wheel is still there, sometimes the pit in which it turned gapes emptily. At Steeple Barton in Oxfordshire nothing remains of one mill but a tiny wheel wedged between the banks of a small channel, and of another, the earth mound covering the ruins and the stone-facing of the riverbank beside which the wheel turned. The second mill was driven by the current of the stream itself and consequently its presence is much harder to detect than the other, for the artificial channel of a mill stream and a mill pool are easy to recognize even when they are overgrown with weeds, or when the mill stream is nothing but a dry ditch cutting its way purposefully across the meadows (Fig. 21). The other Steeple Barton mill, with its small undershot wheel near the ruins of the deserted village street, is obviously a very ancient one, long abandoned. In the midlands, where so much water has been drawn from the countryside to feed the factories, dry valleys, or valleys with only a trickle of water in them today, show traces of old mill streams, though the buildings have vanished completely.

Sometimes a clue is provided by a well-made causeway leading across the meadows, or a lane leading directly to the river bank. Such a place of common resort as a mill usually had several approaches, especially in the south-west, where lanes may converge from hamlets at every point of the compass—on nothing, it seems, but yes, on a bulge in the river bank—on a mound in a lonely field—on the site of a wind- or watermill.

It is the lonely mills that have gone. Where the mill was the centre of a cosy hamlet, or rumbled away in a corner of the village, it may still be working, otherwise it will have become an attractive dwelling-house with one end beside the pool and the other built out from the embankment alongside the mill-race.

'Many ingenious lovely things are gone.' Of the village industries, all were ingenious and a few of them have left lovely things behind them.

How can we recognize the signs of an extinct village industry?

Generally speaking, villages where an industry has flourished contain a large number of small cottages. In a purely farming community, many of the older cottages were built for peasant smallholders and are arranged in pairs with space beside them for a few outbuildings. For industrial workers, even in a village, this is un-

99

necessary, and so the houses are built in terraces, with or without narrow gardens. Where the cloth-making industry flourished the whole valley is sprinkled with houses, placed so as to take advantage of every stream and rivulet for washing yarn. In the north weavers' cottages are distinguished by the very wide first-floor windows which lighted the loom; in Wiltshire by a well-lighted

FIG. 22. Weavers' Cottages. 1. Wiltshire. 2. Yorkshire.

shed at the back or side of the cottage. In the valley bottoms stand the mills which represent the first stage in the journey of the cloth industry back to the towns. The weavers' cottages belong to the sixteenth and seventeenth centuries, the cloth mill and its retinue of terraced cottages to the eighteenth. These are familiar features of south Cotswold villages.

Many of the cottages of east Leicestershire have the same wide upper windows as those of the Yorkshire weavers. The hosiery industry which flourishes in the city of Leicester today had its forerunner in the frame-knitting carried on all over this region in the eighteenth century. This was knitting on hand-operated machines set up in their cottages by villagers who had lost their occupation on farms converted from arable farming to stock raising. These same villagers again faced unemployment when steam power drew away the industry to the towns; and found their salvation in boots. In the nineteenth century certain processes in this manufacture were farmed out to the dwellers in all the villages within a convenient radius of towns where the industry was concentrated, such as Northampton, Wellingborough, and Leicester. By no means all of these villages are lucky enough to have a factory today.

The terraced hillsides of mining districts present a somewhat similar appearance to those of clothing country, though in them the scene is diversified by old spoil heaps, ruined engine houses, and the like. In west Devon and Cornwall a special feature of the landscape is the ruined flues zigzagging over the hillsides; these were built for the manufacture of arsenic in the first German war from the spoil heaps of disused copper mines. These mines brought a brief prosperity to the villages and hamlets of the lower Tamar valley in the nineteenth century. Calstock and Gunnislake, for example, expanded into little towns, so crowded that the beds were said never to grow cold in them; but now these places are no more than villages again, surrounded by picturesque ruins.

The terrible wildernesses of open-cast workings in the east midlands are not the only scars left by iron mining on the countryside; but the ancient workings near Bream in the Forest of Dean are beautiful and impressive. The waterwheel early became a common feature of the iron-worker's forge, and a few hammer mills are still working by Warwickshire streams in the neighbourhood of Birmingham. The 'flash' ponds made to provide a head of water for stamping and rolling mills in iron-working districts where there was no natural current strong enough have embellished the countryside with many lovely small lakes, such as the Soudley and Cannop ponds in Gloucestershire, or the ponds at Sowley in Sussex and at Abinger and Friday Street in Surrey.

Where the yew grows naturally in the woods look for traces of the iron worker, and where, in Devonshire and Cornwall, you come upon stream beds and watercourses tortured into extraordinary heaps and lumps, piled up and hollowed out, you know you are standing among the workings of medieval tin mines; near some of these sites you may see the ruins of the miners' 'blowing house', the furnace where he smelted his ore. And perhaps you may find, built into a moorland wall, the granite moulds into which he poured the molten metal to cast the refined ore into ingots.

In this chapter it has been possible to do no more than investigate very briefly such village activities as are nearly universal or have written their history most clearly on the village and parish. There are, of course, hundreds of other trades, of which little or nothing has been said here. It would have been pleasant to devote space to such little publicized occupations as the pearl fishing of the west, oyster fishing in the east, or the manufacture of salt round our coasts. In each region successive generations of countrymen have exploited the natural riches which lay to their hands so industriously that it almost seems as if, like characters in a fairy tale, they were able to turn straw into gold, or at any rate into silver. They left nothing unused, and to understand their way of life we must get to know the very bones of the land on which they lived.

BOOKS TO READ

English Farming Past and Present. Lord Ernle. Longmans, 1909.
English Peasant Farming. J. Thirsk. Routledge and Kegan Paul, 1957.
Victoria County History of Leicestershire. Vol. II. Articles on Agrarian History by R. H. Hilton and J. Thirsk.
A Tour through England and Wales. D. Defoe. Everyman.
The Open Fields. C. S. and C. S. Orwin. Clarendon Press, 1954.
English Field Systems. H. L. Gray, 1915.
The Wheelwright's Shop. G. Bourne. Cambridge, 1923.
The English Windmill. R. Wailes. Routledge and Kegan Paul, 1956.
Water Mills: an Introduction. Paul N. Wilson. Society for the Protection of Ancient Buildings.
Rural Crafts of England. K. S. Woods. George G. Harrap and Co. Ltd., 1949.

VI

The Buildings: Villagers at Home

SINCE the first thing we notice about any village is the appearance of its houses and cottages perhaps it is strange that
we should have postponed any discussion of them until our
sixth chapter. But to make an intelligible picture of the life of a
community it was necessary that we should first plant the village
firmly in its surroundings and see how it is to be explained in
terms of the land on which it depends for its existence. Nor is this
method of making acquaintance so unnatural; it is thus that we
usually get to know our friends, seeing them first carrying on the
business of their lives, before we penetrate their homes.

Moreover if we had begun with the houses we should have
come in in the middle of the show. For the cottages gathered about
the village green today are nothing like those the men lived in
who saw Arthur plain, or fought under the great Alfred against
the Danes; nor are they like the houses of the men who gave
reluctant evidence before the Domesday commissioners or
cowered indoors when the 'disinherited' came riding by in the
terrible lawless days of King Stephen. Our cottages have an air
of cosiness and they belong to an age when peace and modest
comfort had been won by the peasant community; when the
arduous days of the pioneers and the perilous struggles with invaders were long over, and when the labour of winning a living
from the soil had become light enough to permit men to look for
something more in their homes than a place to eat and sleep.

In an earlier chapter I have spoken of an ocean of green forest with islands of cultivation in it. Small wonder that the people living in such islands built their houses of wood. The Saxon word for a building was *getimbrung*, and stone building was so rare with them that a stone house or church could give the place where it stood a name: e.g. Whitchurch (a newly built stone church would gleam white in the sun), Stonehurch, or Stonehouse.

Even the parts of England now famous for their building stone were heavily forested once, and everywhere to cut down trees for any purpose whatsoever was to clear much needed land for the plough; nor could there be any comparison between the labour involved in quarrying and carrying sufficient stone for the smallest cottage, and that of building it of wood. To build a wooden house a man need only go into the great forests that surrounded his village and choose and fell one or two suitable trees. When he had got his material together the skeleton of the house would be made upon the ground; then he would call on his neighbours to help him and in a day the frame would go up. Records exist of houses built in this way, and of the ale and meat purchased by the owner to encourage and reward his assistants.

This excellent and convivial method of building survived long in districts where sufficient timber remained available, and was eventually taken to the New World. In America 'Barn-raising' parties are a comparatively recent memory, celebrated in plays and films. You can see timber-framed houses built after this fashion in many an English village. Perhaps stone buildings might never have supplanted them if the supply of wood had not all but run out.

It would have seemed inconceivable to the Saxon peasant that this should ever happen; more difficult to imagine than for us to visualize an England without coal. The Norman kings, passionate hunters and powerful despots as they were, created only one New Forest. A hundred years later, however, disputes were going on about woodland rights everywhere. When a party of villagers went to the woods to get some necessary timber they were likely to come up against the neighbouring magnate's people, and a row would ensue. They were not trespassing wantonly, but the forests had shrunk so much that there was no longer a no-man's-land of unfrequented woodland between one settlement and the next, and a boundary had to be agreed and a ditch dug to save the lord's wood from further encroachment.

The men of Devon paid an enormous sum of money to King John to have their county freed from Forest Law which held wholesale clearance and new settlements in check, and everywhere it was the same story in the thirteenth century. Industry also took its toll of the forests. Miners needed few pit props in those days, but iron smelting consumed vast quantities of timber. The Abbot of Flaxley alone cut down two trees every week in the Forest of Dean for his forges. By the seventeenth century, when the government began to concern itself seriously with the supply of timber for shipbuilding, the country was found to be dangerously short of suitable trees.

As wood became scarce and dear, so stone building came in wherever stone was readily available, and elsewhere brick by degrees supplanted timber construction. The pattern of stone, brick, and timber houses forms a sort of diagram illustrating the geology of the country, and it exhibits a bewildering variety (Fig. 23). There are granite, millstone grit, hard lime, and sandstones, the principal materials of the highland zone, the beautiful oolitic limestones of the lowland frontier from Ham Hill up to Ketton and Barnack, the inferior but workable materials of the south-east, Kentish and Norfolk rag, flint and pebble, Pembridge limestone. The heavily ornamented timber-framed houses of Lancashire, Cheshire, and the west midlands are associated with heavy clays where wood was plentiful, the lighter frames, and the many-shaded bricks of the south-eastern counties, the cob of the south-west, and its near relation, sun-baked bricks or clay lumps of Norfolk and the east midlands are related to fertile soils early stripped of timber.

Even within the various regions, outcrops of different material have an immediate effect on local building. The villages on the south side of Bredon Hill in Worcestershire are built of stone, the good building stone of this limestone outcrop being easy to reach up the gentle southern slopes. The steep northern slope makes the quarries difficult of approach, the accessible rock on the northern face is of a different nature and inferior quality; so the villagers stuck to timber.

There is less variety in roofing materials: Norfolk reed, wheat-

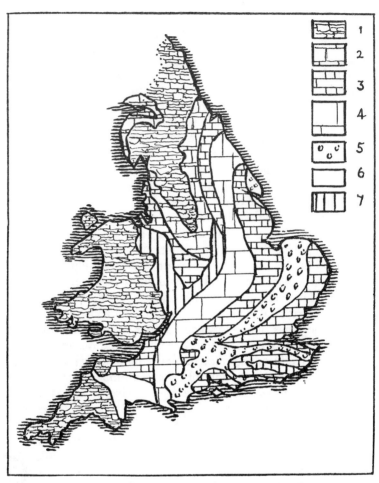

FIG. 23. Building materials of England and Wales.

1. Severe stone buildings. Ancient rocks: magnesium and carboniferous limestones, old and new red sandstone, granite, slate, millstone grit.
2. Some stone buildings, brick, timber. Mainly sandstones.
3. Brick, timber frame, with brick facing, brick nogging, tile hanging. Clays.
4. Fine stone buildings. Oolitic limestone.
5. Sun-baked bricks: timber frame with plaster filling, or plastered over. Flint, pudding-stone, chalk, sarsen stones.
6. Cob; chiefly marl and sandstone.
7. Heavy timber frames especially in N.W., marl, and sandstone.

106

straw, ryestraw, heather or furze for thatch, blue slate, pantiles, or stone tiles such as are used throughout the oolitic limestone belt make up the list.

Fig. 23 refers only to houses built before the Railway Age; red brick and Welsh slate were almost universal in the nineteenth century, even commoner than are factory-made materials in the twentieth.

Wood, then, is the oldest building material.

How can we tell which of the timber houses is the oldest?

'Lord, I am not worthy that thou shouldst come under my roof' said the centurion. From the beginning the roof was the heart of the matter, and the raising and supporting of the roof the most important and difficult part of the builder's art.

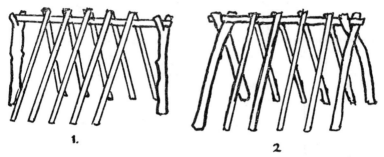

FIG. 24. Supporting the roof: the simplest elements.

In huts of the most primitive type, such as were built in prehistoric times, and put up throughout the ages for temporary shelters, there are alternative methods of carrying the ridge tree and supporting the roof. At each end either a single upright, forked at the top, or a pair of posts leaning together, may be used for the purpose. The rest of the roof and walls are simply made of staves and thatch (Fig. 24). For centuries the houses of the peasantry were simple perishable shacks of this sort. The first was a particularly flimsy method of construction, for the main timbers, having no lateral supports, were liable to collapse in a strong

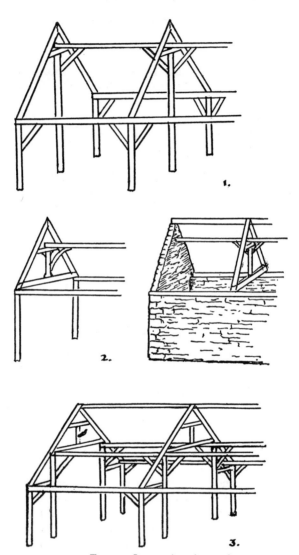

FIG. 25. Supporting the roof:

1. The central arcade as at Mancetter Hall.
2. The central pillars become 'king posts'.
3. The aisled hall.

wind; a tradition exists of one Yorkshire village having been completely carried away in a storm.

The ease with which these shacks could be destroyed and re-built explains the extraordinarily rapid recovery towns and villages constantly made after the visits of invading barbarians. So long as

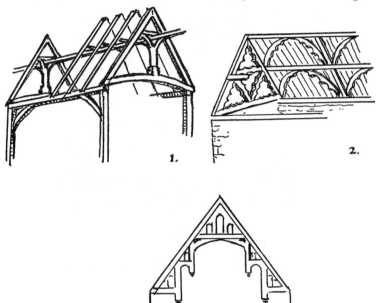

FIG. 26. Supporting the roof:

1. King post.
2. Raking struts and wind braces (see Fig. 27).
3. Hammer beams.

the social and political structure remained in being, physical damage could soon be made good, and the Anglo-Saxons, with their passion for law and order, had a system which withstood the ravages of the Northmen better than that of any other equally exposed community.

The Saxon church at Greenstead in Essex is built of solid tree trunks, split in half. A church, however, was an important building; the houses of ordinary folk could not be so solidly built. For them the stout gable-forks at each end, ridge tree, and rafters reaching to the ground, or to within a few feet of it, provided the necessary frame. The walls were made of light uprights (studs) filled in with mud plaster mixed with straw or horse hair (post and pan), or with woven sticks (wattle) faced with mud plaster (daub).

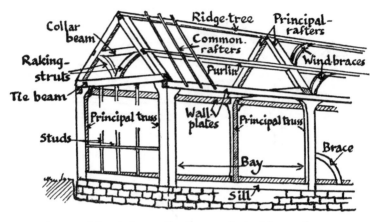

FIG. 27. The skeleton of a 'post-and-truss' house frame.

It is easy to see how the method of supporting the roof on central uprights could be applied to stone buildings. The ridge tree was carried on the stone gables at either end, and, in a longer building, on central columns as well (Fig. 25, 2). Then these columns, instead of resting on the floor, were shortened to rest on a tie beam which carried the weight of the roof on to the walls. These shortened columns are called 'king posts' and there are not many left, but they were common in churches in the seventeenth century. An example of the wooden house with central posts survives at Mancetter Hall in the midlands. Nor was the ridge tree an essential feature. In the south-eastern half of the country there was usually no ridge support, the king post supporting a collar beam between the principal rafters. Originally these were no thicker than the common rafters of the roof, extra rigidity being given to the frame by wind braces morticed into posts and purlins (Fig. 26, 2). Where all the timbers of a roof are of the same thickness (scantling) it is a sign of great age, and generally, the shorter the king post, the more arched the beam on which it rests, the older the roof. Such features date from the fourteenth or early fifteenth century.

The barn at Lordship Farm, Writtle, Essex, displays this method of building to perfection. The roofs of all the great medieval barns and many later ones, still remaining in southern England, are built in this way, sometimes called post and truss framing. The carpenters who made these splendid roofs had come a long way from the primitive huts with their gallows frames, but the underlying idea was still the same.

FIG. 28. Jettying: the overhanging upper storey.

The main timbers of post and truss frames are the four posts standing at the four corners of the house; resting on them the pairs of principal rafters with their tie beams, etc., which meet at the ridge; the wall plates and sills tenoned into the four posts and running round the building at the base and under the eaves (Fig. 27). This basic framework could be lengthened by adding any number of main posts and principal rafters at regular intervals, and widened by the addition of aisles, the posts becoming a double row or arcade of free-standing pillars (Fig. 25, 3); it could be extended to any height. A seventeenth-century manual of construction recommends that the four corner posts should be carried up from foundation to roof. It may have been in the shortage of timbers tall enough for this, and the difficulty of making a rigid join in any other way, that the overhanging upper storey (jetty) originated (Fig. 28).

Tree trunks turned upside down are less liable to rot. In post and truss frames the roots springing from the bole formed natural corbels to support rafters and wall plates (Fig. 29).

In the north and west a sturdier and less elegant method of framing was employed. Samson himself could not have brought down the pillars of a house 'built upon crucks'. Cruck building may have been invented to abolish the need for the inconvenient central column or the aisle arcade in large post and truss framed

Fig. 29. Tree trunk inverted to form a corbel in a 'post-and-truss' house frame.

houses, but it could also have been a natural development from the second of our two primitive methods of supporting a roof: by leaning two posts together (Fig. 30, 2). In cruck buildings these leaning principals are immensely thick, often a tree trunk split in half to supply a matching pair. By selecting a trunk with its main branch at a suitable angle, or a bent trunk, the old builders found the principals could be made to form a graceful arch (Fig. 30, 1), (perhaps they were inspired by the form of a gothic stone arch), and to give more clearance inside the building (Fig. 30, 3). The arched shape was often achieved by inverting the timber so that the tapering branch rested on the sill and the long trunk reached the ridge.

The name cruck simply means 'bent' and may be compared with the shepherd's crook, and the large hooks called 'crocks' used in the west country on pack-horse saddles for carrying hay and similar goods. Crucks are called siles in Lincolnshire, blades in Monmouthshire, forks in Northamptonshire. They can still be seen in ancient barns and farmhouses in many places north of

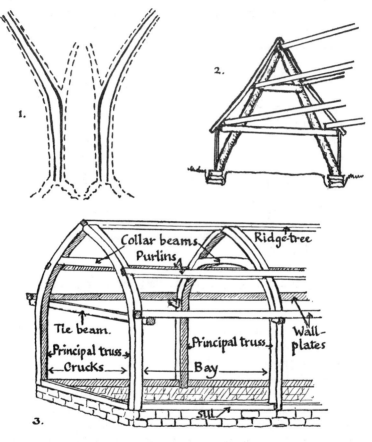

FIG. 30. 'Cruck' construction.

1. A tree trunk split to provide matching 'crucks'; they might be used either way up.
2. Rough work: framework for a barn without stone foundation except under the principal trusses.
3. A fully-developed cruck framework, e.g. for a fifteenth century-yeoman's house.

a line drawn roughly from the Bristol Channel to the Wash, much less frequently in the southern counties, where they must always have been less common.

The method of building was the same for all timber structures. The frame would be made and fitted together in the workshop, and then taken to pieces and brought to the site. In all but the roughest work a stone foundation was laid; then the neighbours would get together and raise them into position. Holes made for levers and dragging chains can sometimes still be seen in the bases of the mighty timbers, and beams and mortice holes are numbered (in Roman numerals) so that the various members could be identified, and fitted into their places.

The skeleton of the building might be completed in a single festive day. A carpenter would take about two months to finish a house 40 feet long by 22 feet wide and 24 feet to the eaves; a smaller man with fewer assistants might take a month or so longer. The walls were finished with a framework of lighter timbers, braces to keep the structure rigid, uprights called studs, or squared panels. These were filled with whatever mode of filling was customary in the district; wicker work and mud plaster some-times mixed with horsehair and cow dung, called wattle and daub, rice and stower, or rad and dab, was a common filling (Fig. 31, 2,); hazel wands set close together and plastered over (clam staff and daub) was another. At Kilpeck in Herefordshire naked wattle can be seen in an old barn, but generally the filling was well covered. In Essex and Suffolk the plasterers commonly amused themselves by combing the wet plaster into a pattern, making rings, inter-laced strapping or even naturalistic reliefs of flowers and fruit in the panels (Fig. 31, 2). This had the practical advantage that a roughened surface resists damp and frost better than a smooth one; it is called pargetting.

When bricks became plentiful they made an admirable filling (brick nogging), particularly when arranged in herring-bone or other pattern, a common feature in Hertfordshire farms and cottages (Fig. 31, 4). Kent and Sussex builders often added a facing of tiles or weatherboarding to an old house whose wattle filling needed replacement, thus completely concealing the ancient framework. Even when they were first built a protective coating of lime and plaster was often put over the timbers. A frame so

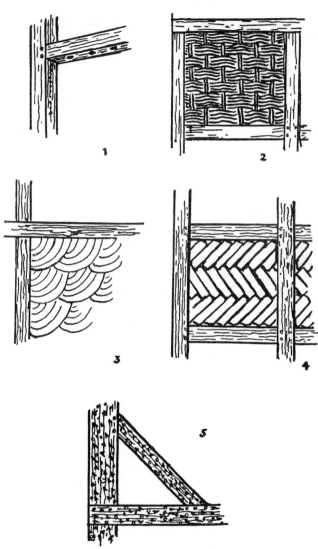

FIG. 31. Filling the timber frame.

1. The holes in the frame made for hazel rods.
2. Half-completed wattle work.
3. Pargetting.
4. Brick-nogging.
5. The framework keyed for a plaster facing.

treated will show a mass of nailheads and small nicks on the surface (Fig. 31, 5), the traces of the 'key' provided for the plaster,
even after this has been stripped off in the mistaken belief that
the building is being restored to its original state. The roof would
be thatched with whatever material was available. Brushwood
might be laid over the rafters first and this would be plastered on
the inside. The thatch, whether it was made of bracken, furze,
heath, wheatstraw, or reed, would be completely covered with
moss or turf. This warded off the attacks of birds and wind, and
served as additional protection against the weather, as did the
coating of asphalt later given to slate roofs in wet districts. The
timber framework was practically indestructible, and many a
flimsy wattle wall has been replaced by brick or stone while the
main timbers stood up and carried the roof through the centuries.

The carpenter's contract included the making of most of the
simple furniture the house was to contain; the board or table,
forms and benches, often made in one with a partition between
hall and entry; a shelf or cupboard for the hall; for the bower or
parlour a bed of planks and perhaps a chest or two.

The defects of cruck building were twofold. First, it was wasteful of large timber since a tree often had to be felled for every
pair of crucks. Secondly, houses so built could only be enlarged
lengthways; even the addition of aisles involved a very clumsy
and elaborate framework. A house might have any number of
bays but its width and height would depend entirely on the span
that could be obtained between the leaning timbers, and a second
floor with adequate headroom was virtually impossible. A 'bay'
is the name given to the space between trusses, that is between
the principal rafters, whether of cruck-truss, or any other type of
frame (Figs. 27, 30). The space varies from ten to sixteen feet.
The cotter would have one bay, the lord three or four; no other
difference was possible.

Timber shortage must have begun quite early in southern
England. Oak was being exported to the Netherlands, and deal
brought in in the Middle Ages, so there was every reason for
economy. Moreover the more sophisticated inhabitants of the
towns probably required, and taught country dwellers to wish
for, houses of differing shapes and sizes with good windows and
several floors. With the demand for an upper storey, cruck build-

ing came to an end, and the carpenters' house came to full flower. This came about in the fifteenth and sixteenth centuries, and reached the humblest type of farmer in the seventeenth.

A Suffolk man wrote in 1618 that timber shortage had enforced 'a new method of compacting, uniting, coupling, framing and building with almost half the timber which was wont to be used, and far stronger, as the workmen stick not to affirm, but the truth thereof is not yet found out soe'. Generally the framework of the oldest timber houses is heavy, with large curved braces and massive corner posts (Fig. 32, 1, 3, 5), with large panels (about four feet square). As time went on the carpenters discovered that a house would maintain its rigidity with a far lighter frame, and used timbers of much smaller scantling. Square panels of two feet became common (Fig. 32, 4), or light studs set close together (Fig. 32, 2), and braces were reduced in size and number. The houses thus appear to contain more timber, but each tree could be cut up to better advantage. In a few parts of England, however, remote from the shipbuilders' yards, exporting merchants and the voracious forges, especially in Lancashire, Cheshire, and the west midlands which were still rich in forest, Elizabethan housebuilders threw economy to the winds and covered the outside of their houses with a multiplication of studs and braces arranged in elaborate patterns, and ornaments carved out of single pieces of timber (Fig. 33, 6, 7).

The new buildings proved to be quite as long-lasting as their more heavily built predecessors, and there are thousands of them in good condition all over England today. They were strong and flexible. Medieval carpenters seldom troubled to obtain seasoned timber, and the frames often warped severely as the wood dried out. The crazy angle of walls and floors in ancient timber-framed buildings is more likely to be the result of this improvidence than of extreme old age. In the salt-mining districts of Cheshire the foundations of all buildings are very liable to subside, but the timber frames seem to be capable of taking almost any strain.

Most of our timber-framed houses date from the sixteenth and early seventeenth centuries, and the older ones were usually modernized at that time. They must have been going up in hundreds everywhere for the new middle class, tradesmen, merchants, and yeomen. They were economical, convenient, and comfort-

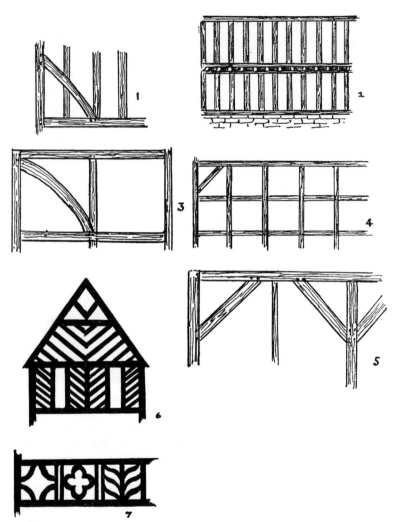

FIG. 32. Studding.

1. Fourteenth century. Compare with 2.
2. Fifteenth–sixteenth century: close studding, often on a stone foundation or lower storey.
3. Medieval square panel, 4 ft. square, compare with 4.
4. Seventeenth–eighteenth century square panel, 2 ft. square, smaller scantling.
5. Thirteenth–fourteenth century framing. Compare with Fig. 25, 1 and 2.
6 and 7. Sixteenth–early seventeenth century, in Shropshire, Lancashire and Cheshire.

able. Their inhabitants enjoyed a far higher standard of comfort than the nobleman in his castle with its dark rooms (for deep window embrasures and embroidered tapestries devour the light) and its cold stone walls and floors. The magnate paid a high price for relative immunity from fire and security from ill-wishers.

FIG. 33. The blessings of peace.

Above: Northumberland yeoman.
Below: Kentish yeoman.

A stone house, however, was a mark of wealth. The lord of the manor had long had one wherever stone was fairly easy to come by. Sometimes the house was lightly fortified and had a moat. On the Welsh border this doubtless had a practical purpose —there are many moated manor houses in Herefordshire—but in lowland England the moat must very early have become a

matter of tradition and prestige. A few last specimens of the fortified manor house were built by eccentric (or perhaps specially
unpopular) notables in Henry VIII's reign. Compton Castle near
Totnes, a curious cross between a castle and a mansion, was built
even later. The Ordnance Survey maps show a moat in many
villages, and this usually marks the site of the original manor
house, but in many cases it would have been no more than a
primitive timber structure within earthen bank and wooden palisade. The ditch merely provided earth for the bank and did not
necessarily contain any water. The house would have been early
abandoned in favour of an unfortified stone house.

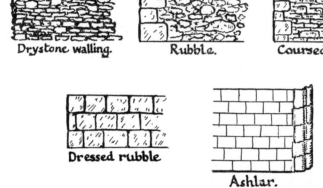

FIG. 34. Masonry.

In the comparatively untroubled heart of England this might
have happened at any time from about 1300 onwards, but centuries had to pass before men could live in peace in the northern
counties. No unfortified house would survive a Scotch raid, and
no unfortified houses more than about two hundred years old
remain in Northumberland and Cumberland. The rich man had
his castle, and the well-do-to their 'pele', a massive two-storey
building with the merest slits for windows and heavily fortified
doors. The cattle were driven into the ground floor during a raid
and the women and children of the small community took refuge
above, while the men would do what they could to save the undefended houses and barns, the sheep and the crops. They were

still living this precarious existence in the fifteenth and sixteenth centuries when many of the 'peles' now used as barns were built. 'Peles' are recognized by their massive walls, the doorways showing the sockets of heavy bars and iron grills; they usually have no chimney. These belonged to yeomen farmers, the rather more handsome structures built by gentlemen often form part of a modern house. Hardly any better illustration of the blessing of peace could be found than a comparison of these gloomy refuges with the house of a Kentish yeoman of the same period with its high, wide hall, light and comfortable chambers at each end, and graceful chimney stack (Fig. 34).

How can we discover the age of a stone house?

The age of stone houses is to some extent determined by looking at the masonry: generally the larger the stone the older the building. Except for arches, quoins, corbels, etc., which were carefully worked, the older masons made use of the largest stones they could find lying about, and filled in the gaps with small stuff. The use of dressed stone, called ashlar, which has to be sawn when it is fresh from the quarry, came in about the fourteenth century. At this date, however, only great churches or the houses of the rich would be faced with ashlar. Most walls would be of rubble masonry, though this was laid with increasing care and regularity, in courses like brickwork, or squared.

All stone not dressed is technically known as rubble. Easily worked stone is called freestone, and the best freestone quarries are and have always been famous. The East Anglian fenmen fetched the stone for their splendid churches and their richest houses from the famous quarries at Barnack or overseas from Caen; Ham Hill stone created a whole building tradition in Somerset, Ketton stone in Northamptonshire; and the Devonians dragged Beer stone all over their difficult roads, because it was almost the only stone in the county suitable for carved capitals, arches, and vaults. The quarries of a district are a key to its architecture, the buildings of a district a key to its underlying structure, and therefore its settlement and mode of life. If you are exploring stone country you should try to find the quarry from which your village was dug.

Since castles, monastic buildings, and many manor houses were built of stone in the Middle Ages, the stone mason already had skill in domestic architecture when he began to apply his art to the smaller type of house. The development of a fine building style depended mainly on the material he had to work with. With millstone grit and granite little could be achieved; the freestones of the great oolitic limestone belt produced a string of handsome villages and a style excellent in proportion and graceful and inventive in detail, which reached its fullest perfection in the Cotswolds.

The humblest of all building materials remains to be described: mud, used in its natural state, or made into bricks. Mud, in the form of puddled clay mixed with straw, horsehair, road scrapings; in Dorset, with chalk loam or sand; in Cornwall, with chips of slate, is the raw material of the cob walls of the south west, finished with a coating of plaster. Cob walls are built in layers of about two and a half feet, each layer, called a 'raise', being allowed to dry before the next is added. The walls set very hard, but the corners are always liable to crumble and are therefore usually rounded. Cob is perhaps the most admirable of all building materials for the small peasant. It makes a house warm in winter and cool in summer, it is very cheap to build, resists fire, and if properly protected from the weather, is very durable. According to a Devonshire saying, cob needs a good hat and a good pair of shoes. Even curtain walls of this material need a stone foundation and a roof of thatch. Cob houses are always treated with rough-cast—limewash mixed with pebbles which serves the same purpose as pargetting.

The sun-baked bricks of which many villages in eastern England were largely built a hundred years ago, were simply large squared lumps of clay, dried hard in the sun.

We now come to the second and more refined way of using mud: bricks which are made of earth baked in a kiln.

Between the collapse of Roman civilization and the late Middle Ages brick-making was almost a lost art. It seems to have been re-discovered in the fourteenth century and bricks were in great demand from the fifteenth century onwards. Different regions have their own colours, in great variety, from the pale yellow of

London stock, made in Kent, to the bluish black made in Stafford-shire which is used so much outside the county for railway cut-tings and bridges. Bricks were used at first to supplement timber, as filling for timber frames (Fig. 32, 3), or to provide the whole lower storey of a house timbered above, and finally timber con-struction gave way to brick altogether (Fig. 35). Long before this transformation was complete bricks had begun to appear in the most unlikely places—even in the pillars and arches of

FIG. 35. A timber string course in an early brick-built house.

churches. It was no longer thought necessary to have dressed stone for window frames, door jambs, dripstones, and cornices, though at first brick surfaces were plastered over to resemble stone. The fashions brought over the North Sea to East Anglia from Flanders, where brick building had early reached the highest degree of per-fection, influenced architects working in both brick and stone all over the country, whether they were planning on the grand scale or making a modest group of almshouses.

And 'this is where we came in.' In the sixteenth and seventeenth centuries when the last of the timber frames were going up and stone houses were becoming common, and when bricks were coming into their own again, the prehistoric skeleton of our villages, the ground plans discussed in an earlier chapter, began to be clothed with the form they have today.

Archaeologists and historians have only very recently begun an intensive study of cottages and farmsteads. The great house, and its predecessors, the medieval manor house, and the castle,

FIG. 36. Houses in disguise.

1. More or less symmetrical arrangement of windows: but note the small ones on the right, and the massive central chimney stack—early eighteenth-century alterations.
2. The timber frame was perhaps always faced with plaster, but new windows have been added on the first floor in the eighteenth century and a bay window in the nineteenth.
3. A timber-framed house tile-hung.

have been amply recorded and described. While the form of a mansion built after the Restoration usually owes little to local building habits, this can hardly be true of the older houses.

A local pattern can only be discovered by taking measurements, and recording every detail of all the old buildings in a neighbour-hood. This can be an exciting occupation, for it is not necessarily the houses which have promising exteriors which are most inter-esting inside. Many of the most ancient farmhouses, dating in part from the fifteenth century, are indistinguishable outside, at first glance, from others built in the nineteenth, because the old frame-work has been completely cased in stone, or brick, or hung with slates, tiles, or weather-boarding (Fig. 36. 3). Inside this casing you may find a stone newel staircase built against a mighty chimney, or the curving limbs of a pair of crucks may be visible in the bed-rooms.

How can an ancient house be recognized and dated?

Perhaps the first thing to look at is the surface of the building, for a curving outline betrays a timber frame or a cob wall. The next thing is the chimney. A large stack, built of rubble masonry, at the end of the building, or along the back, the base ten or twelve feet broad, is a sure sign of an old house (Fig. 40, 3). They built chimneys like that in the sixteenth and early seventeenth centuries, but not, except in very remote places, later than that. If the princi-pal stack is in the middle of the roof so that the base is concealed from outside, look at its size and shape as it emerges from the roof (Fig. 40, 2). A modern brick chimney has often been added to an ancient stack; on the other hand, the brickwork of the stack may be obviously much older than that of the house itself.

Roughly between 1660 and 1800, builders aimed at perfect symmetry, windows matching above and below. To some extent they were able to impose this pattern on the older houses they refaced, but the more modest the house the less would be attemp-ted, so that small windows, and windows irregularly placed, provide another clue (Fig. 36, 2) to the age of a building.

When a second storey was added to an old house the roof was usually too shallow to take dormer windows, and a gable end had to be provided to give light. This explains the type of house known as the Kentish Wealdan house, although it is found else-where. This house with its double floor and gable at each end, and high central hall, well illustrates the first stage in the develop-ment of upper floors. Roof spaces, what we call attics, were not used before 1600, and dormer windows were not invented until upper storeys had become the rule.

Brickwork has its own particular story to tell. English bond was especially popular in the early sixteenth century, Flemish in the eighteenth (Fig. 37, 1, 2, 3). Colour depends much on local variations, but in general the earliest bricks are very light in colour, a pinkish grey; Tudor bricks, though many-coloured, produce a rich red effect; seventeenth-century bricks are a rich red and smooth in texture. Differences in the colour of bricks or mortar often betray an alteration or addition to the fabric even when the new work has been carefully bonded in. Disturbances in the courses show where temporary supports have been put in when doors and windows were enlarged or inserted (Fig. 37a, 2).

Old bricks are small and irregular in shape. In 1770 a minimum size was imposed by statute; in 1784 a tax was levied at so much per brick, the trade responded with larger bricks and gradually the present standard of three by four by ten was established.

Old farmhouses were not pulled down, as a rule, if they came to be regarded as too uncomfortable to live in; either they were incorporated in the offices of the new house, or they were occupied, and remained in use, as stable, cowhouses, or the like. A chimney among the farm buildings is always worth investigating. I have visited such a house at Cudlipptown, a remote hamlet on the borders of Dartmoor. It had only one small window. There was a huge open fireplace with the rusty pot hooks still in position, and beside it the iron door of a bread oven built into the wall. The upper chamber was reached by an outside staircase. Yet this primitive dwelling was lived in by the farmer until the middle of the last century.

Devonshire farmhouses often conceal behind an undistinguished exterior beautiful plaster ceilings dating from the seventeenth century, and even medieval vaults. The attic is the place to look for ancient roofs if you can persuade the farmer's wife to let you go up. You may discover a stone vault or moulded tie beams, cusped wind braces and carved king post, hidden between the attic floor and the thatch. This would be the hall roof of a medieval manor house forming the core of the modern building.

The Council for British Archaeology has issued a report, in the form of an eightpenny pamphlet, entitled *The Investigation*

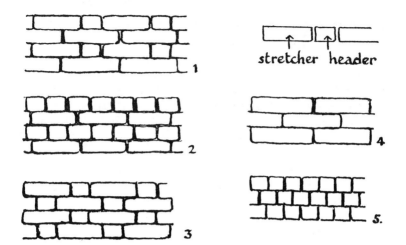

stretcher header

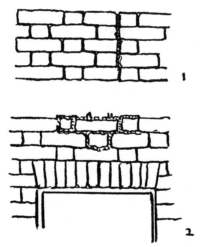

FIG. 37. (above) Bonding.
1. English bond.   2. English cross-bond.   3. Flemish bond.
4. Stretcher bond.   5. Header bond.

FIG. 37a (below) Looking for alterations.
1. Broken bond.   2. Disturbed courses: perhaps a support was
put in here when a new window was made below.

of Smaller Domestic Buildings, which sets forth briefly, but in more detail than has been possible here, how to make an intelligent examination of such houses, and how to record the results. Such records are very valuable now that so many of the old houses are disappearing, and an accurate record would find a welcome in the pages of the local archaeological society's transactions.

At the beginning of this chapter I spoke of a moment in time when our forefathers began to desire something more from their homes than a place to eat and sleep.

What was the first comfort they looked for?

There is no doubt about the answer: after food and shelter came privacy.

There was no privacy in Saxon times. The peasant, huddled in his cot with his family and his livestock, was hardly worse off in this respect than his lord. The timber hall might be warmer and safer, and food and drink might be more plentiful there, but one large apartment, with at best a few low partitions, housed the lord's family, his followers, servants and slaves, and sometimes his beasts as well. The house which stood within many of the 'moats' marked on the Ordnance Survey map was often no more than this. The stone-built hall which took its place in the thirteenth or fourteenth century already contained, at least, a separate chamber for the lady of the house, called a bower, and probably a store room as well. The animals had long ago been moved out, and the farm servants slept with them in their byres. (Though some old houses contained a men-servants' sleeping chamber, lists of household goods still record the presence of beds and bedding in the ox-houses as late as the end of the seventeenth century.) The rest of the household were still sleeping in the hall, and everybody ate and did their business there. In the next two centuries many improvements were added. A screen, that is, a solid wooden partition placed across the bottom of the hall, cut off the door and gave an extra room. A kitchen was added, at first often an entirely separate building, and a chamber would be built over the lady's bower. By the fifteenth century there was frequently a chapel as well.

A house of this sort is often hidden behind a Jacobean façade,

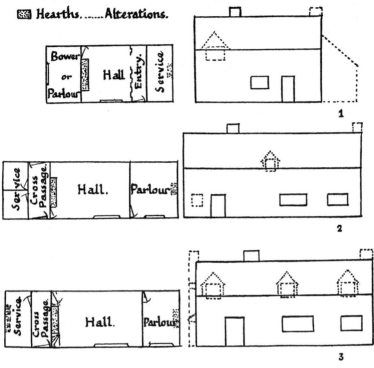

FIG. 38. The farmhouse: how the original plan may be discovered from the elevation.

1. Note the central chimney, position of door and window. An early plan, but already there are two service rooms (domestic offices: buttery, store-room, etc.). Addition: A lean-to kitchen, a second chimney stack, an upper floor, and a gable to light it.

2. Note, the position of door and stack; the long wall between door and old windows. A Dorsetshire yeoman's house of the fifteenth century. Second chimney stack to warm parlour, upper floor, dormer windows, window in the store room have been added.

3. The traditional Westmorland plan as described by James Clark. Note: Compare with No 2 above. Alterations: The service rooms become the kitchen or down house; upper floor and dormer windows.

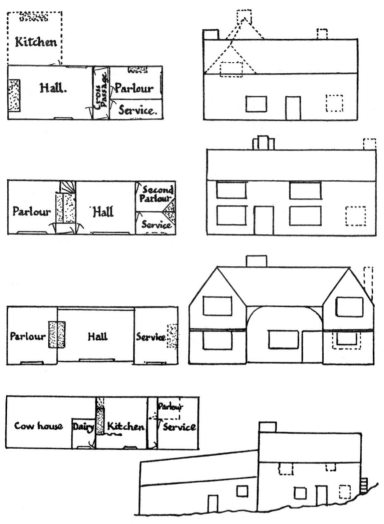

FIG. 39. The farmhouse.

1. Note position of original stack, window and door. A Midland plan; the kitchen wing is characteristic; in a nucleated village a farm may have a limited frontage and the house must extend backwards. Additions: Kitchen wing with gable made on front elevation to light first floor; hearth in parlour.

2. Note the large stack with four flues; door against the stack; contem

but many of them must have been pulled down at that time. Leaving aside the mansions, places like Montacute and Knole, the manor house of a middle-aged gentleman who had fought in the Civil War as a young man would have contained hall and parlour on the ground floor, and upstairs five or six chambers and a garret; the chambers would be over hall and parlour, and over an extensive range of offices. These would include kitchen, buttery, dairy, one or two brewhouses, a boulting house (in which the meal supplied by the miller was sieved to produce a flour suitable for white bread and pastry), and a cheese chamber, sometimes a wash-house. His yards would contain a malt house, ox-house, stables, and three or four barns.

The medieval manor house, if it survived without drastic alteration or enlargement, usually became a farm. Apart from its general appearance of antiquity it can often be recognized by the coat of arms over the door. A floor would be put into the hall about eight feet above ground level and the arched vault or hammerbeam roof in the upper room would be hidden away behind a common ceiling. Many of these houses so remain to this day, particularly in counties of scattered settlement, while others have been bought and restored in recent years by professional people or trust bodies.

The yeoman's house developed more slowly but along the same lines. The living quarters of the family consisted at first of one chamber divided by a screen, then bower and store room were added (Fig. 38, 1). Until the close of the sixteenth century farmhouses continued to be built as part of a long range which included the ox-stall and sometimes the barn, all easily reached from the house, and in highland districts farmsteads were still built in this

porary windows on ground and first floors. An early example of a sixteenth-century farmhouse with two floors, and four hearths, indicating the social standing and wealth of the Kentish yeomen.

3. Note: the double gables contemporary with the main body; position of door window and stack in hall. Known as the Wealdan house but found elsewhere; the house of a very prosperous farmer. (Fifteenth century.)

4. Note: The cowhouse built in one with the dwelling. Position of door, window, and chimney stack. The Welsh longhouse. The traditional plan of an upland cattle farmer. Alterations: the loft made into bedrooms, with newel stair by the central stack. The offices divided to make a parlour, though without fireplace.

way two centuries later (Fig. 39, 4). In 1794 Cumberland farmsteads usually comprised dwelling-house and barn, byre, and
stable, 'mostly built at each end of the farmhouse'. A kitchen and
parlour with bedrooms above had often been added at the back
under the same roof span; this was called an outshot. Another
common improvement was to make a new kitchen, the downhouse, in the byre or stable.

James Clark in a *Survey of the Lakes* wrote this in 1787: 'I cannot
however pass over the method of building each particular house,
especially as it . . . begins of late to be disused. From the front
door an entry runs close behind the fireplace of the better kitchen,
directly across the building to the back door, which opens into a
yard where the byre and stables generally are. On one side of this
entry is the door leading to the downhouse or kitchen where
they brew, bake, etc.; on the other side of the entry is the passage
into the house itself, for so the better kitchen is called, but this
passage is close to the back door so that before you arrive at the
fire you have almost gone round it. . . . Opposite to the fireplace
is the door of the chamber . . . where the master and mistress
sleep' (Fig. 38, 3).

In all these houses, roofs are of a single span; wings had not
yet appeared. Occasionally however the shippon for the cattle was
built in the form of an 'aisle' along the back of the house, under an
extension of the sloping roof, another use of the outshot; frequently today this contains kitchen and scullery. The need for a
kitchen away from the main living room of the house seems to
be the key to these alterations.

Can we discover the original plan of an old house?

There are not many different ways in which three or four rooms
can be arranged. In old houses the chimney is sometimes placed
against the parlour wall, instead of against the entrance passage
(Fig. 38, 1, Fig. 39, 3.); the front door may open into a vestibule
against the stack giving access to the parlour on one hand and
the kitchen on the other (Fig. 39, 2); the house which has only
kitchen and parlour usually has one or two little service rooms—
buttery or milkhouse—beyond the entrance passage. In the midlands the new kitchen often took the form of a back wing (Fig.

49, 1). The placing of old windows on the outside may provide a clue to the original arrangement of the rooms.

Until the middle of the sixteenth century the yeoman built his house of cob or timber, even where stone was to be had; thereafter, riding on a tide of prosperity he began to build in stone or brick and to add to the traditional two rooms—hall and parlour —kitchen and buttery, cellars, and an upper storey. At first the upper chambers were used as storerooms, but soon the children and servants were sleeping among the cheese and lumber, and presently the master and mistress went upstairs too. They often occupied the room at the head of the stairs so that there could be no coming or going without their knowledge. An awkward newel staircase built against the chimney or the merest ladder sufficed at first. A yeoman's house in Essex in 1670 contained a room called the falling door chamber, presumably having in it a trapdoor over the stairs.

When such arrangements were considered adequate by people of some property it may be imagined how miserably the poor were housed. No genuine cottages from this period have survived, for the old labourers' cottages are small farmhouses. Even these, which are often, and justly, condemned by modern standards, are very superior to the kind of shacks sometimes put up even a hundred years ago for farm workers, which might have no more than two tiny ill-lit rooms and a ladder for a staircase.

In 1539, on the eve of a century of rebuilding, for which the name 'the great rebuilding' has been coined, a small farmer's house in the Leicestershire village of Galby had only hall, parlour, and kitchen. A hundred years later a man with a similar farm had a living-room, buttery (probably a kitchen), and entry, and three bedrooms. Improvements on this scale were going on everywhere in prosperous lowland England, but do not seem to have come to the wildest and poorest parts of the country. In the nineteenth century a farmer in the Cleveland district of Yorkshire, who may well have employed more labour than our Galby man, slept with all his children and farmservants in the loft of his house, which was divided with rough wooden screens about four feet high, into doorless compartments; and such was the custom of the district. The men living in these horrible conditions were tenant-farmers, however, inhabiting the houses offered by indifferent landlords; it is not to be supposed that they would have built such places for themselves.

Herrick (1591–1674) describes his parsonage house in Devonshire thus:—

> A little house whose humble roof
> Is weatherproof;
> Under the spars of which I lie
> Both soft and dry;
> Where thou my chamber for to ward
> Hast set a guard. . . .
>
> Like as my parlour, so my hall,
> And kitchen, small;
> A little buttery. . . .

Hall, parlour, kitchen, buttery, one or two chambers above, this was an old-style parsonage. In Leicestershire, in Herrick's time, such houses were being replaced by larger and more dignified dwellings.

Why is the second chimney stack a modern one?

By the middle of the seventeenth century all but the poorest had achieved a modest degree of convenience and privacy, but not warmth; many houses had still only one hearth. Only one house in five had two fireplaces (one other besides the kitchen fire) in Leicestershire in 1670; three out of five had but one. By this date, however, chimneys in the modern sense of the word had become a commonplace. In 1500 even the most antique of what we call open fireplaces would have been a curiosity; a chimney in those days meant a structure of lath and plaster, comprising a hood and flue in the middle of the building which carried the smoke up to the roof. The smoke might escape through a hole in the roof itself or in the gable end (Fig. 40, 1). The tiny gables above hipped roofs often to be seen in old Kentish houses probably existed for this purpose, for they are never present in houses built after the introduction of chimneys. It is not surprising that the earliest kitchens were separate buildings; the dirt and danger of fire must have been very great. Brick and stone chimneys were being added to old houses from the middle of the sixteenth century. Shakespeare makes one of Jack Cade's followers say:

'Sir, he built a chimney in my father's house,
And the bricks are alive to this day to tell of it.'

When brick or stone chimneys became a normal part of every house, a bread oven was usually built into them beside the hearth. These are never used nowadays, but many of them still remain, especially in cottages. Outside the house there is a small rounded projection about shoulder height, roofed with slate or thatch (Fig. 40. 4); in Devonshire it is sometimes merely a bulge in the

FIG. 40. Chimneys.

1. Smoke hole.
2. Ancient central stack.
3. A stack added to an ancient house.
4. Old stack and bread oven.

135

accommodating cob wall. The oven has a small iron door at the back of the fireplace at shoulder level. When baking day came, the oven, which had its own flue, was filled with faggots, and when these had burnt out the bread could go in. As the oven was well insulated it retained its heat long enough to finish the baking. The ovens were not very large and could have no shelves since they had to be filled with fuel; hence the cottage loaf whose picturesque shape was invented to make it possible to bake two loaves in the floorspace of one.

The oldest houses had no glass in the windows. Our Galby farmer of 1539 probably had only shutters or wickerwork screens, his successor of 1740 had small leaded panes in his casements, but the price of glass would still have made it impossible for him to have many windows. By 1649, however, a prosperous yeoman was building handsome, tall windows with many lights, and enlarging old casements (Fig. 41). Those he failed to renew in the seventeenth century were often later replaced by sash windows. The Georgian sashes have small panes; the Victorians introduced plate glass (Fig. 42). The whirligig of fashion has brought casements back, but their first return was disliked by some country people, who regarded sash windows, like white bread, as a mark of social distinction.

One feature of most of the smaller houses of the Stuart period has all but disappeared. Many of them had earth or plaster floors. The labour of preparing floorboards by hand was very great, and with the price of timber constantly increasing, wooden floors would have been a very large item in the cost of building. But when so great a lady as Bess of Hardwick had a plaster floor in her bedroom the fashion was probably not entirely a matter of economy. Earth floors were skilfully made of puddled clay and if lime had been added formed a surface as hard as concrete. They tended to be very dusty, but our forefathers, with characteristic ingenuity, incorporated bullock's blood in the top layer which then polished like black marble. Knuckle bones and the small bones of hoof or trotter were often rammed into the floor in simple patterns to form a pavement. For the upper rooms a thick layer of brushwood, reeds, or coarse grass was nailed to the joists and a few inches of plaster laid on. These floors had two great advantages besides

FIG. 41. Windows.

1. Fourteenth century.
2. Fifteenth century.
2a. Fifteenth century, unglazed.

3. Sixteenth-seventeenth century.
4. Seventeenth century.
4a. Sixteenth-seventeenth century, unglazed with wooden mullions.

137

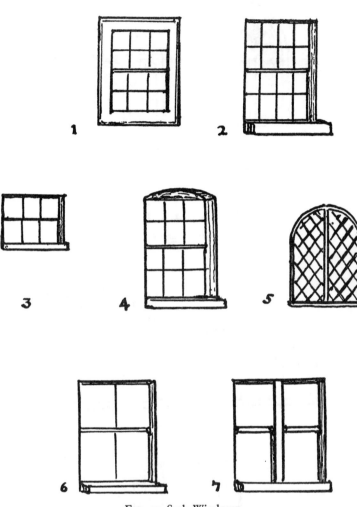

FIG. 42. Sash Windows.

1. Late seventeenth–early eighteenth century.
2. Eighteenth century.
3. Late eighteenth century.
4. Late eighteenth–early nineteenth century.
5. Late eighteenth–early nineteenth century Gothic revival.
6. Nineteenth century (plate glass).
7. Late nineteenth–early twentieth century.

cheapness; they were relatively soundproof, and less inflammable than timber.

Fire was an ever-present danger in houses built of timber and wickerwork. In many villages long hooks were kept for tearing down thatch which had caught alight, and for even more drastic purposes: often the only way to stop a fire from consuming the whole village was to pull down some of the flimsy shacks in its path. The fear of fire must have been a strong argument in favour of stone or brick in the reigns of Tudor and Stuart when so many men were devoting a part of their newgotten riches to the acquisition of greater domestic comfort.

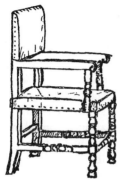

FIG. 43. Joined chair.　　　　Joint stool.

Although bricklayers and stonemasons multiplied in this period, the carpenter was not put out of business, for he still had plenty of work inside the new houses, making panelling, partitions, and furniture, and had, perhaps, more leisure to develop his skill as a joiner. The halls of yeomen's houses were acquiring an ever greater variety of furniture. The household ceased to sit together round the same table. The old board with its benches fixed to the partition was relegated to the servants' use while the family sat at a small 'joined' table, on 'joint' stools, and the master had a great 'joined' chair (Fig. 43). On the 'shelf board' winked a row of pewter dishes and brass basins in place of his father's wooden platters. The oak furniture, like the floor, had often been treated with bullock's blood and presented a surface as black and hard and shining as plastic. Towards the end of the seventeenth century hangings and cushions began to make their appearance; rush and cane chairs, embroidered upholstery, clocks, and (very occasionally) a pair of virginals found their way into the houses of well-to-do farmers, graziers, and shop-keepers.

While many a yeoman flourished and became a gentleman in the seventeenth century, smaller men reached a state of prosperity and comfort which they hardly improved upon for more than a hundred years. As time went on they added a few more chests and cupboards, a spinning-wheel, and a carved cradle to their household goods. Wooden platters (treen) gave way to Staffordshire earthenware before the end of the eighteenth century, and they adorned the mantelpieces with china figures, and china mugs ornamented with topical slogans such as 'God speed the plough' and 'Reform Bill 1832'.

Here is a picture of a village in 1814:

'Uppercross was a moderate sized village which a few years back had been completely in the Old English style; containing only two houses superior in appearance to those of the yeomen and labourers—the mansion of the squire with its high walls, great gates, and old trees, substantial and unmodernized—and the compact, tight, parsonage, enclosed in its own neat garden, with a vine and a pear tree trained round its casements; but upon the marriage of the young squire, it had received the improvement of a farmhouse elevated into a cottage for his residence; and Uppercross cottage, with its verandah, French windows, and other prettinesses, was quite as likely to catch the traveller's eye as the more consistent and considerable aspect of the Great House about a quarter of a mile further on.'

The craze among the sophisticated for 'cottages' was then in its first flush; farmhouses have constantly been 'elevated' in this way ever since. To this period also belong many of the model villages built for their tenants by enlightened landlords with a taste for architecture.

The dissolution of the monasteries had given the new rich of the Tudor period their opportunity to become landowners; the Agrarian revolution, the enclosures, and Victorian high farming brought the most substantial of the eighteenth-century peasants to the top; they became the rich tenant-farmers of the Victorian age. They lived in four-square uncompromising houses of red brick and Welsh slate, planted a monkey puzzle and pampas grass in the garden, and filled their houses with all the paraphernalia of Victorian civilization, the iron kitchen range, the piano, wallpapers festooned with roses, evangelical texts, waxed fruit, and an avalanche of knick-knacks. Their daughters became schoolteachers and their sons rode out hunting on good stout nags.

The labourers inherited many of the older farmhouses, which were often divided up into two or more cottages. They made them cosy with oleographs of the Queen, more china figures, and brightly-coloured rag mats made from the pretty calicos and fiercely dyed woollens that were coming so fast out of the industrial north.

Then a cold wind blew from the New World and very few farmhouses were built between 1870 and 1945.

By the nineteenth century the village trades- and craftsmen were already beginning to lose their importance; in the seventeenth century their houses differed little from those of the farmers. A mason in a small way of business would have the same accommodation as a husbandman—a hall, parlour, buttery, and two or three chambers above, one of them over the shop. He usually had a little yard at the back and a few acres where he kept a pig and a cow, or a few sheep, and some poultry. A blacksmith or a wheelwright often had as good a house as the average yeoman, with the same range of offices equal to those of many a gentleman— the inevitable dairy and brewhouse, malt-house, boulting house, and cheese chamber. (This range seldom, even in the best houses, included a washroom. No doubt the laundry was done in the yard. I remember as a child watching the washerwoman who came in once a week for the purpose, scrubbing our linen in a great wooden trough outside the back door. Many farmhouses in the north of England still have beside the back door the large stone slab called a dais on which such work was done.) The miller and the carpenter were often equally prosperous and comfortable; they invariably had some farming enterprise to rely on besides the profits of their trade.

Not so their great grandchildren; farming had become a whole-time occupation for those who could afford to rent a relatively large compact holding only. The tradesman was a tradesman and nothing else, and he no longer required a range of offices.

He moved while the going was good, into a compact modern house, and his old abode went the way of other unwanted houses; it was usually divided up into cottages.

BOOKS TO READ

The Development of English Building Construction. C. F. Innocent.
The Evolution of the English House. S. O. Addy., ed. Summerson, 1933.
Monmouthshire Houses. C. F. Fox and Lord Raglan, 1951.
The Recording of Architecture and its Publication, and
Notes on the Investigation of Smaller Domestic Buildings. Council for British Archaeology.
Farmhouses and Cottages. Basil Oliver. Batsford.
The Welsh House. I. Peate, 1944.
Midland England. W. G. Hoskins. Batsford.
Old Cottages, Farmhouses and other Stone Buildings in the Cotswold District. Davies and Dauber. Batsford, 1905.
Farm and Cottage Inventories. Introduction. F. S. Steer. Essex Record Office, 1950.

VII

The Buildings: Public Places

FIFTEENTH-CENTURY farmers and merchants, when they made their fortune, usually devoted some of their riches to adorning and improving the parish church. A hundred years later their descendants were faced with the need to replace all the charitable provision for the poor and afflicted which had been swallowed up by the government in the name of reform during the intervening years; moreover the most fervent Christians among them were frequently nonconformists. The generosity of Tudor and Jacobean merchants finds an honourable record in the grammar schools they founded, but the same can hardly be said of their counterparts, the thriving yeomen, waxing fat in country parishes. They had more sympathy for the aged than for the young; they would sometimes leave money for apprenticing boys to a trade but they very seldom founded a school. Those who could afford to do so presented their township with an almshouse, a neat terrace of tiny cottages intended for the old and well-behaved, and usually adorned with a plaque in gable-end or doorway, proclaiming the name and generosity of the donor. Almshouses, linen, blankets, and bread were the most popular benefactions throughout the seventeenth and eighteenth centuries.

A few, more enlightened than the rest, did make bequests for teaching all or some of the parish children, and gifts for this purpose are not uncommon in the wills of their womenfolk, but this usually meant wages for a schoolmaster, or a few pounds to encourage the curate to do the work, running the classes in their own homes, or in an aisle of the church. The familiar outline of the village school is nearly always a product of the Victorian age.

'The school should be faced with red bricks which might be pleasingly varied by interlacings of black heading bricks. . . . The porches, bay window . . . quoins, corbels . . . chimney shaft would be best formed of Caen or Bath stone ashlar, the belfry and ventilator painted and sanded to imitate stone. . . .

'The teacher's lodgings, as usual, consist of parlour, kitchen, pantry, two sleeping rooms over, and scullery, coal room, with a cellar under the stairs etc., the school and house together would cost £350.'

This school was intended for 85 children, allowing 65 square feet per child. It had no playground.

This reads like a description of many of our larger village schools, and such it probably is; for it was made when the *National Society for Promoting the Education of the Poor in the Principles of the Established Church*, founded in 1811, had already been at work for thirty years, and its schools, usually called National Schools, were going up in hundreds of villages all over the country.

This movement marked the culmination of a long, if spasmodic, effort on the part of philanthropists and religious bodies to provide some education for the labouring poor and lessen the wretched ignorance and disorder in which they lived.

Except for those who could gain admission to a monastery there was no education for country folk in medieval England, but the frescoed walls and the jewelled windows of the parish church had supplied some food for the imagination, and the liturgical pageant of the Christian year kept alive the people's interest in salvation. The reformers, intellectuals and politicians, between them swept everything out of the churches most likely to appeal to the minds and hearts of simple men, and by closing innumerable chapels-of-ease in outlying places, made church-going for more than half the rural population a weary business indeed.

In 1698 the *Society for the Promotion of Christian Knowledge* was founded. The S.P.C.K. began its work in London, stirring up the public to found 'charity schools where a number of the poorest children might be taught the three R's and the rudiments of Christianity'. The schools were a great success and the society soon extended its operations to the country. By 1729, 1,419 schools had been founded under its auspices, 268 in Lincolnshire alone.

At first the society was well supported by the various religious bodies and by the gentry, and hundreds of schools were founded by public subscription. Its activities had the further beneficent effect of stimulating the clergy in a duty enjoined on them but often neglected—that of teaching the children their catechism. If many of them were slack in this respect, however, the body as a whole responded nobly to the promptings of the S.P.C.K. But for them, few indeed of our villages would have had a decent school until the nineteenth century; many village schools which flourished for over a hundred years relied on the endowment of a single clerical benefactor.

Allowing for religious differences the aims of the founder of a Yorkshire school begun in 1702 were those of most philanthropists of that time. The master was to be: 'a member of the church of England, a layman of sober life and conversation, able to teach and instruct youth in reading, writing, and the common and useful rules of arithmetic—and once a week to cause his scholars to learn their catechism.'

School buildings of this period are not uncommon in the larger villages, though very seldom used as such. At South Zeal in Devonshire a handsome stone building occupies the island-site in the broad main street. At Bottisham in Cambridgeshire a charming example in brick, adorned with a pair of figures, boy and girl in charity school uniform, survives. At Blockley in Gloucestershire the classical pediment of the old school, defaced by advertisements and the record of several different occupations, still bears the inscription put there by the worthy founder, the vicar of the parish in 1713. There were about thirty such schools in Gloucestershire villages in 1724, about fifteen in Devonshire. Rugged, remote Westmorland stood at the head of the list.

In such a county, full of scattered hamlets and farmsteads, schools flourished in the most unlikely places. The parish of Addingham had a school in the hamlet of Maughamby. This was founded by the vicar of the parish in 1624. He endowed it with seventy-two acres of land, and no doubt the situation of the land determined the site of the school. In 1703 the school property consisted of 'a large school house, a mansion house, a barn and a beast house', and these are still to be seen at Maughamby farm.

In spite of the inconvenience of its situation this school flourished for two hundred years. In 1819 between forty and sixty children were attending it. It was superseded by a *National* school in a more accessible spot in 1866.

In such neighbourhoods, however, the situation convenient for the children of one generation becomes remote for the children of the next, and derelict school buildings are not an uncommon sight. In the parish of Thorneyburn, near the Scotch border, church and school stand alone at the end of a lane which becomes a cart track over the moors a few yards further on.

This seventeenth-century movement soon ran up against three overwhelming difficulties: quarrels between the various religious bodies, lack of staying power among the subscribers, and the indifference or hostility of the rural middle class who thought education for the lower orders at best an unnecessary distraction from work, and at worst an obnoxious incitement to rebellion. The Methodists continued to show a qualified zeal for education, but during the eighteenth century many schools suffered a lamentable deterioration in teaching and in attendance and sometimes they even passed out of existence. (A schoolhouse at Puddletown became a workhouse.) In most cases they survived, however, and when interest in education revived at the end of the century the charity schools and endowed schools became the élite among the schools of the poor, because their scholars learnt to read and write and cast accounts, and therefore joined the ranks of the black-coated workers. The new schools, industrial schools, founded to keep children out of the factories and to teach them a trade in healthier surroundings, and Sunday schools founded (partly at least) to keep working children out of mischief during their scanty leisure, aimed to teach Christianity only for which reading was thought to be necessary, but not writing and arithmetic.

Industrial schools were confined to the towns, but Sunday schools sprang up everywhere, and rather grim little buildings were put up for them. These often still show, over the door, the words Sunday School and a date round about 1800, in faded period lettering.

The modern Sunday school is a pale reflection of the original institution, though it still carries some of the prestige, and is usually fairly well attended. The nineteenth-century Sunday Schools lasted from early morning until late afternoon. The children had to learn even the rudiments of civilized behaviour such as cleanliness and decent manners. The day began with religious instruction and reading, and then the pupils were marched down to the church or chapel in an orderly crocodile. In the afternoon adults pressed in to hear the bible read, and the day finished with Evensong. It was easy to raise money for Sunday schools because they pleased everybody: the poor people and their children who flocked to the schools and found in them the spiritual and mental nourishment otherwise totally absent from their lives, philanthropists who saw how much good they were doing, employers who had no objection to education if it did not get in the way of work, and the rest, who were thankful to have gangs of lawless, pilfering children brought under control and taught a better way of life. Moreover the teaching was largely done by volunteers. The movement owed much to Hannah More, who founded many schools in Somerset and exhorted others to do so, pointing out that 'you need know nothing'. At Kirkstall in 1801 the teacher was a workman, who received a guinea for his services at Christmas and clothes for himself and his children. An elementary knowledge of the Christian faith and the ability to read were the only qualifications. Many devoted women came forward. Charlotte Yonge's novels picture a world in which the excitement and effort that went to the establishment of a village school play a large part.

Apart from these organized if inadequate efforts there was always an unknown and fluctuating number of private schools. The members of a Royal Commission sitting between 1858–1861 turned a cold eye upon them. The dames, they said, were: 'generally advanced in life and their school usually kitchen, sitting-room and bedroom.' The room 'so small that the children stand in a semicircle round the teacher. Indeed I have seen children packed like birds in a nest and tumbling over each other like puppies in a kennel.' The masters: 'None are too old, too poor, too ignorant, too feeble, too sickly, unqualified in one or every way to regard themselves, and to be regarded by others, as unfit for school keeping. Nay, there are few, if any, occupations regarded as incompatible with school keeping. . . . Domestic servants out of a

place, discharged barmaids, vendors of toys or lollipops . . .
milliners, consumptive patients, cripples, persons of at least
doubtful temperance . . . men and women of 70 or even 80 years
of age, persons who spell badly (mostly women I grieve to say)
who can scarcely write and who cannot cipher at all.'

'When other occupations fail for a time, a private school can
be opened. . . . Any room however small and close serves the
purpose; the closeness of the room renders fuel superfluous, and
even keeps the children quiet by its narcotic effects.'

In 1820, 5,500 parishes in England had only schools like these,
3,500 had none at all. Only about fifteen villages in Devon, and
twenty in Gloucestershire had some endowment for education.
Even in Westmorland only one child in seven attended school.
Allowing for the fact that some apparently unsuitable people
might have made good teachers by the standards of the time, and
received the respect and love of their pupils, seen against this
background, the village school, which will, in many cases, soon
be replaced or closed, appears as the triumph of enlightenment it
undoubtedly was when it was built a hundred years ago.

By 1830 the National Society had 3,670 schools, and they
aimed to provide an education at least as good as the charity
schools promoted by the S.P.C.K. had done. The Society continued to build and to improve their curriculum throughout the
century. In 1819 reading, writing, and arithmetic were taught at
Maughamby, with classics optional. In 1868 when the school had
been taken over and was being run on *National* lines the curriculum included geography, history, English Grammar; and one
child was learning mensuration. The classics had been dropped,
and less than half the children stayed at school long enough to
learn geography, history, and English. National Schools were
assisted by Government grants as they still are, for these are the
Direct Grant and Grant-Aided schools of today, and they are still
working, mostly as Primary and Junior schools, in a high proportion of villages. The Education Act of 1870 which made education
compulsory and caused a school to be built in every village merely
filled the gaps in an established system.

In the early centuries of the life of the village the churchyard
and the church formed the centre of communal life, alike for
social and religious purposes. Since the school was built it has

become the scene of every sort of secular activity; bazaars, socials, whist drives, dances, meetings, lectures, and elections all crowd in under the same convenient roof.

Between the church and the school as a place of meeting, comes the inn. There much parish business has always been transacted, there the villagers met to make their complicated arrangements about the cultivation of their common fields, there the inquest would be held on any unfortunate who came to grief, there clubs and friendly societies came together. If the innkeeper is not always the most popular man in the world with travellers, he usually enjoys an honoured place in his own community.

Nowadays few villages have more than one or two unpretentious pubs, what our forefathers called alehouses, or later, beer shops, but before their number was restricted by the Licencing Laws, alehouses were numerous in every place, many of them wretched themselves and spoiling business for others.

Nevertheless it was in the alehouse that the comfortable tradition of the 'local' was bred.

When Margaret Allen died in 1724 at Rothwell in Essex an inventory was made of her house and goods; she had a hall and a parlour, three bedrooms and some attics, the offices included three butteries, one of which was presumably the bar or tap room, and a brewhouse. There was a shuffleboard in the parlour. The following description, though taken from another source and a slightly earlier period, might stand for her.

'If these houses have a boxe-bush or an old post, it is enough to show their profeshion. But if they bee graced, with a sign compleat, it's a signe of good custome: In these houses you shall see the history of Judeth, Susanna, Daniel in the Lyon's Den or Dives and Lazarus painted upon the wall. It may bee reckoned a wonder to see, or find the house empty, for either the parson, churchwarden, or clark, or all are doing some church or court businesse usually in this place. They thrive best where there are fewest; . . . Hot weather and thunder, and want of company are the hostesses griefe, for then her ale soures: Your drink is usually very young, two daies olde: . . . if either hostesse or her daughter, or maide will kisse handsomely at parting, it is a good shooing-horne or bird lime to draw company thither again the sooner. Shee must be courteous to all . . . She suspects tinkers and poore soldiers most . . . She must keep in touch with three sorts of men that is; the maltman, the baker (for yeast) and the justices clarkes. Shee is merry, and half mad, upon Shrove tuesday, May-daies, feast dayes, and morris dances. A good ring of bells in the parish helpes her to many a tester . . . a bag-piper, and a puppet-play brings her in birds that are flush. Her ale, if new lookes like a misty morning, all thicke; well if her ale be strong, her reckoning right, her house clean, her fire good, her face fair, and the towne great and rich; she shall seldome or never sit without chirping birds to bear her company, and at the next churching or christning, she is sure to be ridd or two or three dozen of cakes and ale by gossiping neighbours.'

Margaret Allen's house could well have provided food and lodging, but we are not told that she was an innkeeper, and without an innkeeper's licence she would not have been allowed to do so.

In practice ale-houses often supplied meals and innkeepers sometimes refused, and it was the duty of the magistrates to keep them in order. For the sale of intoxicating liquor has always been the subject of interference by authority from the seventh-century Laws of Ethelbert of Kent to the Defence of the Realm Act of 1917 which established the opening times in operation today. Before 1872 beer could be sold all round the clock, and what beer! If the ale-wife's liquor fell below the required standard, the village ale-taster or constable was there to make trouble for her. The ale-tester used a homely test. He would come into the ale-house unannounced, clad in leather breeches, and call for a glass of ale. When it was brought he would pour a puddle of it on to the bench and sit down in it. There he would remain for thirty minutes by the clock, talking and drinking but immovable. When the time was up, he rose to his feet if he could, for if the ale had been adulterated with sugar his breeches would have stuck to the bench. There was enough natural sugar in the malt without the additions which would make the drink heady and unwholesome. The ale drunk in village inns must have been a valuable food to people whose diet otherwise contained very little sugar.

Many contemporaries of Margaret Allen's ale-house are still in use today as inns, especially in villages off the beaten track, where it is not worth the brewers' while to build a showy modern house.

The presence of a large and handsome old inn may mean that the village is a decayed market centre, like Codicote mentioned in an earlier chapter which has a fine Bell Inn, or it may mean that a modern road has by-passed a place which once derived a modest prosperity from passing travellers. A perfect example of this is to be found at South Zeal in Devonshire. This quiet village was once a small market town and has an ancient, stone-built inn, the Oxenham Arms. The decaying town received the *coup-de-grace* when a turnpike trust took over the Exeter-Okehampton road, the main road into Cornwall, making a new stretch running round the shoulder of the moor and eliminating the headlong plunge and steep ascent which took the old road through South Zeal. Devonshire is a good county in which to look for traces of the operations of the Turnpike Trusts, and as their work had a profound effect on inns and travellers we may pause for a moment to see what else they did to this one road, A.30, in the thirty odd miles between Exeter and Okehampton. Much of this road has been in use as long as there have been men in Devonshire. Its old course after leaving the city passed through the very high, steep country to the west, through the village of Whitstone, now a remote place, in 1724 sufficiently in the swim to be one of the few Devon villages with a charity school. It was a cruel road for wheeled traffic and a new one was made running easily up a little valley to meet the old road which comes in on the left as it enters Tedburn St. Mary (a village grown up by the roadside far away from its church). Between Tedburn St. Mary and South Zeal no alterations were necessary for the road follows the line of a prehistoric trackway, keeping to the high ground and avoiding deep valleys. These two improvements and a new surface made fast travelling, coaches going at about thirteen miles an hour on the flat, a possibility. Horses, however, could not maintain this pace dragging a heavy coach, particularly in Devonshire, for thirty miles, and in the whole of this stretch, after Whitstone and South Zeal had been eliminated, there was no town, no village, and no inn of any size. As a result, in the tiny hamlet of Crockern-well, $10\frac{1}{2}$ miles from Exeter, there stands a Georgian building with a dining-room large enough for a ball-room, and a graceful staircase, lit by an elegant fanlight, leading to two upper floors. There are many famous coaching inns, but this is not one of them, though it is handsome enough. It serves a tiny community and makes no attempt, as so many others have done in the last fifty years, to revive its greatness by catching the eye of passing motorists.

Travellers in the old days contrived the stages of their journeys so as to come at night to a town and only sought shelter in a village if they lost their way or misfortune delayed them. What sort of reception they would then receive would depend on the figure they could cut and the length of their purse.

A German pastor who travelled largely in England thus wrote in his diary:

'They showed me into the kitchen and set me down to sup at the same table as some soldiers and the servants. I now for the first time, found myself in one of those kitchens which I had so often read of in Fielding's fine novels. The chimney of this kitchen where they were roasting and boiling, seemed to be taken off from the rest of the room and enclosed by a wooden partition. The rest of the apartment was made use of as a sitting and eating room. All round on the sides were shelves with pewter dishes and plates, and the ceiling was well stored with provision of various kinds. . . . While I was eating a post chaise drove up; and in a moment both the folding doors were thrown open in order to receive, with all due respect, these guests, who, no doubt, were supposed to be persons of consequence. . . . The next morning I put on clean linen, and dressed myself as well as I could. And now, when I thus made my appearance, they did not, as they had the evening before, show me into the kitchen but into the parlour. I was now addressed by the most respectful term Sir; whereas the evening before I had been called only Master; by this latter appellation, I believe, it is usual to address only farmers and quite common people.'

The innkeeper of those days was apt to enjoy as dubious a reputation with travellers as the miller did with those who stayed at home. The following broadside or pamphlet on the subject of inns was published in the sixteenth century . . . 'It must not be accounted a small matter to afford house room, lodging, rest and food to the comforts of God's children. Though your house (as an Inn) be open to all men to come unto, yet account honest men your best guests.

'Because your guests are God's children, and their bodies the members of Christ, let their usage for meat, lodging, diet and sleep be such as becomes worthy personages.

'Content yourselves with an honest gain. . . . And for the guests . . . eat and drink for necessity and strength not for lust. At tables let your talk be powdered with the salt of heavenly wisdom, as your meat is seasoned with material and earthly salt.'

This pious advice was much needed. Here is William Harrison who wrote in his *Description of England in Shakespeare's Time*, on the subject of inns.

'And when he cometh to the inn and alighteth from his horse, the ostler is forthwith very busy to take down his budget or cap-case in the yard from his saddlebow, which he passeth slyly from hand to hand to feel the weight thereof; or if he miss of this pitch, when the guest hath taken up his chamber, the chamberlain that looketh to the making of the beds will be sure to remove it from the place where the owner hath set it, as if it were to set it more conveniently somewhere else, whereby he getteth an inkling whether it be money . . . and thereof giveth warning to such old guests as haunt the house and are of the confederacy.'

Customers genteel enough to be shown into the parlour ordered their dinner and had it specially prepared for them.

> 'Oh what have you got for dinner, Mrs Bond?
> There's beef in the larder and ducks in the pond.
> Dilly, dilly, dilly, dilly, come and be killed,
> For you must be served and my customers filled.'

The difference between the reception accorded to Nicholas Nickleby and Smike, on their walk to Portsmouth, from that which Tom Jones received on his travels gives some idea of the improvement of manners which the labours of school-founders, and better communications during the intervening hundred years, had brought about.

'If they be graced with a sign compleat, its a signe of good custome.' What was true in Cromwell's time is true today; an unusual or amusing sign is 'good shooing horn or bird lime' much commoner than a kiss at parting. One may speculate about the curious ones, but after all they generally only reflect the enthusiasm of some dead and gone landlord, whereas the Railway Inn, the Tramway Inn, and the Jolly Bargee may send us looking for a derelict piece of engineering which was once important in the life of the village; the heraldic ones, whether they display a full coat of arms, or a single emblem, like the Bear with a Ragged Staff, may well be the first or only news we shall get of gentlemen who once regarded the villagers as subjects, or even of those who built the inn, at the apex of their fortunes, to house the overflow of servants from their enormous mansions when they entertained their friends.

Our village map will now look much less like the unexplored regions of Antarctica. We have marked in fields, meadows, and commons; industrial sites, and roads created or altered in historic times. The various buildings with their materials and approximate dates might be indicated, and it would be an interesting exercise to place over it a tracing of the geological formation which would show how all are linked together.

BOOKS TO READ

The Charity School Movement. M. G. Jones. Cambridge, 1928.
A History of English Elementary Education. F. Smith, 1931.
Inns, Ales and Drinking Customs. F. W. Hackwood. Fisher Unwin, 1909.
The English Inn. T. Burke. Longmans, 1931.

VIII

The Church

'THE church of St. Michael is a small edifice of stone in the Norman and Early English styles. . . . The living is a chapelry annexed to the vicarage of Churcham. . . '

So reads the entry in Kelly's Directory about the church of Bulley, a small Gloucestershire village. Can such facts have any interest for those who do not care much about architectural styles, and have no personal concern with ecclesiastical organization?

The purpose of this chapter is to show that they have a wider meaning. To understand the series of rebuilding and alteration to which the fabric has been subjected hardly exhausts the significance of the building which has been the centre of the community for so long. The parish notice boards, slightly worm-eaten, and covered with dog-eared local government notices though they may be, should be at least as interesting as any tympanum or capital, however finely carved, for they are the gateway to some little explored territory. Here, first of all, we shall find the dedication of the church, the list of services, the status of the incumbent (whether rector, vicar, or perpetual curate), a notice about the repair fund, local government notices (they are there because the church was once in effect a Town Hall), diocesan notices; and all these lifeless announcements are threads in the fabric of history. The dedication perhaps links up with the Dark Ages, the status of the incumbent with the reign of the Plantagenets; the local government notices recall the Elizabethan settlement, and the new framework given to village life by Tudor and Stuart. The

list of services shows the yeast of Victorian church reform still
working, and the repair fund—ah, that is an old story! It may be
a new debt, but the trouble began when the church was built.

In considering church dedications, Bulley makes a good start-
ing point, with its church of St. Michael. The Archangel was very
popular with Celtic Christians. The common Welsh village name
Llanvihangel, whatever the present dedication of the church, pro-
claims him, and he has many churches in Wales, and round its
borders. Bulley itself may not be a case in point, but a dedication
to St. Michael would fortify any other evidence there might be
that the village-story reached back into the Dark Ages and beyond, particularly if St. Michael's church stands in some low-
lying spot. Such a church would have had its beginning in the
cell and attached oratory of some holy man.

The archangel's association with hill tops (St. Michael's Mount,
St. Michael's Brent Tor, to name two obvious instances), though
to us it seems an appropriate one, is a later development, and St.
Michael shares with St. Catherine all the most exposed situations
in Great Britain. This St. Catherine, the saint of the wheel, was a
maiden martyr of Alexandria, and perhaps because Alexandria
owned the most famous lighthouse of the ancient world, chapels
where a light was kept burning for the benefit of seamen or other
travellers were usually dedicated to her. The famous chapel at
Abbotsbury in Dorset where girls used to pray to the saint for a
rich and handsome husband, provided a warning light on the
dangerous Chesil Bank under Portland Bill; St. Catherine's lighthouse in the Isle of Wight is the successor of St. Catherine's
chapel whose ruins still stand on the downs above. St. Catherine's
Hill at Winchester was probably used in the same way by travellers
in the New Forest. The ruins of St. Catherine's chapel still crown
the ferocious rocks of Hartland Point.

Another saint of high places is St. Edward, the martyr, elder
brother of Ethelred the Unready, a youth who, notwithstanding
his canonization by popular acclaim, seems to have been an even
less satisfactory character than his half-brother. His shrine at
Shaftesbury, which is a notable landmark, probably inspired the
founder of the church at Stow-on-the-Wold in a rather similar
position, and perhaps some others.

The idea that every church should be dedicated to a particular patron is not an immemorial one. Some of our churches acquired, and some changed their patrons, within historic times. St. Thomas of Canterbury's churches, for example, must originally have had another dedication, and it is thought that devotion to St. Helen, the finder of the true cross, was brought home by the Crusaders, or by the numerous pilgrims to the Holy Land for whom they opened the way. The fact that many of her churches seem to lie along the old main arteries suggests another possibility. Did villagers living by a main road think a church dedicated to one of the pilgrims' special saints would be good business? Rebuilding or enlargement may have been the occasion for a change. Crooked churches, that is churches where the chancel is not aligned with the nave, or where the tower is out of line with the body of the church, are thought to be a sign of changed dedication. It was the custom, in the ages of faith, for the people to spend the night before their patron's feast watching and praying, and when the sun rose they noted the spot where it first appeared and built their church facing towards it. This explains the fact that few churches face due east.

It is possible sometimes to hazard a guess at the original dedication. Many villages still have a feast day—the 'revel' it is called in Devonshire, 'wake' in the north—and this is usually connected with their patron saint without, however, allowing for the eighteenth-century alteration of the calendar; thus the feast of Ashton in Northamptonshire is kept about the 11th of October, a fortnight after St. Michael's, the patronal feast. If the date of the feast bears no relation to the saint's day even when the fourteen days' time-lag, due to the alteration of the calendar two hundred years ago, is allowed for, it may relate to an older patron. Unfortunately for this line of research, the saint may have disappeared even from the Roman Calendar.

The precise connection between the Celtic saints and the churches dedicated to them can never be fully known. In some cases, the saint or his disciples may really have visited the place, but very often the naming of the church only reflects the favourite devotion of the man who built it, or the activities of a monastic body spreading the cult of its patron, or even a pious fashion. St. Nectan's church at Hartland is an example of the first, Rumonsleigh, also in Devon, of the second of these reasons.

We may suppose that the Norman Conquest swept away the names of many Saxon saints. The supreme crises in the nation's history leave more mark in the church than in the fields. If very few churches bear a dedication to King Charles the Martyr very many show in their fabric the scars inflicted by the winning side in the Civil War, news of the Reformation is written large everywhere, and no church is without a memorial to the catastrophes of our own day.

'The living is a chapelry annexed to the vicarage of Churcham.'

What light does this statement throw on the history of the neighbourhood?

In 1292, when this chapel of St. Michael at Bulley first appears in recorded history, it was merely a chapel-of-ease within Churcham parish. The men of the hamlet would have been obliged to carry their dead to Churcham for burial and to go thither also to marry and baptize their children. Fortunately it was not a long journey. The people of Dowdeswell in the same county had to carry their dead three miles over the wolds to their parish church at Withington; the inhabitants of Moreton-in-the-Marsh waited till 1516 to obtain from the pope permission to bury their own dead, pleading the hardship of carrying them over the hills in winter to their mother church at Blockley, between three or four miles away.

All over England in the Middle Ages, the funeral cortège and the bridal procession must have been a common sight in lanes and highways; and perhaps in stories told of haunted lanes and ghostly lights there lingers some folk-memory of those days. Perhaps in some place which 'no horse would pass' a coffin was once tipped over by bearers who had fortified themselves too thoroughly for a long and arduous journey; or in another, where flickering lights were seen, a drunk, startled from his sleep in the ditch by a passing funeral, swore ever after he had seen a ghost.

Bulley and Dowdeswell have long been separate parishes, and if they have not each a parson of their own today, they share his ministrations on equal terms with a neighbouring village.

Between 1292 and 1535 seventeen chapels-of-ease in Gloucestershire attained the status of parish churches; nevertheless before the earlier date the network of parishes had nearly reached the state in which it was to remain for six hundred years. There were some gaps in the high wolds, and on the heavy forested clays of the Vale, and Dean still lay in the grip of Forest Law, its miners and foresters living in the small settlements round the fringes. Two parishes, Pinnock and Roel, in existence in 1292, had vanished by the later date, and one chapel (at Beachley) on the banks of the Severn had been swallowed up by the river.

The ruins of Roel Church remain among the buildings of Roel farm, and since churches are solid structures some trace of a vanished parish is usually to be found. Sometimes a tradition about the mother church lingers on, or some items in the parish registers provide a clue. The people of Shurdington in Gloucestershire returned to their mother church of Badgeworth when their own church was destroyed in 1641, and their registers were kept there for two hundred years.

Where the parish boundaries reveal that a larger entity has been carved up, the mother church, probably, though not certainly, identifies the parent settlement. Some accidental circumstance may have given one of the offshoots some extraordinary importance. St. Peter and St. Paul, Blockley, the mother church of three or four parishes, was merely a woodland clearing belonging to Batsford until it came into the possession of the Bishop of Worcester. The parent settlement is a tiny village situated in the extreme corner of a small parish, all that remained after the original unit had been divided; a division made not long before the Norman Conquest.

Between 1292 and 1535 the country's chief wealth had been her famous sheep walks, hence the steady development of dependent chapelries into separate parishes, and the appearance at the later date of a number of entirely new parishes and chapels. Before 1535, however, the emphasis had already shifted from wool to finished cloth, and therefore from the wolds to the valleys, to the banks of the streams which drove first the simple fulling mills and later more complicated machinery. New settlements and old expanded and flourished throughout the fifteenth, sixteenth and seventeenth centuries in the South Cotswold valleys, which still produce some fine and famous cloth. But when the hungry sheep in these new villages looked up the pastors who fed them were mainly nonconformists. Only two Anglican chapels, at Chalford and Pitchcombe, were built in the valleys between 1535 and 1834.

By 1834 the Church of England had already stirred itself, and in the next half century two hundred years of neglect were amply made good. The Victorians built and endowed 43 new churches and chapels in the Gloucestershire countryside and repaired hundreds of dilapidated wrecks. They restored desecrated chapels (among them the chapel of Little Badminton which had been used as a barn for many years), and even the lost chapel-of-ease at Beachley swallowed up by the Severn so many hundreds of years before was replaced. It is no longer the fashion to despise their taste in architecture, but perhaps justice is even yet not done to their zeal and piety. It cost them a considerable effort to build those churches which are now often an embarrassment to their successors, whose present task is to create workable units comprising several parishes. The wheel has come full circle, and these units may be compared with the districts served of old by the Saxon minster.

'The living is a chapelry attached to the vicarage of Churcham. Great tithes . . . are paid to the Dean and Chapter of Gloucester.'

That every parish should have its resident minister supported by the revenues of the parish is an ideal which has never been quite capable of fulfilment, nor were the parish revenues originally intended solely for this purpose. In Saxon times, before the parochial system had come into existence, a tax called church scot, and a more or less voluntary contribution called tithe, were paid to the mother church or minster of a district not unlike an enormous parish, and staffed by a body of clergy who served the surrounding country. Churches called minsters and place-names incorporating the element *minster* sometimes indicate the situation of one of these centres; but unfortunately the Saxons used the same word for a monastery; and many churches which were 'minsters' have long ceased to bear the title.

Church scot was a money payment, but tithe was rendered in goods, especially corn, and both were used at the discretion of the clergy, as much for the relief of the poor, and for the support of religious bodies, as for the upkeep of the mother church. At this time many villages had no church, only a hallowed place of assembly to which the priests of the minster came, others had little chapels called 'field churches' built and owned by the landlord, who could close them or pull them down if he chose.

As the payment of tithe became a legal obligation, so it came to be recognized that a man who had built a church on his estate, and was supporting a priest, should devote his tithes and those of his tenants which he was responsible for collecting, to its maintenance. Certain rights were usually reserved to the mother church, notably that of burying the dead. Hence the arrangements already described which lingered on for several hundred years. Blockley, which has already been mentioned, had a nimbus of six or more parishes, and we can discover several more such centres in the same county—at Bibury, Deerhurst, and Withington for example. All these churches, except Blockley, still have some Saxon work in them.

Eventually control of the parish church passed from the owner to the bishop of the diocese, and its revenues were again frequently diverted to the use of the church at large, especially to the support of monasteries. Licences were often granted to religious houses to 'impropriate benefices', that is, to take over the revenue of churches on their estates. A condition was usually attached that a vicar should have a part of the income, or be paid a stipend for living in and serving the parish. He might be a young priest beginning his career, or a man without cleverness or influence enough to get on. At the dissolution of the monasteries the enjoyment of the tithes and endowments passed to the lay purchasers of monastic property, and such parishes are served by vicars to this day.

Most vicars and perpetual curates have at all times been obliged to live in a very modest way. In the Middle Ages they lived very much like the peasantry from whose ranks they were drawn, farming the church land to eke out their stipends and offerings. After the Reformation they generally ceased to have this resource, but relied on a growing amount of petty legal business in connection with the parish government, acting tutor to the squire's son, or running a small school. Their best hope of obtaining an adequate living was to get preferment to more than one benefice (called holding in plurality); then, indeed, they were quite comfortably off and could hire a curate to share, or sometimes take over, the work. A curate might be paid in the Middle Ages from £2 to £5, as little as £5 in Queen Anne's reign, in Queen Victoria's from £50–£70 per annum. The ideal of a resident parson in every parish was nearly achieved towards the end of the nineteenth century when prices were so low that it became possible for a man to live in modest comfort on the stipend of one parish, particularly if he had a little money of his own. This state of affairs did not survive the first German war and since then the amalgamation of parishes into rational working units has been going on. The twentieth-century pluralist holds his livings around him, not scattered, as sometimes in former ages, up and down the county, or even beyond it.

How large in all those early arrangements loomed the burial of the dead! A church with a graveyard was a minster controlled by the bishop of the diocese, and served by a body of priests. A field church had no graveyard and was dependent for its very existence on the whim of the man who built it.

How comes the right of sepulture to be the mark of full parochial status?

To this day some part of the body of a saint reposes beneath every Catholic altar; even the portable stones that missionaries and chaplains use have some small relic enclosed in them. In every church built before the Reformation it was the same. St. Gregory had instructed his missionaries to consecrate the familiar places of worship, pagan though they were, by burying in them relics of the saints. This would not have seemed strange to the natives, who were already in the habit of holding all important gatherings or religious ceremonies on a tumulus, the grave of a departed chief, or of hallowing a place of meeting by a burial. The Christian use of relics was not so much a take-over from paganism as an idea deeply rooted in the hearts of men.

Many churches were built on the site of old burial mounds (Fig. 44), or within the confines of a pagan place of meeting, the circular moot, for instance, which many British villages had (the Cornish Rounds and the moorland stone circles are examples of these). Many of these were probably still in use, for the Saxons had a word, *ciric*, derived, apparently, from the Latin *circus*, which they immediately applied to the Christian church, or, more probably, to the Christian graveyard which preceded it. The Saxons were familiar with the sight of an amphitheatre; King Edwin of Northumbria (616–632 A.D.) modelled the timber seating for the assembly of his thegns at his court at Yeavering on the form of a

FIG. 44. A church built on a prehistoric burial mound.

Roman circus. In the same place excavation shows the church to have been built in the existing cemetery. It is easy to understand that between the coming of Christianity and the building of a church, the ground made sacred by the bones of their fathers would be the place chosen by Saxon and Briton alike for religious rites. Some of the furniture and vestments of the church have their origin in the assumption that the ceremonies will be conducted in the open air—the cope, for instance, which is but an outdoor cloak, and the canopy over the altar. The first structure erected within the perimeter of the graveyard was in many cases merely such a canopy, to protect the sacred vessels.

The magnificent stone crosses which we sometimes find in the north of England were presumably set up to mark the consecrated place long before a church was built. The shape of the cross-head, where it survives, will show whether it was set there by Angle or Northman. Scandinavian crosses have wheeled heads and crude though lively sculpture with a mingling of pagan and Christian symbolism; simple cruciform heads, stately figures and highly formal designs of interlaced strapping, leaves, and beasts mark English or British handiwork.

The simple crosses common in churchyards were, however, market crosses, set there in the Middle Ages, when it was thought to be no desecration, but a guarantee of honesty, to do business in the shadow of the church.

The oldest churches contained the living quarters of the priest. The circular enclosure which ultimately became the churchyard sometimes started as the tiny domain of a holy man containing only his cell and oratory. The priests at Deerhurst lived in the tower. At Bradford-on-Avon the priest seems to have lived in an annexe. A room over the porch may have been used for this purpose and even, occasionally, a room over the chancel, reached by the so-called rood stair; but this last was early forbidden by church law. One or two such lofts survived, however, to be used much later as dovecotes by the incumbents.

The chancel, then, is the original church—the shelter for the altar, with or without the priest's living quarters attached, with the congregation gathering around and standing outside. To this day the chancel is the responsibility of the parson, the nave that of the parishioners—if the people want shelter while they attend Divine Service, they provide it for themselves.

If the priest lived in his part of the building it is hardly surprising that the people should think of secular uses for theirs. In exposed districts they built towers like fortresses, able and obviously intended to shelter them in time of trouble. Such is the tower of Shalfleet in the Isle of Wight, a refuge from pirates sailing up the Newtown river; the tower of Garway on the Welsh Marches is another example. Church towers in Northumberland sheltered their people when the Scots were on the move. The round flint towers on the coast of Norfolk and Suffolk (Fig. 45), where even the entrance is several feet from the ground, were built when the age-old terror of raiders from the sea was still alive and real.

In settled districts, however, the Saxon built his church of wood and it has long ago been replaced by one of stone. In course of time the tower became the permanent repository of a good deal of secular equipment used for the community, from the chest containing the documents on which the efficient running of the parish depended, to the hooks used for tearing down burning thatch.

By far the greater number of church towers witness to fourteenth- and fifteenth-century piety either towards God, or towards the centre alike of their spiritual and material lives. For the church fulfilled the function of the village hall, the school, and even to some extent the inn. It was the focus of all that was most profound and most frivolous in village life, from the parish mass to the church ale (ancient counterpart of the Whist Drive and Dance), a highly secular entertainment got up for a good cause, 'to be held in the churchyard on the morrow of Whit Sunday', a contemporary poster might have run, 'in the church if wet'. The grotesque faces which glare or mouth from the capitals in the nave, or the homely figures caught there by the sculptor in some all too human predicament, would have provided an appropriate setting for such gatherings.

No wonder the village people were prepared to pour out their money in order to improve the little dark buildings of an earlier day, and to scrap some of their favourite frescoes to make room for large windows in the modern style, to make the church dark as Aladdin's cave with jewelled glass, and then to flood it with light again by adding a clerestory.

The use of the church for secular purposes explains also the larger additions: the extra aisle added to the church already large, and the porch. Such aisles were often built by parish guilds (mutual benefit societies rather than craft guilds) for their meetings.

The church porch was used for the swearing of all solemn contracts, from marriages to deeds of sale. Nevertheless, though the motives of the makers may be comprehensible, when we are confronted by some masterpiece of building in a village of some four or five hundred souls we may well ask:

Who paid the bill, and how?

Most of the original churches had been built by the local proprietor, but the whole parish contributed to enlarge and beautify them. The size and beauty of the church, and the style and period of the improvements, is a sure record of the fortunes of a village, between the Norman Conquest and the Dissolution of the monasteries. Even if the land was owned by some magnate willing to

FIG. 45. Contrasts in flint.

1. 'Terror from the sea.' A Norman defensive tower with a fifteenth-century parapet in a small, poor parish.
2. 'The golden fleece.' The steeple of Eye built in 1475.

FIG. 46. Spires: 1, 2, 3, from Northamptonshire, and one from over the border (4). Bloxham in North Oxfordshire.

FIG. 47. Spires: local styles. Two from the Fenland.

do his part, the people of a poor upland parish could never achieve a handsome church; they would hardly manage more than one or two new windows, and perhaps an extra storey, with battlements and pinnacles, on the tower (Fig. 45).

There is one exception to this generalization: a monastery or other religious body might flourish on poor soil, and leave behind a church built on the grand scale. The nave of such churches was frequently used as a parish church, and it was therefore bought, usually without the choir (which was pulled down or fell into ruins), by the parishioners at the Dissolution.

No doubt the element of competition had its share in the decision to rebuild and improve. The men of one parish would hardly bear to be outdone by some despised neighbour, to whom they

FIG. 48. Towers: local styles.

1. Wiltshire and Berkshire.　　3. Gloucestershire.
2. Suffolk.　　　　　　　　　　4. South Devon.

169

would give the sincerest form of flattery. Contracts frequently provide that the various features of the building shall be copied from one or more neighbouring churches: 'a new steeple sixty feet high, the thickness of the steeple of Framsden, string courses as Framsden but in the style of Braunston . . . the other wyndowes and boteracies of the sd stepyll after the facion of the stepyll of Braunston.' This was at Helmingham, Suffolk. Round about Bloxham there are a number of copies or precursors of its beautiful spire—at Adderbury, King's Sutton, and Middleton Cheney, for example (Fig. 48). Rutland has its characteristic blunt spire (Fig. 48), and the beautiful specimens at Ketton and Louth are each members of a numerous family. Spires seem to have been in fashion in the thirteenth and early fourteenth century, and are therefore commonest in the parts of the country enjoying great prosperity at that time, such as the hinterland of Boston which then exported more wool than any other port in England (Fig. 47). A hundred years or so later, when wool was being made into cloth at home, and was bringing riches to different parts of the country, towers had become more popular and many a western village was able to find the money for a tower in the perpendicular style, with battlements, pinnacles, and buttresses. In these also local styles developed. Devonshire has tall slender towers with a pronounced turret staircase (Fig. 48); the noble Somerset towers, especially on the limestone belt, have elaborate pierced battlements, tall pinnacles and large windows (Fig. 49), the richest Gloucestershire towers are crowned with a parapet of blind arcading, with elaborate pinnacles. Herefordshire, Shropshire, and Essex produced their own distinctive, but rather similar belfries, often containing much timber (for those counties were still rich in woodland). The glorious carving of screen and roof in Devonshire and Norfolk reflect alike the triumph of the English sheep; one side of a medal which has a deserted village and an out-of-work labourer on its other face. Each region, if not each county, has its own characteristics, but few proclaim their origin so clearly as the little church at Cranham in Gloucestershire, built between 1292–1535, which sports a pair of clothworker's shears on one buttress of the tower.

The absence of good building stone merely acted as a challenge to a rich community. The unpromising local flint, transfigured by arches, quoins, buttresses and window tracery of freestone brought from far away, provided the bulk of the material for some of the most glorious Suffolk churches. The men of the eastern marshlands fetched stone from Barnack, away in Northamptonshire, or overseas from Caen, and wood from the midland

FIG. 49. Contrast in granite.

1. Tin mining boom.   2. Poor moorland parish.

forests to build, in the middle of a peat bog, their soaring towers and spires and breath-taking timber roofs. At Widecombe in the Moor a tin-mining boom enabled the people to add a graceful tower to their handsome church, built of their own unfriendly granite.

What did it cost to build a parish church?

Labour is usually the largest item in any estimate, and about this we have some intelligible information.

William Horwood, the mason who built the nave and steeple (a lantern tower) of the church at Fotheringay, a noble building on the banks of the river Nene, contracted to do the work for £300. This was in 1434. This sum included the wages of his workmen, but all the materials were to be provided. The contract contains detailed specifications for the building which was to match the existing choir.

'And either of the said isles shal have six mighty botrasse of free-stone, clen-hewyn; and every botrasse fynisht with a fynial . . .

'And the clerestory both withyn and without shal be made of clene asheler growndid upon ten mighty pillars, with four respounds. . . .

'And in each of the said isles shall be five arches abof the stepill, and abof every arch a wyndow, and every wyndow of four lyghts, according in all points to the wyndows of the clerestory of the said qwere. . . .'

This work was done to the order of a high and mighty prince, the Duke of York, and the contract contained a clause that if it were not finished in the time agreed, William Horwood should be imprisoned and his goods confiscated. The common people could impose no such sanctions, although their contracts usually contained a time clause, and the work often came to a standstill. 'To the fabric of the church of Chesham, £6 13s. 4d. on condition that the parishioners on their part carry out at their own expense the work, recently begun, of restoring the church, and not otherwise,' runs a clause in a medieval will.

Two contracts for the building of church towers at Arlingham in Gloucestershire in 1372 and at Dunster in 1442 may be compared; the towers are similar. The mason at Arlingham was paid quarterly at the rate of 17s. and a bushel of wheat for every foot of height, and hay for his horse. He was to build twelve feet a year for three years to finish a tower already begun. The mason at Dunster was to build the tower from the crossing, a hundred feet high (Fig. 50), to the design of another mason (architects were not so called in those days) and he was to be paid 13*s*. 4*d*. for every foot completed. The work was to take three years in both cases. In both places the parishioners were to supply all material and the necessary tackle, and deliver it in the churchyard. At Dunster they would help in moving any stone too large for two or three men to handle; at Arlingham a workshop was to be made available. A present-day stone-mason would probably recognize all the tools in that workshop, except the dogfish skin used for finishing.

FIG. 50. *Left*: The tower of Dunster church. The mason was paid 13*s*. 4*d*. per foot. *Right*: The S. Herefordshire-Worcestershire type of tower—a district with plenty of timber and no building stone.

The mason who built the tower at Helmingham undertook to make good any defect which might appear within twenty years at his own cost.

A carpenter contracted to provide a wagon roof for the choir at Halstead in Essex containing at least thirty couples of rafters, finding all material and labour for £12 13*s*. 4*d*. He made a separate agreement to have the walls inspected and raised three feet and the roof tiled. For this he was to have the old roof, £1 6*s*. 8*d*, and stuff for a new gown. This was in 1413.

Raising money for the upkeep of the church is no modern preoccupation. Perhaps the chief recourse was the 'church ale'. For this gathering, held usually at one of the great feasts, the church-

wardens would beg malt from the farmers of the parish, brew a
vast quantity of strong ale, and call upon the people to come and
drink it. Some parishes had a fixed tariff—a family man paid so
much, so much for a bachelor, so much from a stranger from outside the parish, but all were expected to contribute. The ale was
brewed in the church house, if the parish could afford to build
one. It stood close by the churchyard, and when not being used
by the churchwardens was frequently leased to an ale-wife and
used as an ale-house. Such indeed it frequently became after
'church ales' had been abolished.

'The Steeple of Eye (Fig. 45, 2.) was built in anno 1470 as
aperith by the book of Accompt. The church wardens gatheryd
that year partly with the plough, partly in Church ales, partly in
legacies given that way, but chiefly by the frank and devoute
hartes of the people the some of £46 in litell odd money. They
obtained 25 cwt of lead from the Prior to be repaid in kind or
else to pay for the same at ye Sturbridge fayre next followinge.
They remain indebted for all the flynt stone to ye work or for a
gret parte thereof bought by Mr Hynnyngham.'

The broken shaft of a market cross in the churchyard recalls
the time when the precincts of the church hummed with activity.
When the churchyard was the proper place for an honest man to
do business, when the school and the court were being kept inside
the building, and the churchwardens hurried between it and the
churchhouse, preparing for a gigantic festivity intended to raise
money for mending the roof or building the tower, the churchyard naturally became a fairground on occasion, stalls and sideshows were set up, and the villagers danced and played among the
fresh graves. Fresh they were, for no one lay long in a medieval
churchyard. Hardly had the flesh dissolved in dust before the soil
was turned again for a new tenant. Those who could afford to
purchase for themselves an undisturbed resting place were buried
within the church. There might be a few flat altar tombstones
outside, but the familiar headstone must have come into fashion
after the secular business had been banished. Headstones conform
to the pattern which governs all the rest of man's handiwork in
the village, first the material quarried within the neighbourhood
adorned with as much of the taste and fashion of the period as had
filtered down to the village stone-mason, then the factory-made

article brought in by rail, the same in Thanet or Wharfedale. The memorials inside the church owe less to local craftsmanship. Even the earliest effigies, whether carved in stone or alabaster, come from workshops with a wider, sometimes a national reputation, and few villages would have had a foundry capable of producing a monumental brass in the fifteenth-century style. Even the slabs of slate popular in the sixteenth, seventeenth, and eighteenth

FIG. 51. Two Somersetshire towers. The one on the right is from the Gloucestershire border, cf. Fig. 48. 3. When a Somerset man became Archbishop of York, he introduced the style in the Ridings.

centuries, which may have come from a local quarry, have often been carved by a craftsman highly skilled in lettering and heraldry, obviously a specialist.

We may be sure that much of all this rebuilding and beautifying would never have been undertaken if the old church had not been falling down. It is a mistake to suppose that the Norman builders never did a shoddy piece of work, or that the sheer weight and bulk of masonry in which they put their trust always stood firm.

The reports of the periodical diocesan inspections, called Archdeacon's Visitations, show that the fabric often began to give trouble long before it became venerable. Nor did the villagers always embark on repair and improvement with enthusiasm, and they often found it difficult to raise enough money to finish the work. Nevertheless in prosperous districts the work of modernization went on right up to the Reformation. The stones of some of the guild aisles and porches must still have been white when the revolution came.

Thereafter few additions were made, and only the most necessary repairs performed, and these were usually made to harmonize as much as possible with the existing structure. Simple window heads, gothic in form but without tracery, are easily distinguished as post-Reformation work.

Churches were built in the contemporary style only when the whole fabric had been destroyed or a new parish created, for instance, when some of the enormous parishes on the Scottish border were carved up, and simple churches traditional in shape but more or less up-to-date within, made their appearance among the moors.

The eccentricity of the squire sometimes endowed his village with an architectural curiosity—a church in the Moorish, the Palladian, the Lombardic manner—but if his interests lay in other directions the fabric fared worse. The maintenance of the church fabric has always been a costly business, and in the seventeenth and eighteenth centuries incumbents and parishioners seldom had either the money or the enthusiasm for the work. The application of one parish, Saleby in Lincolnshire, for a licence from the bishop to carry out repairs illustrates the general attitude.

'Sheweth that the West End of the Steeple and Church of Saleby being chiefly erected of Wood and Timber and although they have been frequently repaired, yet by length of time, they are so ruinous and decayed, as that they can no longer be repaired but must be taken down and rebuilt. That your petitioners propose to rebuild the Steeple with Brick, the Expense whereof is estimated at the Sum of forty pounds and upwards. That your petitioners, being Farmers at rack rent cannot afford to raise so large a Sum amongst themselves without injury to themselves and Families. And whereas there are two cracked Bells which have laid by,

FIG. 52. Spires: local styles.

1. Rutland.
2. Sussex.
3. Essex (a heavily timbered county). North Herefordshire has a very similar type of wooden belfry.
4. Home Counties.

entirely useless for many years, the weight thereof is about one hundred pounds; they purpose to sell those and reserve a large one with a Saints Bell [a corruption of Sanctus Bell], to assemble the parishioners at the usual times of divine Service, and by the Money arising by such Sale they will be better enabled to rebuild their Steeple and put their Church in thorough repair.'

This small parish was doing its best, but in many the work was very much neglected and one cannot avoid the suspicion that the parson neglected his part, the chancel, even more than his people did theirs, for the chancel has undergone drastic alteration far more often than the body of the church. If it sometimes seems that the Victorians wantonly removed all that was most interesting from the churches they restored, it is to be remembered that they often inherited a dilapidated wreck, which only the most drastic treatment could make fit for use; and that the healing operation was performed at a time when the Church itself was undergoing an internal revolution which transformed church furniture almost as much as the Reformation itself had done.

The religious upheaval of the sixteenth century had the effect of fossilizing the shell of the church and transforming its interior. At first it took the churchwardens all their time to keep pace with the swing of the political pendulum. Here are entries in the parish records of All Hallows, Hoo, Kent.

1557	Items for canvass and paynting of the roode clothe	viis. vid.
1576	Recevede of Mayster gladwell for one paynted clothe	xxd.
1557	To Burbyge for making the altar	11s. iiiid.

Then Elizabeth I came to the throne.

1560	For takying down the altar	viid.
1571	Ye forms for ye Communion Table	xid.
1565	Item paid for all manere of deuties as in retornying the chales into a cuppe for the church according to the lord Bysshope commandment.	iiiis. vd.

By the middle of the seventeenth century the Church of England was getting into its stride, and the pulpit and the reading desk had supplanted the altar as the centre of interest. The church already contained benches for the most distinguished parishioners, but now the whole congregation must have seats. Galleries became popular and every church was fitted out with pews, some superbly elaborate as at Old Warden, Bedfordshire, many simple and elegant, and most in the plain style to be seen in the old church at Parracombe in Devon. The squire's pew might be enclosed with a panelled screen six feet high and contain comfortable chairs and even a fireplace. Thirty years ago the Carr Quick pew in

FIG. 53. Bench ends.

1. Medieval (Eastern England).
1a. Medieval (Western England).
2. Post-Reformation pews.

3. Post-Reformation bench.
4. Victorian bench.

179

Newton St. Cyre's was still furnished with a table with blotter and inkstand upon it, so that the family could note down the preacher's most pregnant remarks or doodle away the sermon time—usually an hour at least.

Most of the arrangements were repugnant to Victorian ideas. On the one hand the sacramental revival brought about by the Tractarians turned men's eyes again towards the altar, on the other, the ardent spirit of reform which filled them made them eager to see what their neighbours were about, and most willing that their example should be seen. The pulpit raised high above the destructive damp of the floor often survives in the humbler position allotted to it by the reformers, but in most churches the other fittings were chipped, worm-eaten and rotten, so they were swept away and replaced by low pitch-pine pews. Painstaking copies of medieval benches only came in later, when the worship of progress began to give way to a rather indiscriminate reverence for antiquity. Not that the Victorians had no veneration for the past. If they tore up medieval brasses from the floors it was to replace them, and the cracked and sunken paving around them, with tiles of medieval design, and when they filled the windows with highly coloured glass they were consciously, if unsuccessfully, imitating an ancient fashion. For the new roofs they used a new timber in which they had confidence but the form of the roof was supposed to harmonize with its surroundings. They even tore the plaster off the walls in many places because they believed, mistakenly, that the walls had originally been bare.

At Ashton in Northamptonshire the rector's son who acted as his father's curate noted the progress of restoration in the parish register. The floor had been repaved during the eighteenth century. In 1848 the tower was rebuilt for £500. £100 was subscribed by the Duke of Grafton, who owned the village, the rest was to be raised by a church-rate over a period of forty years. In 1853 the pulpit was moved from its position of pre-eminence to one side. In 1854 the nave was re-roofed and an arch added between the nave and chancel. In 1868 the north aisle was restored and re-roofed, and oak pews provided. In 1893 the gallery was removed and an organ installed; the old choir, consisting of a few village musicians with their instruments, ceased to function. In 1898 the graveyard was tidied up and extended.

No doubt this was a typical sequence of events.

We may be able to find out a great deal about all this alteration and repair if the parish chest still contains the documents it was designed for.

The old chest is still to be found in many churches, an object unmistakably ancient though seldom handsome. Some consist of hollowed-out tree trunks, others are carefully made by an expert joiner and fitted with an elaborate system of locks, requiring three keys in the possession of three different people, the parson and the two churchwardens, to open them. This clearly shows the importance of the contents. The chest was traditionally kept against the north wall of the chancel—as far as possible from the door—occasionally in the church tower. Some old chests have a slit in the lid for alms, however, and these no doubt stood where everybody could see them.

There should be three main groups of documents inside, the churchwardens' accounts, vestry minute books, and parish registers. The registers are always distinct, but items which belong to the other two groups are frequently jumbled together. The parson or the curate filled in the register and looked after it, whereas the church business which belongs to the churchwarden's account, and the civil business recorded in the Vestry minute books usually fell to the lot of the same two or three worthies. The churchwardens' accounts may go back into the Middle Ages, the registers may begin at any time after 1538, and the Vestry minute books after about 1600.

The churchwardens' accounts, if they survive, are nearly always the oldest documents in the chest. Medieval parchments would be written in Latin of a straightforward elementary sort, and in a hand which will require much practice to decipher. There are two little books called *Some Examples of English Handwriting, Twelfth to Seventeenth centuries*, and *More Examples of English Handwriting, Thirteenth to Eighteenth Centuries*, by Hilda Grieve, published by the Essex County Council, at Chelmsford, which have been written for beginners. They give photographs of the scripts with a printed transcript of the documents illustrated, and explanatory notes. With their help, anyone who knows a little Latin and has sufficient patience will learn to read such documents. From these we can learn much about the care of the fabric and furniture of the church, of rushes for the floor, wine for the altar, oil for the lamps, and repairs to the roof, and of how our forefathers solved the problem of raising money for these objects.

The churchwardens' accounts of the seventeenth century are written in English fancifully spelt and in a hand hardly less difficult to decipher than the medieval ones. They continue through the centuries to record the upkeep of the fabric; the renting and apportionment of seats inside the church; the provision of fittings such as the tables of commandments, and the Royal Arms, and receipts from church rates raised to finance these objects; the expenses of the ringers, now obliged by statute to ring on all important public occasions as well as Sunday, and needing a good deal of ale to help them do it; the administration of charities, the leasing of lands belonging to the church, and sometimes the care of livestock on them, and other farming interests. The churchwardens had power to impose the church rate on the parishioners for the upkeep of the church, and were required only to present an annual account of their expenditure at a public meeting held in the church about Easter. It was sometimes said that they engaged in costly and unnecessary repairs in order to make a profit out of the rate; one can hardly believe that all the galleries erected in the seventeenth century were required to seat the villagers of that time.

The churchwardens, then, came upon the scene very early in the parish history, supervising the finances of that part of the church and its affairs, which by immemorial custom were the responsibility of the laity. We do not know precisely how the voice of the parish, 'the vestry', came into being. The contract for Arlingham church tower is made in the name of the vicar 'and all the parishioners of the church of Arlingham both named and unnamed', which is a common form; 'all the parishioners of—' 'the vicar and A, B, and C,' are alternatives. The vestry emerges into the clear light of day under Elizabeth I whose government invested it with new and wide powers of local government, but it is evident that these powers could only have been given to an existing body, not to one created for the occasion.

From the earliest times there must have been a mass of secular parish affairs requiring regulation. If one manor embraced the whole village such matters naturally came up for discussion at the manorial court, but single-manor villages formed the minority. Commonly the lands of several manors, each with its own officers, would lie intermixed in the village fields and pastures; in such a case a gathering of villagers outside the manorial framework, making decisions about fields, crops, livestock, and kindred matters binding on all, must have dominated the local scene.

> 'Of all the ills the human heart endures
> How small the part that laws and kings can cure.'

I think that quotation might be applied to the feudal framework of such villages. The status of a peasant, free or unfree, in the feudal system must have been of less importance to him than the byelaws controlling his use of the fields and commons and his obligations to repair a part of the churchyard walls. Many men owning freeholds also held land which rendered them liable to taxes connected with servile status; sometimes in more than one manor. This might give rise to legal arguments which have echoed down the ages, but meanwhile the daily routine of life in the fields went quietly on and the 'lawful and sufficient' men of the village managed their own affairs and were able to speak their minds on many matters. Here are the sidesmen, representatives of the parishioners, reporting at a Visitation in 1301.

'They say that their parish priest is of honest life and good conversation, and hath been there 22 years, honestly fulfilling his priestly office in all that pertaineth to a parish priest, but he is now broken with age and insufficient for the care of the parish.'

By the time their records become numerous the parishioners are styling themselves 'the inhabitants', 'the inhabitants in vestry assembled', 'the parish', 'the town meeting', 'the principal inhabitants', and so on, and their decisions affect every aspect of parish life, religious, moral, and secular.

Presumably important decisions had always been taken by a representative body rather than by a truly democratic assembly of all the villagers, but as time went on this body became more and more exclusive until 'the principal inhabitants' became far more accurate than 'the town meeting' as a description of the 'Vestry' whose minute books form our second block of documents in the parish chest.

Tudor legislation created two officers, the Overseer of Highways and the Overseer of the Poor, who with the help of the churchwardens, and subject only to the spasmodic supervision of the magistrates, wielded enormous power in the village. These offices fell in·rotation upon the most considerable householders, yeomen and tradesmen such as the miller or the innkeeper, and the vestry minute books contain the record of their doings mixed with other parish business such as the administration of schools and charities.

Their duties consisted principally of the care of the roads and streets, and the whole machinery of public assistance.

It was on this last that by far the greater part of their attention was concentrated. The system created by the Poor Law of 1601 with all its subsequent additions and alterations made each parish an independent entity, subject only to some supervision by the magistrates, in its dealings with people in need of assistance. The money to relieve any poor, sick, aged, or unemployed people resident within its bounds, and the immediate wants of passing strangers who came to grief, had to be raised within the parish. This was done by the imposition of a Poor Rate levied in effect by the Overseer of the Poor, and much of the business of Poor Law administration consisted in desperate shifts to avoid increasing this burden. Many parishes were far too small to form a suitable unit and the system was in consequence very wasteful and inefficient, and often so cruel in its effects that a benevolent magistrate would intervene.

The Vestry minute book often paints rather a grim picture of the activities of 'the principal inhabitants of the parish'. To the poor who were resident in the parish a good deal of help and comfort was given. The parish bought medicine and petticoats and made allowances to families afflicted with smallpox or other misfortune. They would sometimes help a man on to his feet by providing a loom, for instance, in a cloth weaving district, and the amount of food that went into the parish workhouse would have provided a sufficient diet for the inmates, if they really received their share. But the books also record the beating of vagrants, both men and women; the outrageous endeavours of the parish officers to prevent women tramps from producing babies within the bounds of the parish who would thus become entitled to parish support; the 'moving on' of all unfortunate individuals who could not, by right of birth or long residence within the parish, make out a claim to remain, much less to be relieved there; the apprenticing of pauper children in industries far away from their homes, sometimes under brutal managers. Not all apprenticeships spelt misery for the children, however; sometimes the parish would organize the apprenticeship of labourers' children in farms, which might mean a second home for them. A Devonshire farmer in the early years of the nineteenth century, when this system was still functioning, would expect hard work but he would take some care of their morals and education and they would have good food—far better than they could hope for at home. If they were ill-treated they had the right of appeal to the magistrate and, so long as they remained near their friends, public opinion was on their side.

The administration of charities by the churchwardens is also recorded in the Vestry Minute Book. They would distribute cloth or coal, engage a schoolmaster, or look after a piece of land, according to the terms of each bequest. Records of these charities were sometimes hung on the church wall. Boards of this sort usually date from the middle years of the eighteenth century even when the charity is older. At that time the Overseers of the Poor were turning greedy eyes upon them. They were designed for the Poor, whose relief was the Overseer's business; they might as well become part of the Overseer's funds, the argument ran; and many of them were swallowed up. A permanent record of the terms of the bequest, put up where everybody could see it, was the best means open to descendants and friends of the benefactor to safeguard his intentions.

The parish registers, often the largest body of documents, and the only one which is almost always there, contain less of human interest than the Minute Books. Their purpose is to record all the births, marriages, and deaths occurring in the parish. The law which brought them into being was passed in 1539 but very few parishes have a complete series beginning at that date.

The earlier volumes sometimes contain notes on events of public or local interest.

'About this tyme begann ye warre, and therewith began disorders, this Register not being carefully kept till ye happy coronacion of King Charles ye II. . . . .'

'Loke, the fox will eate no grapes, and whi he cannot get ym so at this towne thei loue inglesh serviis because thei can have no other, as apperith bi the candelbeme and roodlofte, as I think: iudge you by me. Nicholas Nemo A.D. 1594.'

Slipped among the leaves there may be an interesting description of the seventeenth-century parsonage house showing how many rooms it had, and how it was built. By far the majority, however, contain little beyond the rather lifeless list of names, most of them disappointingly unfamiliar to anyone expecting to find the ancestors of the present inhabitants there. Except in very remote, large parishes where communications were exceptionally bad, three or four generations will usually see the beginning and end of one family's connection with a parish. The number of families belonging to the village for more than a hundred years is very small indeed, and this seems always to have been the case. The tombstones in the churchyard tell the same story. It is rare to find a long series belonging to one family or more than one family having such a series at all. A few improvident sons or a large family of daughters will soon undermine prosperity; the farm is sold up, the family moves away, and their name appears no more in stone or book. Among the poor life is far more precarious. The parish registers bear witness to the horrors of the plague in the seventeenth, and the cholera epidemic in the nineteenth centuries, as well as to the familiar fact of the cruel death rate among children in former times. (As late as 1901 in the village of Corsley on average every labourer's family would lose a child.) But the registers are for genealogical research rather than random study.

The parish chest may also contain occasional notices and proclamations from the outside world. Appeals for public charity on the occasion of some public disaster, and for other good causes authorized by the bishop, known as briefs, are noted in the register. One other most interesting document is occasionally preserved in the parish chest. This is the Enclosure Award, the allotment of the land of the parish by the Enclosure Commissioners already described in an earlier chapter. It will give a detailed picture of the parish before this catastrophic change took place, and to find this document is one of the most rewarding discoveries a local chronicler can make.

Of what denomination is the chapel?

With all this secular business centred on the church, rates, tithes, and obligations due to the parish from all, whatever their religious beliefs, nobody could escape from its influence. Indeed while the zeal for reform and religious argumentation were at their highest and politicians vied with one another in persecuting their opponents, the nonconformists could not even build themselves meeting houses. It was long before they had the right to marry and bury their own people.

By the middle of the seventeenth century the Presbyterians, the Baptists, and the Independents had got a foothold in the country, the Presbyterians rich, powerful, and intellectual, 'learned and polite men', the Independents making up what they lacked in these respects by their zeal and fire, the Baptists perhaps more devout than either. The remnant of the Old Faith and the Quakers remained underground. By the middle of the eighteenth century the Presbyterian body had virtually collapsed, torn asunder as a result of its leaders' attempts to maintain certain fundamental beliefs; its members joined either the Independents, afterwards called Congregationalists, or the new sect, called Unitarians. Catholics and Quakers had been able to emerge from hiding. A few villages have a Quaker meeting house, but very few have a Catholic chapel dating from this time, since the faithful congregated as far as possible round the few great houses which had been able or willing to keep the spark alight. These houses, with their legends of heroic resistance to persecution, and their secret hiding places, have a fascination all their own.

The old meeting houses which survive in our villages, therefore, will date at earliest from the first half of the eighteenth century. Since at first they differed little from a dwelling house in appearance, they are difficult to trace (Fig. 54). Chapels built as the century advanced have a more formal appearance, and are more easily identified. Early chapels, belonging to Baptists, Congregationalists, or Unitarians, will mostly be found in the heart of the village. In Devonshire, for example, Congregational chapels are very numerous because there Puritanism took a firm hold. In parishes of scattered settlement the dissenters often established themselves by supplying the religious needs of hamlet people whose small chapel of ease, conveniently at hand, had been closed since the Reformation.

Where the chapel is an old one, and the church Victorian, we can be fairly sure that the settlement came into being after the Reformation. When the Methodists came in the second half of the eighteenth century to sweep the country with gale force and gather into their fold all the devout enthusiasm the age could produce, they reaped a particularly rich harvest in industrial districts which had grown up in the last hundred years and been largely neglected through the apathy of the Established Church, and the soul-searching doctrinal squabbles of the dissenters.

FIG. 54. An old meeting-house.

The Methodists founded many chapels among people who had been living without any organized religion, but they also encroached on the preserves of the older bodies. People left the sober old meeting house to attend the new chapel of red and yellow brick where the preaching was new and ardent too, and the conventicle went out of use. It is worth looking for the old chapel, which may be disguised as a smithy, a shop, or a dwelling-house. At Blockley the old Baptist chapel, built at the same time and in the same style as the charity school given by the rector, is now used as a parish hall. It only held about fifty people, and its congregation soon grew too big for it, for Blockley was a prosperous place in the eighteenth century with a thriving silk industry, and Baptists were numerous among them.

In their heyday these congregations carried on a life in many respects parallel with that of the Established Church. They kept their own registers and often their own graveyard, and built their own schools. From the first the ministers were chosen by their flock, and therefore supported with rather more enthusiasm than the parson could look for. They often eked out their incomes, as did their brethren of the Establishment, by schoolkeeping. Debarred from any form of public office, they never had any standing comparable with the parsons', but sometimes a far more pervasive influence over the lives of their people, and these in the early days often included persons of consequence in the village community. Nonconformity gradually lost ground among the upper classes because of the disabilities attached to it. No dissenter could become a magistrate and wield the power and influence which lay within the grasp of any landed gentleman on the morrow of King Charles's restoration—a power which more and more of them reached out to take. So nonconformist gentlemen who wished to live on equal terms with their own kind tended to soften their religious opinions into a sufficient conformity and their children gave up the meeting-house altogether. Religious enthusiasm came to be disliked and feared by the upper classes, and the Church of England seemed to have no room for evangelical fervour.

Thus it came about that the nonconformist ministers, especially the Baptists and the Primitive Methodists, were themselves simple uneducated men, drawn from the classes they preached to; and in due course they naturally became the leaders in the movement to secure better conditions for farm labourers. Joseph Arch, the founder of the National Agricultural Labourers Union, the first farm-workers' union to have some brief success, was a Primitive Methodist preacher, and many of his meetings were held in chapels. The sudden outbreak of strikes by farm labourers in 1872, especially in the midlands and East Anglia, called the Revolt of the Field, were his work, and the organization he set on foot to enable labourers to emigrate into manufacturing towns or overseas gave new impetus to the drift of young people away from villages, which is still going on, although the new possibility of finding work in factories round about has done something to arrest it.

The alliance of the clergy of the Established Church with the

farmers in the struggle to keep down farm workers' wages undoubtedly weakened their hold, never very strong, on the
allegiance of the poorest parishioners, and undid some of the
effects of the increased care and zeal which the Victorian clergy
showed to their flocks.

The church which once meant so much in the life of every
person in the parish is now often in danger of becoming nothing
but an ancient monument. One parson has to do the work of two
or three parishes and very few people attend the services which
he labours so hard to take. Depopulated villages find it quite
impossible to keep up the crumbling fabric without outside help.
On the other hand in the more populous villages the necessity of
supporting the church (in a physical sense) perhaps provides a
salutary unifying aim to a people who look mainly outside the
village for their livelihood, and anywhere rather than to the
parish fields for the necessaries they buy with it. While this is so,
one may hope that the church may some day become again their
spiritual home.

BOOKS TO READ

Building in England Down to 1540. L. F. Salzman. Clarendon Press.
Looking for History in British Churches. M. Anderson.
The Parish Churches of England. Cox and Ford. Batsford, 1947.
Local Style in English Architecture. T. D. Atkinson. Batsford, 1947.
The Circle and the Cross. A. Hadrian Allcroft. Macmillan, 1927.
The Parish Chest. W. E. Tate, 1946.

IX

Power in the Land

AFTER the houses of the village folk, farmers, tradesmen, labourers, and the church at last we turn to the mansion of the squire. Once it would have been inconceivable that his house should be the last to be visited; but that was before the social revolution. Now even his house may be gone. Every year a few are pulled down by owners who cannot keep them up and are unable or unwilling to find a purchaser, and many are in the hands of public bodies. Country squires, reigning comfortably over their villages, are now more easily imagined than described. Their houses stand aloof within their parks like palaces, some sombre, some elegant, some massive, others merely dignified, some pretentious and unwieldy, others displaying domestic building at its fullest perfection. All have about them the suggestion of power, but the power has gone. Even if the family is still in possession, the master of the house has lost the wish and seldom has any opportunity to play the village tyrant. He may still be called the squire but he has lost what seem to the imagination to be the essential trappings of squiredom. What were they? According to the Oxford Dictionary a squire is 'a country gentleman or landowner, especially one who is the principal landowner in a village', but the word has overtones which suggest something more than large possessions, a dignity and official status not inevitably associated with wealth. The dictionary goes on to say 'U.S.A., A Justice of the Peace,' and here we approach the heart of the matter; it was the office of magistrate which transformed the country gentleman into a 'squire'.

How and when did this happen?

The record of our village in Domesday Book might include something like this:

'Ranulf holds Aston. In King Edward's time it belonged to Ailsi.'

We have no means of knowing much about Ailsi; perhaps a faint pattern of mounds and ditches may show where his wooden hall stood; a crude window high up in the north wall, or a severe narrow arch, or a piece of stone carved with astonishing fluency and grace may remain, though very rarely, from the church he built. He may have been an important person, who had a bailiff to look after his interests in the village, or he may have been a small landlord whose ancestors had cleared the land and had run the village ever since. Perhaps his grandfather built the church and dedicated it to some saint whose aid he had invoked with good results when he was in difficulties with the Danes.

Nor do we know what had become of him by 1086. Was his corpse mouldering quietly at Stamfordbridge or Hastings; or was he there, glowering, among the nameless army of villagers (*villani*) at the Hundred Court where the Domesday Commissioners collected their evidence, wondering, perhaps not for the first time, but with new bitterness, why his ancestors chose such a wet and windy place to hold their meetings?

At all events Ranulf was in possession, an upstart, Ailsi might think, whose grandfather had been nothing but a heathen pirate. It wasn't that there would be so much innovation; the motley collection of Normans and adventurers who formed the Conqueror's army had no political system to impose comparable to the old Saxon one, which if it never made the country strong enough to keep its frontiers intact, yet held it together through crisis after crisis. But the Saxon system was going to be made to work overtime; the king would squeeze the last ounce of wealth and power out of it; and his followers would do the same.

Ranulf didn't live in the village. He put in one of his followers, or left it to be managed by his steward. If he gave it to one of his men the knight would not be absolute master of the place. He would depend to some extent on Ranulf's good will. Never, while the feudal system lasted, could a village become so self-contained a unit as it was later to be. The lord of the manor was bound on the one hand by certain obligations to a distant over-lord, and in his relations with his tenants by the complicated net of manorial custom; while the church held a watching brief, and a reserve of power, and took care of those who came to grief. Even a resident proprietor could not lord it over his people as an eighteenth-century squire might do. Everybody in feudal society was bound to those above and below him by a series of known and limited obligations; it was regarded as a mark of serfdom that a man should not know at night what work he might be called upon to do in the morning, but even a serf knew that he only had to work a specified number of days in the week, and conditions for harvest, carting, or other work outside the normal routine, were clearly laid down.

Moreover the lord, however great he might be, had no rights over the humblest individual living in his village if that person happened to belong to another manor. The system of personal obligations on which order and government depended trans-cended geographical circumstances. The roads of medieval Eng-land carried a crowd of magnates, bishops, abbots, abbesses, and smaller landlords, and their servants, travelling to and fro between their scattered estates. Medieval society asked of the villager, whose man he was, but the villager might seldom or never have set eyes on his lord's face. At the end of the Middle Ages, only one Leicestershire village in seven had a resident land-owner. Only six of the country gentlemen who sat on the magis-trates' bench in Gloucestershire at the end of the eighteenth century had lands which had descended in their families since the Middle Ages, nearly thirty had estates built up by their forefathers during the fifteenth and sixteenth centuries when the feudal structure was tottering.

Although the idea of feudal and manorial structure has taken possession of men's minds, and is constantly thought of in con-nection with village life, it has left few physical relics behind. Commonest perhaps are the stocks, often proudly preserved on the village green. A few villages boast an ancient lock-up (Fig. 55, 1), and some have a pound (Fig. 55, 2), a small enclosure for

FIG. 55. Traces of the Manor.

1. Pound at Elsdon, Northumberland.   2. Lock-up in Leicestershire.

194

keeping stray cattle until their owners were identified and fined. The size of these pounds will give an idea of the principal farming interests of the district. The pound at Elsdon on the Scottish border would hold a small herd, that at Shorwell, in the Isle of Wight, not more than three or four beasts.

When the feudal bonds which William the Conqueror had drawn tight had weakened and collapsed, the Tudor government substituted the Commission of the Peace as a cement for society, an ancient office which they raised to new importance, placing the charge over a multitude of affairs now covered by the term Local Government, as well as a wide field of criminal jurisdiction, in the hands of small landowners (an estate worth £20 was the only qualification for the magistracy). This set the seal of an official position on the new gentry whose rise about this time has been noted in a previous chapter, and gave them the power which we associate with a squire. The power of the manorial courts and the manor officials passed to the Justices and their new parish officers. If the old courts continued to meet their proceedings rapidly became an empty form regarded as such by those who attended them. By the eighteenth century 'a manor' in common speech meant sporting rights—game preserves and the like.

The relations of the squire with his tenants are often described as feudal; the medieval villager would hardly have called them so. The law did not ask a seventeenth-century villager whose man he was, but where he lived. On the other hand his landlord lived near by, and wielded the enormous powers of the Justice of the Peace. Technically a freer man, the cottager might find himself at least as firmly in his lord's grasp as ever his great-grandfather had been and by the law of settlement as much bound to the soil of his native place.

Sir Tunbelly Clumsy had no overlord, and manorial custom had gone with the wind; either his own cousin or some despised and powerless curate was installed at the rectory. If one of the tenants committed a petty offence, he would be judged before his landlord sitting in his capacity as magistrate in the front parlour of his house. Well for such a villager if the magistrate were an enlightened and virtuous man; if not, the victim had no redress. A malignant or stupid Justice had an appalling power to inflict misery and harm on his poor neighbours.

A rich counterpoint of high civilization and sordid brutality runs through eighteenth-century life. There is plenty of evidence that some of the magistrates exercised their power irresponsibly without scruple or remorse, even if we disregard the characters Fielding drew (we should perhaps be sorry if future ages should judge us on the evidence of our own fiction writers); others were humane and honourable men. A contemporary writer says: 'The power, which is almost irresponsible, could not be endured if it were not controlled by a sense of private honour.'

Some magistrates only used their commission to hold their own domain in the hollow of their hand, but there were generally a sufficient number intelligent and public-spirited enough to attend the Quarter Sessions regularly and to do a considerable amount of work of many kinds for no recompense except the pleasure men have in public affairs, and the opportunity to eat a good dinner among friends. Nothing could have been more unimpressive than these meetings, nine or ten gentlemen at most, gathered together most often in an inn parlour, and attended only by their clerks, but the Quarter Sessions formed the apex of the unpaid government service which really ran the country. It would be impossible to describe their business in detail here; apart from the criminal cases which came before them they had the care of prisons, of public assistance, of licensing, the upkeep of roads and bridges, the making of byelaws, and even the fixing of wage rates; and much else besides.

The magistrates who attended the Quarter Sessions formed a governing clique, a closely-knit and exclusive body, and discovered through these meetings a new loyalty—to their county—which found expression in antiquarian and historical interests. In time their manner of dealing with their business became less haphazard as the accumulated experience of local government over a hundred years or so began to tell. Some would become specialists in a particular branch of the administration; by the end of the eighteenth century many of them were taking the work in the most serious spirit and making it the business of their lives, as the following quotations from private correspondence show:

'Sir I would not ask the honour (the magistracy) for my only child were I in the least distrustful of his Ability but as he had the advantage of a Liberal Education, has good parts and is an Honest man, he may by Application and Addition of my assistance while I am living become duly qualified for that office.'

'I want your opinion about the time of my beginning to act as Magistrate. . . . Now I confess I think myself full young for it at present . . . but on the other hand I conceive I shall get more useful knowledge of the business by acting with you for a month than by acting by myself for three, may it not therefore be a matter of importance to me to begin immediately and pick your brains for as long a time as I can.'

Country gentlemen had not as a rule much opportunity of receiving new ideas. Very few of the Gloucestershire magistrates already mentioned had been to a university, and their town house, if they had one, was no further away than the county town, but spas such as Cheltenham, Clifton, and Bath, as they became fashionable must have brought in fresh life to country society by enabling the local gentry to mingle with people of wider views. Squire Westons continued to exist, but their number declined. In the end it was their zeal for the reform of the public services under their care which brought the magistrates down. Reform costs money, in their case money from the rates; demands for money to rebuild the prisons, to take the lunatics out of the gaols and poor-houses and form separate asylums for them, were coldly received. It was easy enough for critics to pick holes in their amateurish administration, and in 1835 a large part of their powers was taken away.

For nearly a century afterwards their hold on their villages remained on a solid foundation of long tradition and economic supremacy.

Squire, then, is the name given to a landed proprietor enjoying unique and extensive powers both judicial and administrative over the affairs of the county and the lives of his tenants.

In what did this power consist?

The powers exercised by the Bench of Magistrates had never been vested in the central government. Some were taken over from the feudal structure, others from the church, others were constantly being thrust on them from above. First in point of time came the care of the roads, but of far more importance in the life of the village was their administration of the Poor Law. The office of Overseer of Highways was created in 1591, that of Overseer of the Poor in 1597 by an Act which with numerous modifications governed the whole machinery of public assistance for over two hundred years. The Justices of the Peace appointed these two officers and supervised their proceedings, and they immediately became, together with the churchwardens, the key figures in the parish. Their labours were unpaid, and the work was sometimes very troublesome, involving them in disputes with their neighbours. The offices went in rotation among the principal farmers and tradesmen of the community; the rates they were empowered to collect were by far the heaviest burden of taxation country people had to pay, and they themselves and their neighbours the principal contributors. Small wonder that as the burden became heavier, the system became ever more inefficient and oppressive.

The Justices appointed an Overseer in every Parish to inspect the roads, organize maintenance, and with their permission collect a rate within the parish to finance necessary repairs. It was the Overseer who estimated what it would be necessary to collect from himself and his friends, and under his care the roads rapidly became nearly impassable except in dry weather. There was perhaps less traffic on them than there had been in the Middle Ages and therefore less interest in keeping them up. The parish officers devoted such funds as they could raise to caring for the lanes most used by the villagers rather than to the main highway. The squire's power was useful to him here; we may be sure his own approach road was always kept in tolerable condition, but unless he had interested himself specially in this matter he would probably be content to let the parish economize elsewhere. The Overseer, moreover, felt himself entitled to recoup himself for his trouble out of the Rate. This system completely broke down; by the middle of the eighteenth century the care of most of the main highways had been vested in private bodies, the Turnpike trusts, each operating individual stretches of road and financing their operations by a system of tolls. These bodies were largely manned by the landowners and principal tradesmen of the neighbourhood. Something has already been said of their activities and the far-reaching effect they might have on the fortunes of the village. The cottages built for the men who collected the fees at the toll gates added a new feature to the landscape. You will often find one on the outskirts of a village lying on the main road, a little house, obviously designed with more care than a labourer's cottage, jutting out into the street with a window placed obliquely to enable the occupant to overlook approaching traffic (Fig. 56).

FIG. 56. Two Devonshire Toll houses.

Devonshire toll houses have a distinctive style, as if every Trust had employed the same architect, or used standard designs. In an age when private rights were flaunted unchecked and might have been expected to exclude the possibility of corporate action, private individuals thus combined to undertake road-engineering works which the modern state hardly surpasses, replacing bridle paths with carriage-ways ten to sixteen feet wide and by-passing gradients too steep for wheeled traffic (Fig. 57). The magistracy, with all its faults, taught men to combine and to act. The Overseers retained the charge of any roads not operated by a Trust and they were very ill-kept unless a magistrate who had made it his hobby to look after roads and bridges had the matter brought before the bench at Quarter Sessions; the parish would then be fined and ordered to undertake repairs.

The turnpike roads were not good by modern standards, but they revolutionized wheeled traffic. The curricle in which the Squire's son delighted to drive about, the farmer's gig, the post-chaise, and the stage-coach all travelled at a speed inconceivable in the seventeenth century. A young Frenchman imprisoned during the Napoleonic War at Norman Cross on the Great North Road expressed his astonishment at the speed and quantity of the traffic. Only the coming of the railways brought the turnpike system to an end. Overnight, as it were, the revenue at the toll gates disappeared and some other means had to be found to keep

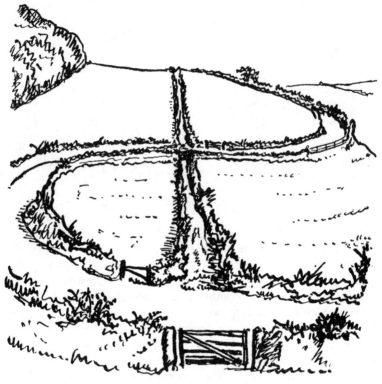

FIG. 57. The Turnpike and the old road.

up the roads. But the name lingered on, and even at the beginning of the present century country people still referred to the turnpike.

The importance of the Overseers of the Poor suffered no such decline, and although the effect of their activities on the landscape of the village was largely negative (the absence of eighteenth-century cottages other than divided farmhouses in purely agricultural villages may be attributed to them), they loomed so large in the lives of the people that something must be said of them here.

During the Middle Ages the church had provided with more or less faithfulness and efficiency for the needs of those who came to grief, providing hospitals for the sick and bread for the needy. A religious body applying for licence to take over the revenues of a church on one of its estates would often give as a reason the need of funds for this purpose; a layman, giving a leper hospital to his parish, would put it in the hands of the church. When the greater part of this provision had disappeared, and a century of social and economic upheaval had increased the number of people in need of assistance, there came a time when even a Tudor government could not feel that the subject had been fully dealt with by ordering that beggars and vagrants should be whipped until their backs were bloody, and set in the stocks by the village constable. The act of 1597 already mentioned was passed to deal more efficiently with unemployed, sick, and poverty-stricken people. Under its terms an Overseer of the Poor was to be appointed in every parish and supervised by the magistrates. Their task was to set the able-bodied to work, and to relieve the wants of those who could not; later they were obliged to keep a workhouse for those under their care who had nowhere else to go, and in these unhappy places, some of them still standing in the village, as a local name will occasionally reveal, the aged, orphans, lunatics, sick people, and whole families of paupers lived together. The parish workhouse is described with all the angry passion of a reformer in the opening pages of *Oliver Twist*. The inmates were supposed to do some form of work which would produce a profit and so lessen the burden on the rates, but the system seldom worked. To finance all this the Overseer was to collect the Poor Rate from the parishioners, but he himself was unpaid and could not refuse the office. The magistrates in Quarter Session had to sanction the Rate, but if they refused the work would not be done; the parishioners were entitled to hear the accounts read (this was often done in church about Easter time) but could not refuse to pay. The Overseer of the Poor was a person of consequence. However, 'In parochial administration the ostensible minister, the nominal Overseer, is sometimes a person of inferior rank; but the King of the Parish still acts behind the scene, and the Overseer does not alter his arrangements. Happy is the parish that has a good King'.

Under the Settlement Act of 1662 only those born or settled within the parish were entitled to assistance; outsiders could be moved on, or sent back where they belonged, that is to their parish of origin. An Overseer of the Poor could be indicted for manslaughter if he allowed anyone to die of want who had appealed to him, but otherwise he could do as he pleased unless the magistrate chose to intervene. The Poor Rate lay so heavily upon the parish, that rather than allow strangers to come in who might become a burden on the rates, the parish officers would bribe them to go, or pay to have them 'conducted', as the term was, out of the parish. For this last a licence had to be obtained from a magistrate, and with it the unfortunate would be sent into the next parish, where the parish officers would repeat the process, and so it would go on until the victim reached the place of his birth. Landowners would even pull down cottages for fear they should be occupied by people who might eventually need parish assistance. Nobody would build any new ones, and squatters who attempted to put up shacks for themselves on waste ground were fiercely resisted. These measures, if pushed to extremity, could make paupers of men able and willing to work, by denying them the right to go and look for it. A single man could move about fairly freely, but a married man with a family would be driven out, unless he came with a certificate of settlement by which document his parish of origin admitted responsibility for him and his family if he fell on evil days. If cottages were pulled down, labourers had to live herded together, and the result was an ever-increasing number of bastards for whom the parish had to provide.

The poor would flee from the harshness of the parish officer to the squire, who in one case might refuse the licence to conduct, in another insist that the Overseer's meagre allowance be increased.

'Whoever thinks himself neglected has nothing to do but take a walk to the first Justice of the Peace and make his complaint.' ....'the country gentleman consults only those feelings which give him pleasure, and which Nature has taught us to admire,' wrote Arthur Young.

Nevertheless it is impossible to read the records of Poor Law administration which remain in the parish chest without some indignation, and one has to remember that the plight of the poor would have been even worse without the assistance the Overseer did provide to those legally entitled to it.

Whether he were benevolent or indifferent, the squire both as magistrate and landlord was deeply implicated in all this. When the Commission of the Peace was first raised to new importance the small gentry seem to have taken a hundred years or so to realize what it meant to them, but by 1700 they had come to understand that it would be to their advantage to accept the office of magistrate. If they did not, someone else would obtain all this power over their tenants and their land. The Poor Rate might not press so heavily on them as it did on farmers and tradesmen, but they would want to have a say in the matter. Some of them, indeed, took on the office of Overseer.

The magistrates also enjoyed the power, thrust on them in 1601, of fixing maximum wage rates. This was soon allowed to lapse because the economic conditions which had been forcing wages up ceased to operate. Throughout the eighteenth century prices crept up, while wages remained more or less steady. Then came the Enclosure movement which threw some agricultural labourers out of work, and deprived others of common rights which had provided them with a comforting allowance of food and fuel; their numbers were swelled by smallholders whose holdings would no longer support them. The Napoleonic wars caused a good deal of hardship. Everything combined to render the condition of agricultural labourers more desperate. The new industrial towns and their 'dark satanic mills' which we look back on in horror held for them the promise of the Klondike. The wages of those who remained on the land no longer provided even a starvation diet.

Once again it fell to the magistrates to provide a remedy for this intolerable hardship, which they did with characteristic amateurishness. The wage which had provided the Elizabethan workman with a modest living had only gone up by threepence or fourpence a week, while the cost of living had trebled. Nevertheless they deemed it 'inexpedient' to revive their powers and fix a minimum wage. At last in 1785 the Berkshire Quarter Sessions, unconscious that they were putting their place of meeting (the Pelican Inn, Speenhamland) for ever 'on the map', worked out a schedule of wage subsidies to be paid out of the Poor Rate, and this quickly became the rule all over England, pinned to the wall in every 'local', demanded as of right by every labourer, and upheld by magistrates everywhere. Thirty years later the Berkshire magistrates reversed these enactments. The Speenhamland system had come in for much criticism and had been found to have a demoralizing effect on the workers. But the magistrates still could not bring themselves to prescribe a minimum; they forbade the payment of subsidies and recommended larger and better workhouses.

Two years later most of their power was gone, and with it went the old Poor Law machinery. The Overseer declined into the Deputy Guardian, the magistrate took his seat on the Board of Guardians which administered the new Poor Law from the nearest town. In this capacity his control of the village poor weakened. The payment of outdoor relief was abolished; the poorhouse was closed down and in time became an ordinary dwelling; its occupants were sent off grumbling to a new workhouse on the outskirts of the market town. Their complaint was that families had been able to keep together in the old place, whereas under the new arrangements men and women were separated, and far from their old homes into the bargain. The shadow of the workhouse hung heavily over the nineteenth-century village. A man had to be lucky as well as thrifty and hardworking to avoid finishing his days there.

The magistrates were supposed 'to have a strict regard to . . . ales houses, masters, servants, and the poor.' While Puritan feeling ran high many of them devoted their energies to rooting out gaming houses, punishing Sabbath breakers, and so forth. The licensing of inns and alehouses remains to this day in their hands. Two or three justices were enough to form a bench for this purpose (the Brewster Sessions). Two justices sitting together might fine or imprison for a number of petty offences, ranging from abandoning a bastard child, or leaving an employment before the expiry of the agreed term, to killing game and taking eggs; three justices sitting privately with no one present but a few witnesses might sentence a man to seven years' transportation for rick burning (in this case the accused might choose to be sent to the Assizes, but if he did so he risked the death sentence).

Alone in his hall the magistrate might issue warrants and summonses, licences to conduct, and licences of many other kinds, he could bind over some offenders to appear at Quarter Sessions, fine some, and send others to the House of Correction —a place of punishment only one degree less terrible than the county gaol. Even in a small country place few days would pass when there was no business to be done.

I have dwelt at length on the squire as magistrate because it was this that made him unique among landlords, and because for two centuries at least, and those not distant ones, the whole organization of the parish revolved round this power of his which was capable of touching at any rate the poorer inhabitants at every point in their lives; and because his office, its voluntary character and amateur status, is the most characteristic example of the English way of getting things done.

Between his duties as magistrate, his wine, women, and sport, the average eighteenth-century squire passed his days. One generation saw the rebuilding of the mansion in as handsome a style as the reigning squire could afford, and each added their portraits and a few pieces of furniture. A few gentlemen made the grand tour, brought back a collection of Italian pictures (usually a poor one), and built a picture gallery to house it; a few others cherished political ambitions and ruined themselves running for parliament. Of the more intelligent and enterprising, some devoted themselves to farming and became pioneers of agricultural improvement, others (mostly the new gentry coming from the industrial world) devoted themselves to social reform; others interested themselves in architecture and landscape gardening. These rebuilt the mansion once again and laid out the park in a fasionable style, with avenues of trees which we enjoy, but which they only imagined; with lakes and summer-houses and stretches of lawn patterned at the height of summer by the ghostly outlines of the parterres, knots, and alleys of the formal gardens they swept away. These grandiose schemes of improvement often involved no less than the removal of the village or part of it from the neighbourhood of the house. The church remained marooned in the grounds and the cottagers were rehoused outside the park gates. The subject was in the news round about the beginning of the nineteenth century. A distinguished architect, P. F. Robinson, wrote in a volume of picturesque designs in 1830:

'Village architecture may at a very small expense be rendered attractive, and a variety of forms and embellishments introduced pleasing to the lover of painting and of charity, by adding to his sources of amusement and interest. In this manner landed proprietors may find delightful employment and add to the value of their estates by improving the condition of the cottagers and their dwellings, here and there adding a porch or a lean-to, or judiciously altering a chimney. Ancient buildings are frequently capable of being made both comfortable and scenic by trifling alterations and additions and more pleasing effects are by such means produced than by rebuilding the structure . . .' but 'the labourer's cottage cannot be too simple in its form and it should br comprised in a very small compass . . the dwelling is only one storey in height, and the rooms are kept to the smallest possible size.'

Naturally it is the squires whose taste ran to architecture who have left most mark on the village landscape with their park gates and lodges, their model cottages and sometimes their romantic toys. The same architect wrote: 'Seen from an adjoining plantation the outline (of the granary) would remind the traveller of the Temple of Venus in the Kingdom of Naples, on the coast of Baia, the roof assuming the form of the Temple of Vesta'. However the idea of picturesque farm buildings never really caught on, perhaps because even as a tenant John Bull was a person to be reckoned with, and he might not have relished the presence of the Temple of Vesta in his strawyard; hermitages, towers, and grottos were more popular.

Others again patronized the arts, collected books, interested themselves in antiquities, undertook excavations, and collected Roman remains; wrote the history of their county, or took up astronomy; these were all gentlemanly occupations. All, sottish or intelligent, were united in believing that the proper end for a well-spent life was a handsome monument in the parish church inscribed with some elegant sentiments and plenty of genealogical detail.

They formed, not a brilliant body of men, but a very stable

element in the realm, and they founded a tradition of voluntary service of which we are right to be proud. If their rule was despotic, it was not aloof; the green baize frontier between the servants and the gentry had not yet gone up. The squire's son began his schooling in the village and went cock-fighting, bull-baiting, wrestling, and prize-fighting along with his tenants whom another day he might throw into a stinking prison for a trifling offence without remorse. They were perhaps more human in their attitude to their people though less humane than their descendants who erected an impassable barrier between themselves and their 'inferiors' but strove to do them good. By the time the good Queen came to the throne, the days were gone when a squire's daughter would share a bed with her maid. Hand in hand with the desire for better quarters and a better mode of life for the servants went a determination to keep them as much apart as if they had belonged to a different order of being.

Rebuilding and enlargement was going on all through the latter half of the eighteenth century when the ranks of the gentry were being swelled by business men who had made their fortunes. At Attingham Park in Shropshire the small gable of the manageable, convenient Queen Anne house remains looking like a doll's house in the vast backyard of a Palladian mansion. The Victorian maxim 'a gentleman lives on what he has' would have seemed strange to an eighteenth-century squire, who apprenticed his younger sons to a trade and hoped that they would need no further help. And if the younger sons succeeded they came back to the country, bought up the estate of some squire who had come to grief, altered the house to suit their fashionable tastes and well-lined pockets, and settled down.

Even the most unenterprising or unsuccessful families altered their houses in the nineteenth century. The large families and large staffs and large ideas of the period demanded at least the addition of a servants' wing and of modern conveniences. At the beginning of the century this meant a large kitchen range in the kitchen, and new grates in the fireplaces throughout the house. Many a well-planned old house became an inconvenient rabbit warren in the course of these alterations. Convenience in fact had ceased to matter; wages were so low and food so cheap that a gentleman could afford to keep a vast number of servants, and feel at the same time that he was helping his poor tenants by taking their daughters off their hands. An architect's handbook of the period recommends that the coal cellar should be as far as possible from the kitchen so that the trouble of fetching fuel should make the staff more economical of it. Building materials were cheap, too. Nineteenth-century architects and their patrons were thus able to give the freest possible expression to taste and ingenuity, unhampered to a great extent by considerations of expense, convenience, or the outmoded preference for symmetry. All this is even more apparent in new mansions put up at this time than in alterations and additions to old ones.

The Victorian squire cut a benevolent figure upon the whole. He wielded his diminished power with determination but with good intention. He could still take dire revenge on a tenant who offended him, and expected the utmost respect to be paid to his rank and possessions, but he was building decent cottages (he would not even have considered the 'picturesque' labourer's cottage containing kitchen, bedroom and wash-house 'in the smallest possible compass'); he was providing clean water in the village street, subsidizing halls, schools, almshouses, and playgrounds, and generally helping the village out of the slough into which the oppression of the Poor Rate had sunk it. He was a good landlord in general, caring for his property, and seeing to it that his land was well farmed; doing all that he conceived to be his duty by his tenants in the way of repairs, perquisites, and consideration and relief in hard cases, fully expecting to pass on to his children's children the good heritage he had received. It is never right to apply the standards of one epoch to the customs of another. The wages he paid his workpeople barely provided them with the means of life, but at least he usually saw to it that they had employment, and any man growing up in the village who did not choose to seek his fortune in the army, or learn a trade, was sure of being taken on either by the squire himself or by one of his farmers. Before the days of agricultural machinery the land could always do with an extra pair of hands.

The squire felt himself to be responsible for his people and his land. The feudal notion of reciprocal obligation had undergone a complete transformation. Manorial officials had served the community as part of the due they owed to their lord, and upon

A GREAT REBUILDING. (1) The winning design for a pair of cottages in a competition promoted in 1864 by the Society of Arts. These cottages were put up in seventeen counties and the style is very familiar.

(2) A cottage design, published in 1837, but erected earlier. Cottages of this type are not uncommon, especially at lodge gates and round about the fringes of parks.

CHILHAM, KENT. An ideal village! The site was inhabited in Roman times. The squire's mansion, built in 1616, incorporating the Norman castle, is on the left. The village was formerly a market town, hence the handsome church. A "National Society" school can be seen left centre; in the foreground, a medieval timbered farm house.

this foundation the unpaid government service had been built. During the centuries of the magistrates' ascendancy what had seemed at first only a new form of dignity and power had become almost a professional responsibility for the life and well-being of the community. When the power was gone a sense of moral obligation remained which found expression in the formation and support of innumerable private bodies devoted to the common good, carrying out work which is now considered to be the duty of the state. The Turnpike trusts and the Society for the Prevention of Cruelty to Children reflect alike the English notion that the proper way to get something done is to found a society of private persons who will devote themselves to it. It is hard to doubt that this tradition had its beginning in stuffy inn parlours where the Justices met and, in their slipshod way, ran the county.

The squire however was not the only person there. The magistrates did their best to exclude anyone not of their order from their company, to the point, in a few cases, of going on strike if the attempt was made to introduce someone they considered inferior; but younger brothers and cousins were welcome, and this let in the clergy; for a benefice of £300 gave them the necessary estate. Among the ranks of the clergy there were many whose talents and energy made them welcome an opportunity for public service, which the few and brief duties expected of an eighteenth-century parson denied them. Clerical magistrates formed the most active and efficient part of the bench, and even, sometimes, the majority of those who attended Quarter Sessions. To their credit stands a zeal for the reform of the worst horrors that came within their jurisdiction, horrors on which the squires usually turned a blind eye. Nevertheless it was a formidable trinity which headed most village communities: church, state, and economic mastery embodied in two men, who were quite often united by ties of blood as well. This state of affairs has entirely passed away. If the squire shines with ever diminishing glory, the parson has undergone a complete metamorphosis.

In fortune and manner of life the parson of today somewhat resembles his predecessor's curate, as he hurries from parish to parish for the Sunday services. Beneath the same tree where the curate used to tie his horse before hurrying into the vestry, and pulling a gown and surplice over his riding boots, he leaves his

little car, which fortunately for modern notions of clerical pro-
priety requires neither boot nor whip. When the day's work is
done he would rather return to a modest house in the village
street as the curate used to do, than to his predecessor's vast
house. Herrick's 'humble roof' would have suited him well, but
it is gone; he could have been comfortable in the modest Georgian
parsonage which took its place, but to this has been added a large
high drawing-room (which requires tons of coal to warm it, and
hundreds of pounds' worth of curtains to keep out the draughts),
a servant's wing, and stabling for three or four horses. Harassed
by all this unwanted magnificence, and enjoying very little of the
influence which used to go with it, his job is no longer regarded
as a comfortable one, but as a true vocation. In this respect he is
more fortunate than the curate, who was treated as a servant.
The parson inherits from the nineteenth century, besides the
over-large house, a character of priesthood which the Tractarian
revival brought back to the Church of England.

The parsonage can be made to yield its quota of parish history.
We can distinguish five types of house, the modern house, the
Victorian mansion, the large eighteenth-century house, the
modest Georgian parsonage with Victorian additions (sometimes
only traces of the old house remain visible from the outside) and the
few which contain some remnant of the medieval priest's house.

Of the modern house, its modest size and small garden an index
of a social revolution now in progress, little needs to be said. The
old rectory (it is nearly always a rectory) will probably still be
standing, inhabited by someone who has money to spend, but you
may look in vain for it within the confines of the village. A house,
however large, if it is conveniently near the church can be divided
into flats, or partially closed, or even have a wing pulled down.
Those distant rectories were usually built by the men for whom
the term 'squarson' was coined, gentlemen of some property,
who owned also the advowson (the right to choose the incumbent)
of their own benefice, and kept it in the family, the eldest son
taking orders automatically in order to inherit the family fortune.
The work was done by a curate, so it mattered little where the
incumbent built his house. Such arrangements were not uncommon in the eighteenth, and even lingered on through the
nineteenth century.

The Victorian reformers found many parishes which had no parsonage, or none fit for habitation. This often happened in very small poor parishes, where the benefice had never been sufficient to provide a decent living. Parishes which came into being in the Middle Ages, during a period of exceptional prosperity; parishes whose church revenues had been made over to a small, poor, religious house; these were often saddled with a large house during the brief Victorian summer.

An ancient priest's house, with its hall and parlour, and chamber above, was even less suitable than a small Georgian parsonage to contain a Victorian family and a Victorian staff. The income of the average incumbent was not high (only a few were ever really rich) but in that golden age a little money would go a long way in building as in everything else, and each man did as much as he could. The poorer the living the more necessary it might be to do something. The religious revival raised the dignity of even the poorest clergyman. Parson Adams's successor married a gentleman's daughter, and he would endeavour to bring his house nearer to her standard, by giving her a drawing-room, adding more bedrooms, and perhaps accommodation for a pony carriage. The Victorian vicarage is far more a monument to low prices and cheap labour than to any sudden access of wealth in the Victorian church.

The clergy of the old school changed their mode of living also. The squire's son endowed with a family living miles distant from his father's house, began to feel it his duty to go and live there, and it was natural that he should alter and improve what had been good enough for the curate before he occupied it himself. This change began about the end of the eighteenth century. Readers of Jane Austen notice that it was already in progress before she finished writing: Henry Tilney is a parson in the old style who only goes and lives in his parish when he quarrels with his father, and whose room is full of guns and fishing rods (I'm sure he made an excellent magistrate when he grew older); Edmund Bertram belongs to the new order, he 'has no thought but of residence'.

The dignified Georgian rectory has another story to tell. Here dwelt one of those worthies who lived in comfort on the income of three or four parishes, sometimes scattered over several counties, with a curate to do most of the parish duty; not a three-bottle man let us hope, but certainly one who loved good living, and lived as he chose. He is good-humouredly caricatured in the novels of Thomas Love Peacock. He was free to be as keen a sportsman as the squire, to join with the churchwardens and the parish clerk in 'purchasing a bull of superior blood and known courage to be baited . . . at the approaching feast', to go away for long periods if he wished. If his tastes were scholarly he had plenty of time to indulge them, to read the classics, to write books, to make collections, to engage in antiquarian speculation or archaeological investigation. If he were public-spirited he would find an outlet for his energies on the Bench, acquire knowledge of the law as it related to Local Government, pilot his heavier witted colleagues through their business, and perhaps carry them along with him in some favourite scheme of reform. Eighteenth-century clergy were not often distinguished by their zeal for souls, and the standard of conduct required of them was not high, but in favour of their piety it may be noted that John Wesley was one of them, and of their learning, that although scholarship was no longer the prerogative of churchmen they still formed the intellectual backbone of the country, and the largest audience for men of letters. We think they and their contemporaries ate and drank a great deal, but they took only two meals a day against our four or five. At the beginning of the century they were foremost among the founders of charity schools (few villages would have got a school from the squire), and towards its close they were sharing with the new gentry emerging from the industrial world, such men as Howard and Paul, the pioneer work of reform in prisons, asylums, and workhouses, and setting on foot the new drive to spread education. Indeed their influence on the Bench seems to have been wholly beneficial, and may gradually have raised the intellectual and moral level of its performance, especially as their intolerance or oppressiveness towards dissenters or towards the pleasures of the poor were more than offset by the indifference and good nature of the country gentry in any matter not touching their pockets or their prerogatives.

Their good work as magistrates may well have done something to restore the position of the clergy; during the seventeenth century they seem to have sunk low in the public esteem. This was due in some cases to extreme poverty. Prices had been rising ever since the Reformation, most of the clergy were supporting a wife and a string of children on a benefice designed for a celibate priest, and the income from all the miscellaneous offerings which belong to the Catholic way of life had disappeared. Some of the clergy were living no better than labourers and had little more education. Their more fortunate brethren were involved in passionate and not always edifying doctrinal argument, and by their support of the Royalist, and later the Jacobite, cause often found themselves on the losing side, in an age when to belong to the opposition might spell disaster. We glimpse them dimly through a dust-cloud of political and religious controversy.

Their houses have been largely absorbed into those of their successors, but we know that in size, quality, and comfort they varied between those of the husbandman and those of the yeoman. The pulpit in which they discoursed Sunday by Sunday is often still in use; one such in a Suffolk church bears a rhyme cut by the carpenter well out of sight:

> 'a proud parson and a simple squire
> made me build this pulpit higher.'

The seventeenth century was the golden age of Anglican preaching: shortly after its close one non-conformist wrote:

'I cannot but believe that if the Established clergy and the Dissenting Ministers in general were to exchange their manner of living for one year it would be the ruin of our cause, even though there should be no alteration in the constitution and discipline of the Church of England.'

He considered Presbyterian sermons too long and too dry.

Never before or since that epoch had the lives of the clergy been so precarious, nevertheless many weathered the storm and lived quietly and uneventfully in their parishes. Here is a letter from a non-conformist clergyman of a type who would probably have found himself in a benefice during the Commonwealth: leaving aside the reference to the 'common temptations of the age' this letter might well have been written by a member of the Established clergy, for school-keeping remained for long a popular way of augmenting clerical incomes.

'My hands are indeed at present pretty full of business; for besides my ordinary ministerial employments I take boys to table and teach. If you know of any, Mr. Johnson, who would have their children instructed in the languages, writing, arithmetic, in good wholesome air, in a country retirement, out of the way of the common temptations of the age, where they should in every respect be carefully looked after and well done to, if you should recommend them . . . I hope . . . you would never be ashamed of it. We are situated pleasantly, at some distance from a little country village . . . near the navigable river which runs between Boston and Lincoln. My wife is particularly well qualified for the ordering and encouraging of children.'

Any small Georgian parsonage, which before it received its nineteenth-century additions usually consisted of a hall and parlour, with a kitchen and buttery on the ground floor, and two or three chambers above, might have housed a little school of this sort at one time. The incumbent of four small Gloucestershire livings who kept a school in a fifth parish, and himself lived in Gloucester, must have been a professional schoolmaster, to whom his livings were simply an additional source of income.

When we have left the church and parsonage behind, there will usually be little else in the village to remind us of them. But there may be a tithe barn, or church farm.

In an earlier chapter the nature of tithe has been briefly described—a tax on property paid until very recently in kind— sheaves of corn, bales of wool, hides, hay, beasts and poultry might be laid under contribution, and if the produce each year made it necessary, the rector would have a barn in which to store it. A 'tithe' barn usually indicates that the rector was collecting from more than one parish; the barn was built at his headquarters. Most ancient tithe barns are connected with monastic or episcopal estates, but it was as rectors of parishes that the abbots and bishops collected the tribute.

Tithe still forms an important part of clerical income but now it has been standardized as a money payment. It is often deeply resented by farmers, especially if they are not themselves churchgoers or even nominal members of the Church of England. Once, the parson was expected to go round and collect his sheaves, and choose his geese and sheep, and in the last century he often had plenty of trouble and annoyance over it.

When the change to a money payment had only recently been made some farmers would still insist on paying in kind, out of malice, and a flock of lambs might turn up on the rectory doorstep, to the great embarrassment of the unfortunate incumbent. The other source of clerical income is land, called 'the glebe'; it may consist of odd fields, farms (hence Church Farm, Glebe Farm), or rows of cottages. These represent ancient endowments, and their name sometimes records their age-long connection with the church. Through many centuries of village history the parson might well be the only man in the village not born, or at least reared, in the neighbourhood. The extent to which he entered into the life of his flock would depend on the worth of the man himself, but the source of his income made it inevitable that he should become more or less intimately acquainted with the life of the land, the farming resources and practice of his parish.

Nowadays the parson usually moves on after ten years or so, but in the old times it was not uncommon for him to remain in one place throughout his working life. He would come to the parish as a young stranger and end his days there fifty years later a familiar and respected figure, as much part of the community as if his father's father had been born there. When he died his friends and parishioners would often subscribe for a memorial tablet to be placed in the chancel which had so long been his. Not for him the tons of alabaster, the recumbent figure, the marble drapery, which did honour to the dignity of the squire's name and family. A modest wall tablet, adorned with an urn, or a weeping figure in low relief, with his name and age, and perhaps his college, and his length of service in the parish, is frequently his monument; occasionally a set of verses records his piety and generosity. Modern inscriptions, however, are always brief and plain.

Fittingly the parsons' memorials and the squires' are far the commonest on village church walls; their prominence, and their relative size and dignity aptly reflect the positions these two occupied at the head of village society, and the ease, security, and power which were normally their lot.

BOOKS TO READ

English Local Government from the Reformation to the Municipal Corporations Act. B. and S. Webb.

The Growth of the English House. Y. A. Gotch. Revised ed., 1928.

X

The Modern World

INTO the closed rural society of squire and yeoman, justice and
pauper, so different alike in modes of thought and manner of
life from ours, there burst, in the second quarter of the nineteenth century, the vanguard of the modern world. Armed with
pick and shovel the 'navvies' employed to build the railways came
tramping down the turnpike. 'Navvy' was an abbreviation of
'navigator', a term first applied to the men who worked on the
canals, which later became current for any man engaged in excavation, and is still remembered and used by the older generation.
In some districts the gangs had been seen fifty years or so before
when the waterways were in the making, but the canals made little
impact upon country life. They were quiet slow-moving freight
carriers only, and even where a canal ran through the parish, the
lonely lock-keeper might be the only parishioner working on the
system.

The first railway was built in 1824; thirty years later the whole
country had been covered. Historians of the railways have, in
general, little to say about the physical work of laying that elaborate network over the face of the land. The quarrels of the shareholders, the plans and disappointments of the engineers come in
for their full share of attention, and some of the most dramatic
incidents in the process of construction are described; but what
it meant to the thousands of parishes on which the railway builders
descended, who the workers were, and whence they came, are
questions passed over in silence. It is as if the coming of the rail-

way could have had no significant effect on the people across whose familiar fields it accidentally passed on its majestic way from one great city to the next.

And indeed the railways did in a sense pass country people by at first. In its immediate effect on the lives of the village-folk the first bus was more important. Journalists might be confident that a new age had begun, but to a farm labourer working from dawn to dark to bring home eight or ten shillings a week it can have made little difference if two miles away there was a station from which he could travel all over England in a matter of hours; he had no money, and usually no wish, to travel. Nor was it expected that he should; some of the early promoters were doubtful about carrying any third-class passengers at all, and philanthropists were afraid that the railways would deprive the poor of their normal means of locomotion—the slow coach and the carrier's cart. On the other hand, the farm labourer is not likely to have objected to the railways since they offered the same possibilities of better paid work that airfields and atomic plants do today. It is not from the common folk of invaded solitudes that the cry goes up:

> 'Is there no nook of English ground secure
> From rash assault?'

Men who live by the soil naturally feel aggrieved when they see good land buried for ever under tons of earth or fathoms of water; some nineteenth-century farmers opposed the railway also from a groundless fear of its effect on their crops; with better reason innkeepers and horse dealers saw in it the knell of their trade. Among the upper classes there were those who hated it as a destroyer of beauty, and those who saw in it only an invasion of their possessions—their fox covers or their privacy. Since the opposition usually attracts more attention than the contented majority, the malcontents, the squire who set his dogs on the surveyors, and the poor prophet who foretold failure and disaster, come more to life in the pages of history than all those unnamed citizens who welcomed the railways as a possible source of future profit and improvement and those who felt (usually with reason) that they had struck a good bargain with the shareholders for the land over which it was to run.

What were the immediate and long-term effects of a railway laid across the heart of the parish?

In a quiet village off the beaten track, where people from a town ten miles off were looked on as foreigners, the effect of the invasion of an army of workmen three or four hundred strong drawn from every part of the British Isles, but owning no loyalty except to the gang, almost defies imagination.

The skilled core of these gangs, drawn originally from the 'bankers' and ditchers of the eastern fen-and marshlands, was gradually augmented by men from the wildest and hardiest stocks in the British Isles—men from the hills of Lancashire and Cumberland, from Scotland, and above all from Ireland. This army of labourers went wherever there was a railway to make, and wherever it went it drew after it a tail of recruits, some working only in their own neighbourhood, and returning to their old employments when the gang moved on, some who left their homes for good, attracted by rough company and high pay, and often, probably, by the splendid physique of the men themselves, and their freedom to go wherever work was to be found.

The villagers locked up their hen roosts when the navvies were about and viewed their pay-day debauches with a mixture of awe and disgust. The older heads among them despised and disapproved of the strangers, but a young farm-hand might well be drawn to a life as healthy as his own, but spiced with danger and comradeship and much better rewarded. A really skilled worker on the railways got 5s. a day, whereas a youth who had begun his working life at the age of ten was only earning about five shillings at week at seventeen and eight to ten shillings when he grew up and married. The beer shops were thronged with great hefty fellows with money in their pockets and meat under their belts, at a time when a slab of meat hung up outside the recruiting office in a country town was the most eloquent propaganda for army life that could be devised. The navvies could talk of adventures with flood and fire all over England, and even sometimes overseas, to men who worked year in, year out, on a diet of bread and potatoes, with a little meat on Sunday if things went well, and whose ambition was to die before they had to go to the workhouse. Of course their presence upset the labour market a little, and of course it upset the girls. Nobody had a good word to say for the navvies, certainly not the employers of cheap labour and the Poor Law officers; even the attitude of railway engineers and contractors towards them was somewhat tinged with fear, although a mixture of firmness and facetiousness seems usually to have sufficed to control them.

The navvies only received their pay once a fortnight at best, often only once a month, and their outbreaks of drunkenness cannot have been a daily menace. As the police force was still in its infancy, troops were sometimes called in on these occasions, but they never had much ado to keep order. The pitched battle which occurred at the mouth of Mickleton tunnel in Gloucestershire was brought on by a dispute between the contractors, not their workpeople; several hundred navvies joined in this affair but only one man had his head cut upen with a shovel and a few were otherwise injured; nobody was killed. This does not suggest a very brutish set of men. They were acknowledged to be loyal to each other and generally to their employers, and to be very generous towards their sick or injured comrades; they were responsive to any efforts made on their behalf (the men working on Kilsby tunnel toiled night and day to restore their temporary chapel after it had been burnt down). Perhaps their poor reputation sprang in equal parts from envy, from a distrust of strangers, from a recollection of small injuries among country folk, and from a 'fear of the mob' which had lingered in the air since the French Revolution, among their employers.

A gang of about three hundred men would normally be employed on a given stretch of line and would remain in the district three, four, or five years. (Most of our trunk lines were built in this short space of time.) They crowded into the villages which already had hardly room for their own growing populations, but still it was impossible to find lodging for all of them. Large numbers, especially married workers, would live in huts provided for them by the contractors. These ranged from squalid shacks of mud and straw into which they had to herd like cattle, to decent wooden huts provided with reasonable amenities. The poorest conditions were deemed good enough for Irish labourers and unskilled men drawn from the surrounding countryside. At that time there were many agricultural labourers in lowland England used to starvation wages and only too glad of an opportunity to earn more money under whatever conditions; moreover the nature of the terrain in that part of the country made highly-skilled work for the most part unnecessary. The lines in south-west England, afterwards incorporated in the Great Western system, were mostly laid by men of this type. Only when there were difficult excavations and embankments to make, or when it was deemed necessary to work by night, would the aristocrats of the navigtors' world be called in in large numbers, and for them better conditions were provided. During the building of the Midland railway in 1838 there were dwellings for 2,000 navvies on Batty Moor; their settlement resembled 'the gold digger's village in the colonies. Potters' carts, brewer's drays, and traps and horses for hire might all be found, besides numerous hawkers who plied from door to door.' There were shops, public houses, a hospital, post office, public library, mission house, day and Sunday schools. In this part of the country villages were few and far between, the merest hamlets, and poor. Settlements on the scale of Batty Moor were not provided in the land of large nu-cleated villages which could absorb a majority of the workers, and few extra amenities were provided for them there. The con-tractors would often pay out the wages in a beer shop, and shrug off the responsibility for food supplies on to the village shop-keepers. Whole districts found themselves artificially swollen for years on end, and permanently affected by the strangers. The men had none of the superiority and respectability of the farmer and the tradesman, but they had a scale of wages, and a freedom to move about, hitherto undreamt of by their rural counterparts. Perhaps the smouldering discontent of country folk which came into the open after 1870 had its beginning in these contact with another and very different way of life.

Meanwhile the navvies' operations were the wonder of the countryside. 'At night huge fires that blazed on the summit of the ridge lit up the rugged outline of the gangs of men and gave a strange and lurid colouring to the spectacle.' (Before the days of acetylene and electricity a bonfire was the only way of lighting the work at night.) Huge crowds gathered on the cliffs between Folkestone and Dover to see the blasting of the chalk from the great cuttings there; even in lowland England the making of cuttings, embankments, and bridges involved almost acrobatic performances on the part of men and horses. The operation of tipping to form an embankment is thus described. 'The horse that draws it (the truck) is made to quicken his speed, and then to trot and gallop . . . when they have approached very near to the edge, the driver loosens the horse from the wagon, gives him a signal which he has been taught to obey, and both leap aside at the same instant . . . while the wagon rushes on by the speed it has acquired, till it is suddenly stopped at the end of the embankment (by a piece of stout timber) the shock makes the hinder part to tip up, and the load is discharged. . . .' Débris was removed from cuttings by 'running'. Planks were laid up the sides of the cuttings on which to wheel the barrows. 'The *running* is performed by stout young men round the waist of each of whom a strong belt is attached, fastened to which is a rope running up the side of the cutting and turning on a wheel at the top, while to the other end a horse is attached . . . the horse (is led) quickly out . . . into the field and thus the man is drawn up the acclivity . . . the horse being led back the rope is slackened and the man runs down the plank . . . the barrow . . . is at once rendered unmanageable by any irregularity in the motion of the horse.'

There were from thirty to forty horse-runs in the great Tring cutting in the Chilterns, but only one fatal accident occurred. The men stubbornly opposed the engineers' efforts to devise a safer method. Navvies worked hard and recklessly, and accidents were fairly common; contemporaries describe the housewives of a Northamptonshire village crowding round to see and touch a mangled limb. Tunnelling was always a source of wonder and excitement. During the making of Kilsby tunnel so much water came into the workings on one occasion that the gang was only saved from drowning by means of an extemporized raft, towed to the nearest working shaft by the engineer swimming with the rope between his teeth.

At last when the line was laid the navvies moved away, and although there was no band to play, and their accoutrements were not of the kind that flash and jingle on the highway, we may be sure they left behind some red eyes (the Overseers of the Poor complained of more lasting tokens of affection). Some of the more spirited maidens had followed their lovers and some of the young men had left the plough. At Ashton in Northants one of the village girls who married a navvy and went away with him returned after he had been killed in an accident to settle down with her old sweetheart; the story is still remembered in the village.

When the glorious day came for the opening of the line, a crowd gathered to see the first train come through. Sometimes the village children were given a free ride down the track, and a few of them, probably, never set foot in a train again.

After the first excitement had died down the closely-knit self-sufficient village community sailed on unaware that it had taken aboard a cargo that would split its seams. The children ran down to the railway cutting to wave at the passing trains and sit on the pleasant bank of turf and flowers which soon covered the raw gashes in the landscape, and a new job, that of railway worker, ganger, signalman or porter, better paid than work in the fields, became available to their parents; the villagers found the trains a more comfortable mode of travel for their rare journeys than the coach had been, but it can hardly be said that new horizons opened before them in their daily lives. It was not the passenger but the goods train which quietly undermined the old order.

The goods train brought in cheap building materials, and red brick and Welsh slate began to gleam rawly in a landscape which had hitherto known only the colour of the native rocks. It brought coal. Fuel had become a real difficulty in eastern England. In Lincolnshire they used cow dung for firing. The coppice wood in the new hedgerows planted after the enclosures was as yet barely large and plentiful enough to be useful and cottagers had lost their time-honoured resources of turf and brushwood from the commons. The old bread ovens described in an earlier chapter were going out of use in the homes of the poor, who lived mainly on bread. Even when corn was very dear and the people reduced almost to starvation potatoes never became popular because it was hard to find fuel to cook them. The railways changed all that. Cheap bright factory goods began to arrive to dazzle the eye and put the sober local craftsman out of business, and smart agricultural machinery to revolutionize the immemorial routine of the fields.

Nor was it a one-way traffic. The goods train took out of the village quickly and cheaply whatever its people had to offer to the world outside. Corn and wool had always been exported from their various regions by wagon; cattle and sheep had gone on their feet, snuffling their way slowly along the ancient drove roads of England; but the railways opened up a market for perishable goods as well, for garden produce and above all for milk. The immediate neighbourhood of the great cities had long been devoted mainly to the production of these commodities, but now the whole countryside became their reservoir of food. Then began the characteristic rattle of milk cans which still resounds on country roads, for the milk trade depends entirely upon rapid transport and is the creation of the railway age. In those days each farmer had to transport his own milk to the station twice a day, and had specially built carts and strong fast horses for the purpose. The middleman's truck which tears around the lanes today has enabled even the remotest farms to engage in this lucrative enterprise; a wooden platform for milk-cans by the farm gate was becoming common in the 'thirties of the present century, and became universal during the late war.

Fishing villages sprang to new life when the railways put them in touch with distant markets and brought back a crowd of holiday makers in the summer. For them the chain of development was complete when the old village hidden up the valley, and the medieval harbour which grew up when the fear of raiders from the sea died away, were linked together with a Victorian High Street, with a station hard by, and new roads lined with villas reaching out into the country.

When the twentieth century began there were men alive in remote villages who had never made a train journey, but the effects of the railway were manifest in even the most secluded spot. In a community where few had travelled further than the neighbouring market town more than once or twice in their lives, everybody now wore factory-made clothes and boots, used mass-produced tools and domestic utensils, cooked on an iron range of standard make; and most people read a weekly newspaper. One of the blacksmiths had gone out of business, the cobbler had given up making boots, the tailor was an old man and there was nobody to succeed him, the farmer's wife had given up cheese-making and the mill was falling down. Of all the prophets at the

coming of the railways, the innkeeper had been most accurate in
his intimations of disaster: a trance had fallen on the roadside inn,
its dining room empty, its bedrooms dust-sheeted, its only
customers the neighbours in the bar. Even its importance among
the villagers had suffered a decline. The numerous meetings
which from time immemorial had been held in the inn parlour
now took place in the school or the Jubilee Hall. During the early
part of the previous century every village had at least one Friendly
Society, a mutual benefit club, whose place of assembly was invariably one of the village inns, the landlord frequently acting as
treasurer. The club night was a cheerful weekly or monthly
occasion and the annual 'walk' an important event in the villagers' year. Armed with their wands of office, a brass emblem on
a wooden staff, the members would perambulate the parish and
finish up with a dinner at the inn. The professed object of the
clubs was, of course, to help members when they fell on evil days,
but their funds were usually so small that the assistance they provided was of little value. Consequently as the century advanced
the great national societies such as the Manchester Oddfellows
gained ground in country places at the expense of the local institutions, which also came under fire from reformers and temperance
advocates on account of their connection with the inn. Very few
of these clubs remained by 1900, but their staves are to be seen
in antique shops, and may occasionally be found in lumber rooms.

Nor would the parson and the squire any longer think it becoming to conduct their business as magistrates in the inn parlour.
The large town breweries were already supplying farmers who
had given up making their own beer, and they were buying up
country inns, so that the landlord from being the owner of his
business and a craftsman became merely a manager and retailer.
In this process the beer itself declined in social status as well as in
strength and flavour.

This was on the debit side; on the credit side stood a restored
church, rows of neat red brick cottages, a well-lighted school,
and often good, clean water piped to taps or pumps in the village
street, a dusty but fairly well paved highway.

Horse dealers had been wrong in their prognostications; the
railways had brought them an increase of business. Traffic on the
trunk roads was a shadow of its former self (the whole coaching

VILLAGE FRIENDLY SOCIETIES' POLE HEADS. The members carried the poles in their annual procession, called a walk. Surviving specimens are all from the West Country.

Horse Runs in Tring cutting. The work of giants! The men with their barrowloads of débris were drawn up the side of the cutting by horses and ran back with the empty barrows.

interest had vanished overnight), but the railway station acted as a magnet to the wagons and drays of local traders, the gentleman's carriage, the carrier's cart, the farmer's milk float and the village 'fly', and the surface of the roads was kept in good condition for light horse traffic. It had a smooth white surface of granite or other suitable stone chips, thickly coated with dust which blew up around every passing vehicle and covered the hedges, and even the lower branches of the trees with a floury film.

'White in the moon the long road lies'—

and beside it marched the poles and wires which connected the village once and for all with the outside world.

The use of the newly invented telegraph for signalling purposes followed quickly upon the building of the railways, and soon private companies began to exploit it, and to erect their poles along the roads. By 1900 in most large villages one of the shopkeepers had cleared a corner of his counter for use as a post and telegraph office, and displayed a modest black and white notice to this effect outside, among others of painted iron less modestly advertising tea and farming necessaries. Small or remote places had only a letter-box, or a skeleton service of stamps and postal orders in one of the shops. The introduction of Old Age Pensions in 1906 must have greatly increased the need for post offices. This was an event of the utmost importance to poor people, since it lifted the gloomy shadow of the workhouse from their lives. Flora Thompson in her delightful trilogy *Lark Rise to Candleford* describes how old women used to collect their money with tears running down their faces and bring flowers for the girl behind the counter. The telephone and the telephone kiosk made their appearance between the wars of 1914 and 1939, and little telephone exchanges, tiny buildings about the size of an old wellhouse, have come within the last few years.

The village shop still houses the post office; it has maintained its importance although its character has changed. The shopkeeper is no longer regarded by the village women as an arbiter of fashion, but she is still expected to keep all the necessities of life, except dresses and hats, even now when this term has come to include so much that our grandfathers never dreamt of.

Of course it would be a mistake to attribute all this change solely to the coming of the railways; much of it, the new cottages, the water supply, the school, the restored church, can be imagined as happening under different conditions. But it was cheap and rapid transport which determined the physical form these changes took, and the appearance the village was in future to wear.

The aspect of the village today reveals four epochs of domestic building: the yeomen's farmhouses, and the husbandmen's farmhouses now occupied as cottages; terraces of eighteenth- or early nineteenth-century cottages occurring only in villages where an industry has flourished; Victorian farmhouses and cottages; and council houses. We have already discussed the farmhouses in an earlier chapter; for them and for the houses of the gentry the 'great rebuilding' as it is sometimes called, occurred in the seventeenth century. Another 'great rebuilding' came in the nineteenth century, this time to the homes of the poor.

What have Victorian cottages to tell of village life in the nineteenth century?

The occupant of a Victorian cottage worked long and hard and brought home very little money at the end of the week. Only if his wife and children were at work would he be able to live in reasonable comfort. Children began bird-scaring and stone-picking at the age of nine or earlier, and a smart boy of eleven would be expected to manage a pair of horses. Women often worked in the fields hoeing, weeding, stone-picking, and harvesting. Picking stones off the surface of a ploughed field to be carted to the roadside for repairs was work one would do in order to pay the shoemaker's bill, but, as an old man who remembered it remarked, 'it was slavery'. Hoeing and weeding were hard but not unpleasant work, and harvesting was pure joy.

While his children were too young to work the cottager had to struggle to keep body and soul together. His fortunes reached their lowest ebb in the 'hungry forties' after the abolition of the Speenhamland subsidies, and before the repeal of the Corn Laws brought cheaper bread.

Great landowners had reached the summit of wealth and power and began to take a more generous view of their responsibilities to their poorest tenants. Counties where most of the land was in the hands of small squires and freehold farmers fared worst.

If a small squire was content to be the king of his parish all was well, but if his tastes ran to politics, cards, or horse-racing, if he had extravagant sons, or an ambitious wife and a large number of marriageable daughters, he would have to economize on the estate in order to find the money to pay their debts, make an allowance to a son in the army (his grandfather would have sent this boy to make a fortune in the City), to buy a benefice for another son, and to provide a London season for the daughters. Even in the reign of Victoria it took a large rent-roll to sustain this kind of thing.

Farmers as a class have never been noted for openhandedness, and as employers in the last century their main virtue seems to have been a willingness to take on any surplus labour there might be—for a wage on which a family could barely live. As landlords they were no better. If they had to build cottages it was done as cheaply and meanly as possible. More often, however, where there was no squire, a few poor cottages would be run up by the local builder, or one of the village tradesmen, as a speculation. Cottages were let for a tiny rent, and were sometimes free, but it was not unknown for a man to be charged rent by a farmer, if he were injured in the course of his work and obliged to be absent for several weeks. When the Reverend Edward Girdlestone arrived in Devon in 1863 he found the labourers miserably housed, and earning only a starvation wage. Private remonstrance proved useless, so he denounced the employers in his sermons, telling them that the disease raging among their cattle was God's punishment for their treatment of their workpeople, and when this brought him only unpopularity and persecution, he organized a scheme for helping labourers to leave the countryside; he campaigned all his life, and not entirely in vain, on their behalf.

It must be said, however, that if farmers expected their men to live miserably, they sometimes fared little better themselves. Richard Jefferies draws a striking picture of the old-style farmer (this was at the close of the century) resisting every modern invention in his fields, and denying himself every comfort in his rage for saving money.

Happy the tenants of a great lord! As an old woman who lived

227

in one of the Duke of Grafton's villages said, 'If you lived in one of the Duke's cottages you were safe for the rest of your life'. Railway workers at Hatfield, whatever their politics, hoped to end their days in one of the Marquess of Salisbury's cottages. Though by no means all the aristocracy showed humanity to their tenants, the majority set a good example. Many kept their cottages in hand instead of letting them with the farms, so that tenant farmers should not have a stranglehold upon their workpeople, and these cottages were usually well built and comfortable. By the middle of the century cholera epidemics, and the publication of such books as Charles Kingsley's *Two Years Ago* had had their effect upon public opinion. The Duke of Bedford, who was considered to be the richest man in England with an income of over £300,000 a year, set a particularly high standard. Each cottage had two rooms downstairs, and two or three bedrooms, one with a fireplace; every cottage had a kitchen range and copper, and coal, wood, and tool sheds, and for each group there was a communal oven. Very few, even among like-minded peers, thought it necessary to provide comfort on this scale. The Prize Essay on 'Cottages' in a competition run by the Royal Agricultural Society in 1843 advocated kitchen and pantry below and two rooms above, and no fireplace upstairs. Thatch is recommended as being warmer than slate or tile in the unceiled bedrooms.

The author thought brick or stone was to be preferred to 'stud and mud' or cob, and this opinion prevailed. Hence in most Devonshire villages only one or two of the traditional whitewashed, thatched cottages survive, and in the midlands red brick completely ousted the black and white tradition. Only on the great limestone belt did the rebuilding of the villages make no obvious break with the past.

Victorian cottages have acquired the patina of age, and even the brightest of red brick harmonizes well enough with the older dwellings. As they often have small windows and low roofs, colour is the only important difference between new and old. Those small windows were never opened, and the little light they gave was usually obscured by luxuriant pot plants. But, except in bad weather, the door stood wide open. If there were tiny children in the house a screen two feet high would be dropped into grooves to keep them from straying; and they might be seen hanging over

the boards to watch the passers-by. The older cottages usually
had a half door, the lower part closed, and when her work was
done the housewife might survey the scene, or gossip with the
neighbours leaning over it. From this customary use of the door
for light and air comes the expression 'to darken the door': a
person crossing the threshold of an old cottage would dim the
whole interior. It is a reminder, moreover, of the miserable hovels
which preceded these cottages. Eighteenth-century writers
describe shacks of mud and straw with perhaps a few pieces of
broken glass embedded in the walls to give light if the door had
to be shut, and even in 1842 the sanitary commissioners found
many whose windows were stuffed with rags or blocked with
clay—one-roomed cabins with earth floors below ground level,
always damp and muddy, and often flooded. It is with such as
these that the meanest Victorian cottage should be compared.
The prize cottage of 1843 would not have done twenty years later.
When the Society of Arts offered a prize for a cottage design in
1864 the winning entry conformed to, or surpassed, the Duke of
Bedford's standard; two of the three bedrooms, for example, had
fireplaces, and each cottage had its own oven. The cost of a pair
was £260. In the next ten years the successful architect erected
these cottages in seventeen counties, and during that time the cost
of building them nearly doubled (Plate 5. No 1.). By 1874 economy
had again to be considered and he had prepared a design of which
he says 'The plan is similar to the last but not quite so large; the
roof gables and porches are plain and inexpensive, the roof being
flat-pitched and slated. . . . Of course a flat-pitched roof with
slates could not look so well, and if the cottages are to be placed
near the park it would not be desirable to have this exterior, but
for general use on farms and in villages this plan would answer
every purpose.

'Where occasion may require, a few pounds spent in barge-
boarding the gables and dormers and putting hoods over the
doors would greatly improve the external appearance.'

In 1874 simplicity was not considered picturesque; cottages
of this period are loaded with barge-boarding, overgrown
chimneys, fancy tiling and variegated brickwork.

The oldest council houses, dating from the early twenties, are
beginning to look as if they truly belonged to the village scene,

but their plan generally derives from a suburban, rather than a rural, tradition, and they represent as well as anything the break-up of the old order and the invasion into parish affairs of the Rural District Council and the County Council, bodies which, between them, since 1878 have taken over most of the functions of the vestry, and in recent years have superseded the squire as provider and patron.

Nearly all Victorian cottages had a garden, and their occupants often had an allotment as well. Allotments came into fashion in the first half of the nineteenth century as part of a somewhat half-hearted effort to improve the lot of the labouring poor. The vestry would occasionally devote parish land, or purchase a field, for allotments, and let it out at a very low rent. In 1887 and 1890 the Allotments Acts gave power to County Councils to acquire and let land for this purpose. That rather shabby piece of ground, with little huts set at crazy angles dotted over it, once meant the difference between a starvation diet of bread and potatoes, and a rich variety of home-grown fruit and vegetables with a surplus for sale, or better still, where the fruit and vegetables could be grown in the cottage garden, the allotment would produce pig-feed. Decaying styes which once housed the cottagers' most cherished possessions are still to be seen in cottage gardens. The pig was enormously important. Bringing up a family of ten on ten shillings a week you could seldom afford even two or three pennyworth of butcher's meat; before the invention of margarine lard flavoured with rosemary was the countryman's substitute for butter; alternatively the pig, or half of it, could be sold to pay the shoemaker's bill. The more comfortable family still prided itself on the its home-cured hams, the sides of bacon always ready, the glorious feast after pig-killing, and the power of giving something worthwhile on those occasions to one's friends.

Sanitary regulations and higher wages have emptied those styes. It is sad that home-cured bacon should be a thing of the past, but the old village undoubtedly needed cleaning up. Before 1860 few landlords would have thought of providing their cottages with decent privies; there was no public drainage at all and the air stank of decaying cabbage, leaky cess-pits, and pigs. Much of the village water supply must have been unfit for human consumption by modern standards, and the cottagers owed their relative immunity from water-borne infection to a lifelong process of acclimatization and to their natural preference for tea and beer.

The tiny dwellings built in Victorian times would never have held a Victorian family if all the children had stayed at home, but they seldom did. At thirteen, or even earlier, the girls went into domestic service and never slept in their parents' house again except when they came home for a holiday.

FIG. 58. An old farmhouse in Westmorland with a spinning gallery. In more hospitable country the women worked at their front doors.

This was a state of affairs largely brought about by the triumph of steam. So long as machinery depended on water power, industry remained in the countryside, and often provided occupation for a host of out-workers. In one Wiltshire village at least, where the cloth industry throve until the middle of the century, the wage subsidies prescribed at Speenhamland were never demanded. Spinning-wheels whirred, looms rattled, wire and blade workers' mills thudded, and the countryman had some alternative to work on the land. This was even more important to his wife; innumerable industries flourished among the women-folk. But when the machines moved away to the coalfields, and became ever more subtle and efficient, the women lost their markets; they were driven to work in the fields, where they had never been seen before, and where the presence of their cheap labour still further undermined the economic position of their men. Even where local industry survived it became ever less profitable. The lace dealer, for example, had ceased to visit Buckinghamshire villages before the nineteenth century was out. Straw-plaiting for millinery lasted a little longer. In 1900 women were still making the long tramp from outlying villages to St. Albans market, their goods carefully carried in a pillowcase, en-joying the day's shopping when they had sold their plaits, and returning tired and satisfied in the evening, but local markets such as that at Codicote had already disappeared, and the work no longer commanded a fair price. Many cottages in Hertfordshire must still have on their mantelshelves the notched yard-mark used by these workers to measure their pieces. These two indus-tries survived longer than most.

When the factories had taken over, women could no longer contribute to the family income except by working in the fields, or going into service. Luckily the swelling army of tradesmen and clerks required plenty of servants. So away the girls went as soon as they had learnt the rudiments of their job in a local farm-house, and though they were able to send valuable contributions of money and clothes to their families, the village must have been a sadder place when they were no longer there to dance at the Wake, or dress the May garland.

Perhaps it was for this reason that during the nineteenth century so many time-honoured customs, sports, and pastimes came to an end. The disappearance of all the craftsmen and husbandmen who had been their own masters, and able to take a day off if they wished, no doubt had its effect too. At all events the maypole, once so much loved and honoured, came down—what good was it if there were not girls enough to make up the set? A few villages still proudly cherish their maypole and the children are carefully taught to skip round it, but the weaving colours and taut ribbons, the contracting, panting circle must have had a different meaning when grown men and girls did the dances. The song 'Come Lasses and Lads' reminds us that dancing round the may-pole was an amusement for courting couples, rather than for schoolchildren. When the daughters of the village had gone away into service young men could find wives among the domestic servants in their neighbourhood and court them on Sunday on their way home from church, but these girls had learnt sophisti-cated tastes from their employers, and neither taught nor en-couraged their children to play the old games.

All the ceremonies connected with the first of May have a pagan origin, but the puritans seem to have thought the maypole especially shocking. Magistrates during the Commonwealth were ordered to be strict in abolishing it. It was set up again after the Restoration, however, and probably most of the other forms of amusement which came under fire under the 'rule of the saints' were revived and lingered on into the nineteenth century, to perish for social and economic, rather than religious and moral, reasons.

The villagers managed to keep the Wake or revel going, how-ever (their patronal feast, though few of them probably remem-bered the fact). These celebrations had an origin almost infinitely remote. St. Gregory, in his famous letter of advice to St. Augus-tine's followers, bade them allow their converts to set up bowers of greenery in the churchyard and make a feast instead of a pagan sacrifice. The medieval fair in honour of the saint to whom the church was dedicated followed this traditional pattern. Stalls were set up in the churchyard, and dancing, feasting, and sport were the order of the day. The custom of roasting an ox whole continued in some places until the eve of the late war. The fair, of course, had been turned out of the churchyard, but it continued to flourish on the village green or in a nearby field, and by the nineteenth century to the home-made entertainment had been added a fun fair with roundabouts, swings, shooting-galleries, and all the popular sideshows, and every child, however poor, had a few pennies to spend. The stalls were always getting fewer, however, and as the villages dwindled it was no longer worth the showman's while to bring out his vans.

The skittle-alley behind the inn, with its neat clipped hedges and wooden benches, is a thing of the past; but the sport survives, kept alive by the contest for a pig, fought out at all good villages fêtes. Skilled performers come to these from all over the district, and the event retains its excitement and interest, although the pig has lost his importance in cottage economy. Bowls are still popular, but occasionally a field name will show that a village has allowed its green to go out of use.

At least one village still has a quintain. This was an ancient game, the rustic version of a knightly tournament. The tall post remains with the swivelling arm grown stiff from disuse. One end of the arm carried a target, the other a bag of flour. If the rider hit the target fair and square with his staff he would pass out of reach in time; if he hit it wide he would be brought up short, and the flour bag swinging round would empty itself over his head.

The more brutal the sport the harder it died. While maypoles quietly lost their devotees, and morris dancers' bells and ribbons tarnished in disuse, only legislation could do away with cock-fighting and bull-baiting; the former is still carried on in secret. A cockpit is a small grassy amphitheatre sunk in the ground behind the inn, or in a quiet corner of the park. This was a sport for men of all classes; bull-baiting attracted both sexes. The bull post was set up on the village green or in as public a spot as possible and everybody, the parson, and the squire, women and children, turned out to see the sickening fun. Not many villages still cherish the stake to which the victim was tied, but in some the English love of tradition has got the better of the modern Englishman's tenderness of heart.

Tenderness of heart found little place in village life before the nineteenth century. Besides cock-fighting, bull- and bear-baiting, badger-baiting, and the even simpler amusement of beating or stoning animals to death were enormously popular; prize-fighters fought till neither party could stand up, shin-hacking contests were one of the mildest forms of village rivalry, and people walked miles to see a public execution.

The work of tempering this natural savagery in country places fell mainly on the clergy, and on their womenfolk, who, by reviving religious life, teaching in Sunday schools, teaching music, concentrating interest and energy on building schools and restoring churches, gradually effected a genuine change of heart, and introduced their parishioners to more civilized forms of amusement.

The closing years of the nineteenth century saw a golden age of home-made entertainment. Socials, concerts, lectures, penny-readings, and theatricals were got up regularly in the school; there was, as one old body said, always something going on.

Indoor amusements flourished exceedingly during the long winter evenings. Outdoor games necessarily had less importance among men at work during the greater part of the daylight hours; nevertheless many villages first had a cricket club about this time, and in some, especially in the great cricketing counties, the game took root. In others its existence is only spasmodic: a gentleman farmer takes an interest in the game, forms a club, helps it to build a gay little pavilion, and cricket flourishes for perhaps a generation; then it is abandoned and the pavilion may be seen quietly rotting under the dripping trees. The same fortune frequently attends the village tennis courts.

Many villages still rely on the school to provide them with a large room for whist drives, dances, sales of work, and flower shows, the only forms of home-made entertainment which are popular today; but some have a hall built to commemorate the end of the 1914–18 war, or King George the Fifth's Jubilee, or some other public event. In small villages the Women's Institute often has a hut (built usually shortly before the late war) which can be used for these purposes; but many villages are now too small to have any social life.

In Victorian times the village population was increasing.

Where and why have the people gone?

Cottage life in the nineteenth century was undoubtedly very poor and hard by modern standards, especially while the children were too young to work. Labourers had little share in the farmers' golden age, and when the influx of corn from the New World brought that to a sudden end about 1875 depression settled on the countryside. Machinery was just beginning to affect the agricultural routine, so that farmers were no longer willing, in hard times, to employ any able-bodied man who asked for work. The richest cornfields were often the first to go, and as the green carpet crept back over the parish the labourers knew there was nothing for it but to get up and go. Thousands emigrated, and many more drifted away into the towns. From one village alone five families went overseas in a single year. There had been an even greater exodus forty years before from the eastern counties, when most of the families had gone to Canada or Australia, but some had gone to manufacturing towns and trickled back if they could not find work. But now the countrymen who left went away for good. The teachers up at the village school insinuated the notion that farmwork was no occupation for a promising boy, and mothers who had learnt something of middle-class life in their years of service told their sons: 'I don't want you to work on the land.' They wanted their sons to learn a trade and to rise for ever above the ranks of unskilled workers, and above the drudgery (as they thought it) of the fields; but the ranks of the country craftsmen were dwindling too, so that to follow a trade a boy had to leave home.

When the twentieth century began in Corsley, a Wiltshire village, the average labourer's family contained four or five children. Of these, one would probably not reach manhood; some or all the girls would marry outside the district, one of the boys was likely to leave the countryside, and one was destined to fall in the 1914–18 war. It seemed as if no one would be left to work the land, and as if the tide of prosperity would never turn. But salvation from an unexpected quarter was already announcing its approach with a faint 'poop-poop' on the highway. It would be another twenty-five years before the words 'Good Stabling' painted over the arch in the inn yard would be allowed to become chipped and faded. before the wheelwright turned his shop into a garage and the horse-dealer bought a bus. I well remember the inn yard at Exeter where we stabled our pony for the last time in 1922, how our trap was pushed into its place in a long row of farmers' dog-carts—thirty or forty of them, for it was market day; how not more than four years later the carts had disappeared; their place was taken by a row of snub-nosed Morris and Ford cars. Tarmac, which is too slippery for horses, was rare in the deep country in the 1920's even on main roads; side roads retained the colour of the local soil, and the bare humped surface produced by the endless passing of iron tyres and horses' feet.

Horses continued for some years more to provide the main motive power on the farm. There would be from four to twenty horses in the stables, according to the size of the farm, and according to the soil from two to four would go to make up a plough team. In a large field four such teams might be seen working at once, the creaking of their harness as familiar a sound as the putter of a tractor is today.

The machine age may be said to have begun on the farm the day (round about 1830) the farmer left his old pearwood ploughs to moulder under a hedge, and harnessed his teams to iron ploughs, made indeed by some enterprising local blacksmith, but with material brought in from outside instead of with trees cut from his own hedgerows. The blacksmith took a wooden plough for his model, imitating features unavoidable in a wooden construction (for example the lower right handle) but meaningless in iron. A few of these locally-made iron ploughs may linger about field corners in very remote places, and even a wooden plough may occasionally be found in an old shed.

Machinery made very slow progress in the south; threshing machines were common in Lancashire by 1813 and the 'gingangs' described in an earlier chapter were built for the horse-wheel which drove them. In the south they found little favour, and in 1842 farmers were still using 'miserable machines' by northern standards if they used any at all. Horsetracks are fairly common on Devonshire farms (they are not called *gingangs* there) and one or two were still in use on the eve of the last war. In the north their original use had been completely forgotten.

By 1879 the most progressive farmers had introduced a steam-driven thresher of the type still in use. It was a large, wooden-cased machine drawn and driven by a steam engine commonly called a traction engine. A similar engine was used to drive a steam plough, an excessively cumbrous contraption which had only a very short life. Horse-hoes and drills were already in use, though many farmers still preferred broadcast sowing, and by the beginning of the twentieth century the horse-drawn reaper and binder was not uncommon. This was to revolutionize the harvest, but the corn still had to be built into stooks, and the great horse wagons still had to bring the harvest home. Mowing and tedding machines came in about the same time, and elevators only a little later. These machines, slightly improved, are still in use. Many farmers still relied on the traditional methods altogether or in part, and as by this time they had weathered the first shock of New World competition they were again ready to give employment to any likely lad growing up in the parish. Women, however, disappeared from the fields except at harvest time, and children were shut in school till the age of eleven.

FIG. 59. A tractor of the 'twenties.

After the 1914–18 war oil-driven tractors made their appearance (Fig. 59). Modelled on the steam engines already in use, they were too heavy to work efficiently in the fields, but by 1930 the design had been so much improved that they were fast displacing horse and steam engines on all the largest and most progressive farms. Only the depression which still hung over the countryside prevented smaller men from making the change. The old machinery was easily adapted for use with the tractor, and new apparatus began to make its appearance in the fields. The manure spreader lightened one of the farmers' most laborious tasks, the baler simplified harvest work, and the four- or six-shared tractor-plough biting deep into the soil transformed the slowest, heaviest, and most fundamental of all farming operations.

Occasionally you may meet with an old iron tractor or steam engine lying abandoned in the field, or a pair of old iron wheels in the yard (Fig. 60).

Combine harvesters began to appear in England before the

last war, and today they have almost displaced the reaper and binder. For them field and farm gates are widened and hedges grubbed up. The rickyard stands empty, no longer filled with great stacks of unthreshed corn, but farmers are filling up the empty spaces with grain-drying equipment. The man who works these machines would probably not recognize a flail if you showed him one.

FIG. 60. Tractor wheels, old and new.

Highly mechanized farms require little labour, but a man need no longer leave home to find other work. Life is coming back to the countryside, its harbingers the electric grid which began to bestride the country in the late 'twenties, and the village bus. Since electricity reached out into the country industry need no longer cling to the coalfields, and light and power have greatly lessened the relative discomforts of country life. And since the bus service began villagers who hitherto had merely welcomed or suffered the intrusions of the outside world are able at last to explore it for themselves and to find work and entertainment within a twenty-mile radius of their homes. People who cherish

239

the relics of the past dislike the village bus almost as much as they do Hodge's new motor-cycle, and call it unbeautiful, undignified, a disrupter of the old self-sufficient community, and a slayer of wholesome home-made entertainment, but the atmosphere of happiness and good humour which pervades its progress, crammed with housewives, school-children, and workers, suggests that to the people who use it it has been a bringer of good tidings, and that the drift away from the country may now come to an end.

BOOKS TO READ

Our Iron Road. F. Williams, 1883.
British Rural Life and Labour. F. G. Heath, 1911.
Life in an English Village. M. F. Davies, 1909.
Hodge and His Masters. R. Jefferies. Methuen, 1937.
Small Talk at Wreyland. C. Torr. (Abridged edition), Cambridge, 1926.
Lark Rise to Candleford. F. Thompson. World's Classics.
The 'Revolt of the Field' in Lincs. R. Russell. National Union of Agricultural Workers, 1956.
Ask Mamma. R. Surtees, 1858.
Two Years Ago. Charles Kingsley, 1857.

XI

The Spoken Word

HUMAN testimony is notoriously unreliable; two honest people will give totally different accounts of the same incident. That is why the evidence of buildings, ruins, and plots of ground, imperfect though it is, should be preferred to popular tradition. Nevertheless we would give much for one conversation with a thirteenth-century peasant or an eighteenth-century justice. The last hundred years, or even a little more, are covered by the memories of the aged, since these often include the stories their parents told them of things remembered from their own youth. Such memories are fairly reliable on all matters relating to the day-to-day business of living such as working conditions, customs, tools, food, and clothing. The narrators saw in their youth the teams of men mowing with scythes, and followed their mothers across the hard, wintry fields, picking off the stones; and they can tell when the first reaper and binder, or tractor, made its appearance on the village farms. They know where the people got their water before the pipes were laid, and whose barn was used for celebrations before the school or hall was built. They can describe those celebrations in terms which make the modern world seem drab to the listener, and then make his blood rise with indignation by telling the stories their fathers told them, of life in the 'hungry forties'.

They can tell, or have heard their mothers tell, when, for example, the 'undertaker' ceased his rounds of Norfolk villages collecting home-weaver's work, or the lace factor his tour of the

Buckingham district. They know when bicycles were introduced and the difference they made to labourers who might have to walk five or six miles to work and the same distance home at night. They know all the houses in the village, and which of them may be worth exploring, and they can tell which was once a shop or an inn, an old school or a chapel. They are usually very ready to talk about the squire and his family, and to recount with a kind of relish, almost amounting to pride, the number of horses he had in his stable, and how he ruled the village. The parsons are spoken of with interest, but with less respect; exhortations from the pulpit to be contented with their wages, to work hard, and to be good Tories, would destroy the good-will built up by half a lifetime of faithful pastoral care.

Much of what these old people remember, especially of customs and methods of work, came down to them from distant generations; the old ways of life have already perished, and when they die even the memory will vanish. Today it is still possible to hear a woman tell stories of a mother's childhood who was born before Waterloo. First-hand pictures of village life in those days are so rare that any story, however trivial, lights up the scene.

Flora Thompson describes in *Lark Rise* life in the hamlet where she was born. It is a wonderfully fresh and vivid account of cottagers' lives at a time when England was at the summit of her wealth and power. There was an old woman in her village who could remember keeping geese on the commons before they were enclosed (soon after 1800). This woman's father had been one of the small farmers or husbandmen who found their share of the common land after enclosure less valuable than the free range had been, and his daughter and her husband had been unable to keep the farm in being. The husband had sunk to the condition of a labourer, but they had kept the house and perhaps a tiny reserve of capital, and lived better than their neighbours. This was not an unusual case; it was often said that the Enclosures were unjust to the poorer members of the village community, both to husbandmen of this type, and to cottagers, who though they had no right to use the commons had been permitted to do so for fuel, and for a few geese, or an occasional cow or donkey. No doubt these opinions had been heard by some of the villagers, and discussed at leisure in the pub, and the tradition had grown up within two generations that the commons had been given to the poor of the parish in the remote past, and that the squire and the farmers had stolen it from them. In fact theirs was a squatters' settlement which had been planted on the common about a hundred years before, and it was the squatters who had 'robbed' the whole village community of the land on which their little township stood. The memories of unlettered peasants are not so much longer or more accurate than those of other men.

Popular traditions have to be regarded with caution; the truth they contain is frequently much distorted. Moreover a miasma of romantic fancy often enshrouds them, manifesting itself chiefly in a dreary preoccupation with druids, or with erring monks and nuns. This used to infect the work of otherwise serious and scholarly local antiquaries as well as the village gossips. Therefore if the old gardener tells you that the vicarage was a nunnery, check his statement in some standard work of reference, such as Knowles and Hadcock: *Medieval Religious Houses*. If he tells you that it is connected by an underground passage to a monastery three miles away do not believe him at all. In this case someone has probably discovered an old drain and embellished it with details taken from a novel left at home by servants visiting their families. (For the perfect example of such an 'underground passage', see the main drain at Hayles in Gloucestershire, a portion of which is exposed beneath the monastery kitchen.)

The villagers may show themselves more reticent about old customs and sayings. Folklore as such is outside our subject, but there are some hints to be picked up in the manners and speech of the people. Fifty years ago Sussex mothers were still frightening their children with 'Boney' to make them behave themselves. Bonaparte's threat of invasion was only a hundred years old. In Oxfordshire, the scene of some fighting and much countermarching, the Civil War was still remembered, and 'Crumell'll get you' was the threat. In some parts of the country, if they have attended a funeral in another parish church than their own, the people go to that church the following Sunday, a folk memory, certainly, of the requiem mass which would have been offered there before the Reformation. Traditions connected with the ancient faith died slowly in some districts. In Cleveland a hundred years ago, the bridegroom customarily put a handful of coins on the service book during or after the marriage ceremony, unknowingly commemorating the gift of gold and silver to the bride which forms part of the Catholic rite.

We have seen in an earlier chapter how place-names may bear witness to a foreign invasion which happened fifteen hundred years ago. Local dialects reflect the same features, and often record much later and more peaceful foreign influences. Thus the speech of the south and eastern counties in coastal districts shows the effects of the influx of Protestant refugees in the seventeenth century: such words as the Norfolk *locum* for an attic window (French *lucarne*), and Sussex *boco*, *frap* for *much* and *hit*. East Anglian dialect and sayings even contain faint memories of the Celtic stocks with which Saxon and Dane intermingled, as when the people speak of a Winwaloe wind (Winwaloe was a Celtic virgin martyr).

The English are rather fond of incorporating foreign words into their language, but they never give themselves any trouble over the pronunciation of these outlandish sounds: *beaucoup* becomes boco, Ypres becomes Wipers, *cruc* becomes church. How many British names and words were thus absorbed by the Saxon conquerors?

Our plan of the village is now as complete a record as we can make it, and each feature a thread in the tapestry depicting the village story.

Under the inspiration of the Women's Institutes and other bodies many villages are now engaged in such efforts of reconstruction, and modern-school teachers find their pupils take a keen interest in this type of project, and can use their local knowledge to make a real contribution to it. If I have been able to help them to probe a little deeper into the past, and in collecting material to cast their nets a little wider, to read the landscape as well as documents, books, and memories, I shall have contributed to a worthwhile undertaking. I hope that copies of records thus made will be deposited in the County Library or Record Office.

Countryside and country life are alike changing so rapidly that anyone who loves to understand the past and desires to see a familiar landscape in historical depth must get to work quickly. He must examine the great house before it is pulled down, visit the prehistoric remains before War Office or Forestry Commission get to work on them, inspect the old farm buildings, study the craftsmanship that went to their building and try to understand the type of enterprise they were designed to serve before they are replaced, and collect as best he can from lumber rooms and auction sales 'things forgotten and unprized' (as old inventories used to call them), the tools of vanished trades. A melancholy occupation, some might think, but it has all the excitement of a collector's life, with its lucky finds and arduous pursuits, and as he pursues it, the 'bad old days' or 'Merry England'— whichever myth has hitherto tinged his notions of bygone country life, will perhaps give place to a picture of the past more in tune with reality. He will observe that things which now seem to belong to an immemorial routine were once new and exciting intrusions upon ways of life which then seemed equally stable and permanent; that there was never a time when the old could not grumble that 'things are not what they were' and the young reply that 'times have changed'.

BOOKS TO READ

Ask the Fellows who Cut the Hay. G. E. Evans. Faber and Faber, 1956.

Index

INDEX